THE DIGITAL REVOLUTION AND GOVERNANCE

To the memory of my mother

The Digital Revolution and Governance

XIUDIAN DAI
University of Hull

LONDON AND NEW YORK

First published 2000 by Ashgate Publishing

Reissued 2018 by Routledge
2 Park Square, Milton Park, Abingdon, Oxon OX14 4RN
711 Third Avenue, New York, NY 10017, USA

Routledge is an imprint of the Taylor & Francis Group, an informa business

Copyright © Xiudian Dai 2000

All rights reserved. No part of this book may be reprinted or reproduced or utilised in any form or by any electronic, mechanical, or other means, now known or hereafter invented, including photocopying and recording, or in any information storage or retrieval system, without permission in writing from the publishers.

Notice:
Product or corporate names may be trademarks or registered trademarks, and are used only for identification and explanation without intent to infringe.

Publisher's Note
The publisher has gone to great lengths to ensure the quality of this reprint but points out that some imperfections in the original copies may be apparent.

Disclaimer
The publisher has made every effort to trace copyright holders and welcomes correspondence from those they have been unable to contact.

A Library of Congress record exists under LC control number: 00134806

ISBN 13: 978-1-138-74212-3 (hbk)
ISBN 13: 978-1-138-74211-6 (pbk)
ISBN 13: 978-1-315-18215-5 (ebk)

Contents

List of Figures		vii
List of Tables		viii
List of Abbreviations		xi

1 The Politics of the Digital Age: An Introduction   1

Part I: The Digital Revolution and Governance

2 'eEurope' and European Governance   19

3 Networked Governance for a 'Network Society'?   65

4 New Industrial Policy for the Digital Age: Informatisation and Development   93

Part II: Governance of the Digital Revolution

5 Chinese Politics Online: Implications of the Internet   137

6 Shaping the Screen: The Politics of Digital TV   171

7 Global Governance of Innovation: The Case of DVD   221

8 Conclusion   241

Bibliography   *249*
Index   *261*

List of Figures

Figure 2.1	Selected official documents of the European Commission for promoting the information society	38
Figure 3.1	Information society policy networks and EU regional policymaking	83
Figure 4.1	Mawei Police's application for approval to investigate the IP telephony case	125
Figure 4.2	Fujian Provincial Public Security Authority's authorisation for investigating the IP telephony case	126
Figure 6.1	News Corp.'s digital broadcasting empire	196
Figure 6.2	DVB organisational structure	200
Figure 6.3	Map of DVB worldwide adoption	202
Figure 7.1	The DVD Forum organisational structure	234
Figure 7.2	Map of DVD regional management code	236
Figure 7.3	DVD regional playback control code	236

List of Tables

Table 2.1	Trans-European Telecommunications Networks: proposals for a priority programme	27
Table 2.2	Merger decisions taken by the European Commission concerning the telecommunications sector (February 1995 – February 1998)	32
Table 2.3	Simplification/consolidation of EU legislation on ICTs	35
Table 2.4	Dates of the Europe Agreements and EU membership applications	49
Table 2.5	The economic gap – basic data: 1995	51
Table 2.6	The communications gap: The CEECs and Western Europe	53
Table 2.7	Average waiting time for a telephone line in the CEECs	54
Table 2.8	Computers (hosts) connected to the Internet per 1000 inhabitants	55
Table 2.9	Information society project starting date	57
Table 3.1	The European Regional Information Society Initiative: RISI and IRISI	74
Table 3.2	Membership of the TeleCities network	76

Table 3.3	Information society policy dissemination *via* new policy networks	79
Table 3.4	Multi-regional information society projects (RISI 2)	85
Table 3.5	Selected TeleCities information society projects with EU funding	86
Table 4.1	Government investment in telecommunications, Rmb billion	100
Table 4.2	National telephone exchange capacity	101
Table 4.3	Growth of telecommunications: 1980-1998	101
Table 4.4	China in the world league table: telephone lines and position	102
Table 4.5	Selected foreign firms in the Chinese ICT sector	103
Table 4.6	China's information superhighway: The 22 fibre trunk links (1991-95)	105
Table 4.7	The national grid of fibre optic cable links	106
Table 4.8	China's information superhighway: International links	107
Table 4.9	Administrative authorities of selected 'Golden Projects'	121
Table 5.1	Internet development in China: 1994-1999	141
Table 5.2	Major Internet Service Providers (ISPs) in China	141
Table 5.3	Growth of the ICT sector and GDP in China: 1980-1998	142
Table 5.4	China online: Internet users	143

Table 6.1	EU audiovisual policy on TV technologies and programme making	190
Table 6.2	DVB digital broadcasting standards	204
Table 6.3	Introduction of digital TV in the European Union	209

List of Abbreviations

3G	3rd Generation (mobile communication)
ADSL	Asynchronous Digital Subscriber Line
ADTV	Advanced Digital Television
AOL	America Online
ASkyB	American Sky Broadcasting
ATM	Asynchronous Transfer Mode (or Automatic Teller Machine)
ATRC	Advanced Television Research Consortium
ATSC	Advanced Television Systems Committee
BCP	Big Character Poster
BDB	British Digital Broadcasting
BIB	British Interactive Broadcasting
BSB	British Satellite Broadcasting
BSkyB	British Sky Broadcasting
BT	British Telecom
BTC	Bulgarian Telecommunications Company
C&W	Cable & Wireless
CASS	Chinese Academy of Social Sciences
CCIR	Consultative Committee for International Radio
CCP	Chinese Communist Party
CD	Compact Disc
CDA	Communications Decency Act
CD-i	Compact Disc interactive
CDP	China Democracy Party
CDTV	Compact Disc Total Vision
CEA	Consumer Electronics Manufacturers Association
CEECs	Central and East European Countries
CERNet	Chinese Education and Research Network
CIIED	Centre for the Chinese Information Infrastructure and Economic Development
CND	China News Digest

CNNIC	China Internet Network Information Centre
CNTWC	Chinese National Telecommunications Working Conference
COFDM	Coded Orthogonal Frequency Division Multiplexing
CRT	Cathode Ray Tube
CTV	Colour Television
DBS	Direct Broadcast by Satellite
DCC	Digital Compact Cassette
DTI	Department of Trade and Industry
dTTb	digital Terrestrial Television broadcasting
DVB	Digital Video Broadcasting
DVB-C	Digital Video Broadcasting-Cable
DVB-S	Digital Video Broadcasting-Satellite
DVB-T	Digital Video Broadcasting-Terrestrial
DVD	Digital Versatile Disc (or Digital Video Disc)
EBU	European Broadcasting Union
ECB	European Central Bank
EDI	Electronic Data Interchange
EDTV	Extended Definition TV
EEIG	European Economic Interest Grouping
EIB	European Investment Bank
ELG	European Launching Group
ERA	European Regulatory Authority
ERDF	European Regional Development Fund
eris@	European Regional Information Society Association
ESF	European Social Fund
ESIS	European Survey of the Information Society
ETSI	European Telecommunications Standard Institute
EU	European Union
EUMEDIS	Euro-Mediterranean Information Society Forum
FCC	Federal Communications Commission
FMPIC	Fuzhou Municipality People's Intermediate Court
FPD	Flat Panel Display
GDP	Gross Domestic Product
GI	General Instrument
GII	Global Information Infrastructure
GIS	Global Information Society

GSM	Global Standard for Mobile communications
HD-Divine	High Definition Digital Video Narrowband Emission
HD-MAC	High Definition Multiplexed Analogue Component
HDTV	High Definition Television
HEFCE	Higher Education Funding Council for England
HLGIS	High-Level Group on the Information Society
HSBC	the Hong Kong and Shanghai Bank Corporation
ICANN	Internet Corporation for Assigned Names and Numbers
ICP	Internet Contents Provider
ICT	Information and Communications Technology
IP	Internet Protocol
IRISI	Inter-Regional Information Society Initiative
ISAC	Information Society Activities Centre
ISDB-T	Integrated Services Digital Broadcasting-Terrestrial
ISDN	Integrated Services Digital Network
ISkyB	Indian Sky Broadcasting
ISP	Internet Service Provider
ISPO	Information Society Projects Office (or Information Society Promotion Office)
IT	Information Technology
ITC	Independent Television Commission
ITDLG	Information Technology Development Leading Group
ITU	International Telecommunications Union
JANet	Joint Academic Network
JCINE	Joint Conference for the Informatisation of the National Economy
JHLC	Joint High Level Committee
JSkyB	Japan Sky Broadcasting
LFR	Less Favoured Region
LSE	London Stock Exchange
MAC	Multiplexed Analogue Component
MBFT	Ministry of Broadcasting, Film and Television
MD	MiniDisc
MEI	Ministry of the Electronics Industry

MEP	Ministry of Electric Power
MII	Ministry of Information Industry
MITI	Ministry of International Trade and Industry
MMCD	Multimedia CD
MNC	Multinational Corporation
MOR	Ministry of the Railways
MPS	Ministry of Public Security
MPT	Ministry of Posts and Telecommunications
MPTB	Mawei Post and Telecommunications Bureau
MSS	Ministry of State Security
MUSE	Multiple Sub-nyquist Sampling Encoding
NHK	Nippon Hoso Kyokai (or Japan Broadcasting Corp.)
NIC	Newly Industrialised Country
NII	National Information Infrastructure
NPC	National People's Congress
NRA	National Regulatory Authority
NTL	National Transcommunications Limited
NTSC	National Television Systems Committee
Oftel	Office for Telecommunications
PAL	Phase Alteration by Line
PC	Personal Computer
PLA	People's Liberation Army
PSTN	Public Switched Telephone Network
PTA	Posts and Telecommunications Administration
RACE	Research on Advanced Communications for Europe
R&D	Research and Development
RIIT	Research Institute of Industrial Technologies
RISI	Regional Information Society Initiative
RISSG	Regional Information Society Steering Group
RISU	Regional Information Society Unit
Rmb	Renminbi
SAR	Special Administrative Region
SCIO	State Council Information Office
SCWA	State Commission for Wireless Administration
SD	Super Density disc
SDH	Synchronous Digital Hierarchy
SDI	Strategic Defence Initiative

SDTV	Standard Definition TV
SECAM	*Systèm Electronique Couleur avec Mémoire*
SIC	State Information Centre
simulcast	simultaneous broadcasting
SME	Small and Medium sized Enterprise
SPC	State Planning Commission
STB	set-top box
TENs	Trans-European Networks
TEN-Telecom	Trans-European Telecommunications Networks
TEU	Treaty of the European Union
UN	United Nations
VADIS	Video-Audio Digital Interactive System
VAT	Value Added Tax
VCR	Video Cassette Recorder
VoD	Video-on-Demand
WTO	World Trade Organisation
WWW	World Wide Web
Y2K	year 2000

1 The Politics of the Digital Age: An Introduction

The Digital Revolution and the Network Society

In the late 16th Century William Shakespeare wrote in *A Midsummer Night's Dream*, 'I'll put a girdle round about the earth in 40 minutes.'[1] Five hundred years on, the 'Midsummer Night's Dream' has been turned into a reality for an increasingly large number of human beings living on Planet Earth. Land-based fixed line telecommunications networks, satellite transponders above the earth, terrestrial transmission off the air and submarine fibre optical cables, etc., have been put into place to provide multidimensional and complementary means of real-time communication at any distance. Nowadays, it is a matter of time needed for striking a key on the computer keyboard or dialling destination number through the telephone handset, rather than '40 minutes' for electronic information and communication to 'girdle' round about the earth. With reliable networks, high-speeds make the entire globe immediately accessible and the notion of time and space has changed (Bakis, 1997). If Shakespeare lived today to witness the arrival of the digital age, he might have reconsidered the wording for his play.

It is a quantum leap forward from Shakespeare's age to the 21st Century in terms of advancement in communications technologies. However, this change did not happy over night. Rather, it represents a new milestone in the ceaseless pursuit of new means of communication by human beings.

The first major breakthrough in modern communications technologies is telegraphy. Using different combinations of dots and dashes to represent letters and numbers, the Morse Code, developed by Samuel Morse in the United States (US) in 1937, has led to the development of modern communications networks throughout the world. This was followed by a long list of information and communications technologies (ICTs) over the last two centuries. Among others, the invention of the Bell telephone system in 1876, the Marconi radio system in 1896 (patented in Britain), the beginning of television broadcasting in the 1920s, the success in building electronic computers in Germany, the US and Britain in the 1940s and the birth of the Internet in the late 1960s are some of the major milestones in the history of electronic and electronic communications technologies.

The digital revolution began with the digitisation[2] of the information and communications technologies and the wide application of digital techniques in other industrial sectors. The process of the digital revolution is in part manifested in the introduction of a variety of new information and communications systems. Among others, electronic mail (e-mail), the World Wide Web (WWW), multi-channel digital TV broadcasting, Digital Versatile Disc (DVD), Integrated Services Digital Network (ISDN), Asynchronous Digital Subscriber Line (ADSL) and the 3rd Generation (3G) mobile communications, etc., are typical examples. New acronyms representing a newer generation or of digital technologies and services are being invented at a much faster pace than the general public could digest what they actually standard for. In short, we now live in a world that has become digital (Negroponte, 1995).

The social impact of the digital revolution is profound and, to a certain extent, the contemporary society is heading towards total reliance upon digital technologies. In politics, the American Democratic Party in Arizona successfully held its online local election – voters used the computer keyboard to cast their votes in March 2000. The forthcoming London Mayor election in May 2000 was said to be assisted by computerised vote counting. An increasingly large number of governments – both democratic regimes and the totalitarian alike – are quick to recognise the potential of the Internet in enhancing their governance by launching 'government online' programmes. In economic policymaking, the British government recently claimed in its last 'Competitiveness White Paper'[3] that it would make Britain the best environment for electronic commerce (e-commerce) in the world. At the last European Union (EU) summit in Lisbon in March 2000, heads of the Member States reached a consensus over a new vision, which confirmed the 'Internet economy' would enable the EU to become the most competitive economy in the world. The Singaporean government has been endeavouring to turn the city-state into the 'IT (Information Technology) Hub' in South East Asia.

In the commercial world, the revolutionary role played by new ICTs is even more evident. First of all, it is the mushrooming phenomenon of the so-called 'dot-com' companies – the rapid increase of Internet companies throughout the world. The online bookseller Amazon, for instance, has become the largest bookstore in the world within a short space of time and is poised to render the conventional chains of outlets the dinosaurs of the printing age. Yahoo!, eBay, Freeserve, T-Online, World Online, etc, are just a few examples of a new breed of commercial Internet establishments, which are the recipients of large sums of venture capital investment. Time Warner, one of the largest media conglomerates in the world, could not resist the commercial power of the Internet and hence subjected itself to a merger deal with America Online (AOL) – a young Internet company.

Second, conventional companies, large and small, are either willingly or forced to reshape their corporate strategy with the Internet as a core element. Shortly after commenting on the 'dot-com' phenomenon as a 'hype', Rupert Murdoch, Chairman of News Corp., launched a new strategy to reform his global corporate empire with focus on the Internet. Food retailing stores, such as Tesco and ASDA in Britain, are finding the Internet an important and complementary channel for their business. Having been initially concerned with the possibility that online publishing could wipe out their paper-based news selling, newspapers (both national and local ones) are now among the fast movers to digitally duplicate themselves and most of their Web versions are free to access.

Undoubtedly, for some, the digital revolution produces enormous benefits. Among others, barriers, such as geographical distance, to human communication is being removed; 'paperless office' has been promised; transparent and more efficient government could be created; global democratisation and capitalist mode of production could be promoted in the digital age. Further, the digital revolution even comes to the rescue when politicians in many industrialised countries are bewildered by the thorny issues of unemployment and poverty relief. Seemingly, digital information and communications technologies provide powerful solutions to many social and economic problems. During a visit to the recent Comdex computer trade show, US President Bill Clinton expressed his belief that the information economy holds the key to solving his country's problems:

> I came here today to ask you to set another trend – to devote more time and technology, more ideas and energy, to closing the digital divide. I honestly believe that the new information economy has the potential, at home and around the world, to lift more people out of poverty more quickly than at any previous period in all of human history – and that tapping that potential is actually in our enlightened self-interest.[4]

However, the digital revolution is rolling out at a price. Whilst new ICTs are creating new businesses and new jobs, they are also 'deleting' jobs. The restructuring of the banking sector in Britain is a typical example of this dilemma. On a single day, April 7, 2000, the Barclays Bank closed 171 branches in the rural areas of Britain, representing a downsizing by one tenth of its branch network. In a comparable scale, the National Westminster Bank has cut the size of its network from 3,086 in 1988 to about 1,712 and the Midland Bank, now part of the Hong Kong and Shanghai Bank Corporation (HSBC), has seen its branch network shrink from 2,090 in 1988 to about 1,622. In answering questions during recent media interviews, the Barclays management repeatedly cited the fast growth in telephone banking and Internet-based online banking as the primary reasons for the branch closure:

> Five years ago we had no telephone banking. Two years ago we had no online banking. Can I imagine a future where customers are using the telephone and the internet much more[?] Yes. ... If that continues to gather pace then I can't sit there and ignore it. It would be irresponsible of me to close my eyes to evidence of customer change and shut off the possibility of further closures.[5]

The Barclays affair coincided with the widely discussed Rover case. When BMW, the German parent company of Rover, disclosed its plan in March 2000 to sell off its loss-making Rover branch, the Department of Trade and Industry showed deep concern and exercised direct intervention in an attempt to 'save' the unfortunate Rover business. It is still too early to say whether the government intervention is effective or not. In contrast, in the case of the Barclays branch closure and, indeed, the radical restructuring of the overall banking sector, the British government appeared to be powerless to do anything. In the end of the day, the downsizing of the banking sector in Britain is a child born from the marriage between the new ICTs and market forces. There is perhaps hardly any role which the government could play in this marriage.

The world in which we live today is becoming increasingly reliant upon the normal functioning of digital technologies. Prior to the last change of millennium, literally every part of the world and every aspect of life, from western industrialised countries to developing nations with hardly any exception, had been subject to a common threat: the 'millennium bug' or the 'year 2000 (Y2K)' problem.[6] Fortunately, the world entered into the 21st Century without experiencing widespread disasters caused by the 'millennium bug'. However, the 'Y2K' scare does demonstrate the great extent to which our society relies upon information and communications technologies. As a matter of fact, in addition to the wide use of computers, silicon chips nowadays have been almost universally 'embedded' into other machines and equipment. Children's toys, consumer audiovisual machines, domestic appliances, cars, aircraft, mobile telephone handsets and telephone switches, nuclear weapon control systems and so forth, are all built with computer chips inside them.

Whether we like it or not, the way we live today is already significantly characterised by digitisation. Those who wish to retreat into the woods might be surprised to find that the woods are rapidly disappearing. The *Far Eastern Economic Review* recently reported that the cyberspace[7] has become the meeting place of choice for growing numbers of Korean youngsters who now can not imagine life without e-mail and mobile phones. They are called the 'N-generation', or 'Net-generation', and there is a whole new business and political culture building up around them.[8]

What seems to be a fundamental dilemma faced by individuals, organisations and government policy makers is the necessity to use new ICTs and the difficulties to keep the same technologies under full control. Whilst digital technologies can be used to improve productivity and create convenience, there is always a possibility that the same technologies could strike back against the will of their users or become uncontrollable. It is a common knowledge that almost all financial markets nowadays exist only on computer screens and stock transactions are executed on computer keyboards. On April 5, 2000, the London Stock Exchange (LSE) experienced the worst meltdown in its history and traders were unable to deal for almost eight hours. The halt of the LSE was caused solely by a computer breakdown. The apparent weakness in London's computerised trading system has led to speculation that the German market authorities will take a lead in the proposed merger between the LSE and the Frankfurt stock exchange, a move that could undermine London's status as Europe's pre-eminent financial centre.[9]

The proliferation of new information and communications technologies and their socio-economic impact have become an important area of academic research over the last few years. Among others, a growing number of political scientists, political economists, sociologists, human geographers, specialists in cultural studies and management studies, etc., are trying to define the nature and impact the digital revolution might have pertinent to their own subject area.

The outcome of the digital revolution, as suggested by some writers (e.g., Castells, 1996; van Dijk, 1999), is the so-called 'network society'. Castells argues that, as a historical trend, 'dominant functions and processes in the information age are increasingly organised around networks' and 'networks constitute the new social morphology of our societies' (1996, p. 469). However, 'the basic elements of the *network society* are not so much networks themselves but individuals, households, groups and organisations *linked by these networks*' (van Dijk, 1999, p. 24). Meanwhile, a plethora of similar terms have also been used by academics and policymakers to depicted the revolutionary impact of digital technologies. Among others, such concepts as 'information society', 'information economy', 'informational society', 'digital economy', 'post-industrial society', etc., appear often in the literature. Leonard (1999) argues that, compared with network organisations, hierarchical organisations are ill-equipped to deal with the political and economic demands that globalisation and technological change are forcing upon us.[10]

The phenomenon 'networking' can not be said new. Rather, the invention of every new information and communications technology system adds a new layer dimension of technical networking for storing, processing and disseminating information and communications data (e.g., telegraph networks, telephone networks, TV and radio broadcasting networks and the Internet). What seems new is the pervasive networking effect various digital technologies have produced, which is apparently transforming our society in terms of politics and power, economic and business life, education, law, social structure, media and cultural changes. On top of the fast spread of physical and technological networks of digital communications, individuals and organisations are beginning to wake up to the great potential these networks can offer them and the likelihood of being disadvantaged if they were excluded from the emergent network society.

It is worth mentioning that, although participation by individual users and public sector organisations is growing, the emergent network society is already being characterised by commercialisation in terms of building, controlling and large-scale usage of the new communications networks by the private business sector.

In March 2000 three giant American motor companies, General Motors (GM), Ford and DaimlerChrysler (DC) announced plans to join forces to create a single automotive-parts exchange run through the Internet, the Detroit Exchange. It is expected that many other major motor companies, such as Toyota, Honda, Nissan and Renault, will join the online venture. When launched, the GM-Ford-DC Detroit Exchange will create a centralised online marketplace with a global reach. It is anticipated that the Exchange could handle business worth at least $240 billion a year on the millions of parts needed for building a car and as much as $1 trillion if it becomes a global standard.[11] Optimists estimate that the enhanced efficiency of the motor industry, thanks to the Detroit Exchange, could reduce the costs of new vehicles to consumers by up to $2000 each vehicle. The Detroit Exchange is a typical example of major business organisations taking the advantage of new communications technologies to create networks among themselves to reduce costs and maximise profit making.

Following the Detroit Exchange initiative, six major airlines, including British Airways, American Airlines, Air France, Continental Airlines, Delta Airlines and United Airlines, jointly announced in April 2000 that they would launch a worldwide electronic marketplace in a month's time. The proposed electronic marketplace is designated to handle about $32 billion worth of the six airlines' annual procurement.[12]

In April 2000, Merrill Lynch and Hong Kong and Shanghai Bank Corporation Holdings, two of the world's leading financial groups, have joined forces to create a global online banking and investment services company to serve individual customers across the world. Backed by 24-hour call centres and offices in key geographical locations, the Merrill Lynch-HSBC joint venture will offer customers access from different countries the convenience of online banking and investment services.[13] The new Merrill Lynch-HSBC online deposit account will be launched later in the year 2000 in Britain, Australia, Canada, Germany, Hong Kong and Japan. Other countries will follow later. The big financial institutions have been one of the leading forces behind globalisation by moving capitals across national borders. By collectively building their online financial service networks, these financial institutions, such as Merrill Lynch and HSBC, have virtually eliminated national borders.

Undoubtedly, the large-scale commercial initiatives, such as those proposed by the automotive sector, the airline sector and the banking sector, could substantially transform the nature of global commerce. The launch of these global business networks would also add new features to the development of the network society.

Technology and Governance[14]

Apparently the digital revolution is a significant factor contributing to societal changes. Many believe that changes in technology have always been an important component in the progress of human societies (Coombs, Saviotti and Walsh, 1987). Regarding the relationship between technology and governance, it is argued that technological innovation plays an important role in establishing, transforming, or maintaining states or societies at the macro-level:

> More recently in the United States one role of new technologies has been to provide grounds for the growth of the federal government, through the proliferation of such agencies as the Federal Communications Commission for regulating telecommunications, the Federal Aviation Administration for regulating the airline industry, the Nuclear Regulatory Commission and the Department of Energy for administering aspects of national energy production and nuclear weapons development, and the like (Sclove, 1995, p. 16).

The same trend is also evident in other parts of the world. The digital revolution has in part prompted the European Commission to take the view that each Member State of the European Union should appoint a new minister with responsibilities for the information society and, accordingly, a special Council of Ministers could be formed at the EU level (Bangemann et al, 1994). The British government, among others, has subsequently appointed an 'e-Envoy' for the Prime Minister and an 'e-Minister'. In addition, the European Commission has recently restructured its internal administration by re-naming Directorate-General XIII as the 'Information Society' directorate. During a recent State Council restructuring, the Chinese government has created a 'super-ministry', i.e., the Ministry of Information Industry, to regulate the overall ICT sector. At the global level, despite the absence of a 'world government', the establishment of new organisations, such as the ICANN (Internet Corporation for Assigned Names and Numbers), would certainly help add a new dimension, i.e., global governance of new technologies, to the process of international politics.

Whilst high hopes are being attached to the new digital media in terms of promoting democratisation and facilitating political change, some argue that the arrival of the Internet age will not substantially change the current power structure:

> Rather than acting as revolutionary tool rearranging political power and instigating direct democracy, the Internet is destined to become dominated by the same actors in American politics who currently utilize other mediums. Undoubtedly, public expression will become more common and policy makers will be expected to respond hastily. But the mobilization of public expression will still largely be the creation of groups and individuals who currently dominate the political landscape (Davis, 1999, p. 5).

In the late 19th Century and early 20th Century, the British Empire (and, indeed, other European Empires) promoted and in part funded the construction of international cable networks to facilitate communication between the Empire headquarters and the colonies. Whilst the level of efficiency in governance within the Empire might have been improved due to the use of telegraphic services, the new communications networks alone were not sufficient to keep the Empire together.

State planners in the former Soviet Union did have deployed computer systems to help improve planning efficiency in the 1970s. However, technologies proved far from being a panacea:

> Soviet authorities knew that hierarchical planning led to rigidity and that the

increasingly diverse range of products required not only great flexibility but also more rapid responses by planning agencies. ... The solution, obviously, was computers to speed response and improve the interaction of parallel systems. In 1971 the Party Congress authorised the creation of an 'All-State System for the Collection and Processing of Information for Reporting, Planning and Management of the National Economy', and in 1973 a reorganisation of the central ministries was proposed to facilitate the task of central data processing. However, computerisation of economic planning encountered the same problems which bewildered the economy itself. ... Managers of enterprises at all levels remained unenthusiastic; computerisation did not promise them any tangible rewards but did promise more effective surveillance of their performance – which might hamper their efforts to achieve results with unauthorised or illegal methods (Tipton and Aldrich, 1987, p. 250).

In the Soviet case, computerisation has failed to help solve the fundamental problems associated with central economic planning. Eventually, the Soviet empire as a whole collapsed by the end of the 1980s. In China, communications technologies, such as telephone, TV and radio broadcasting networks and, more recently, the Internet, etc., have been gradually introduced to the public, but the communist totalitarian regime has managed to stay in control throughout. In other words, the technological revolution has not led to the demise of dictatorship, not to mention establishing direct democracy.

In a way comparable with the Soviet case, the present Chinese leadership introduced a major programme on the Informatisation of the National Economy in the early 1990s – using new information and communications technologies to overcome the inefficiency in economic planning and boost national economic development.[15] Would computerised economic governance in the digital age help preserve the centralised planning system, which was created by the communist revolution in China? Given the disastrous Soviet experience, there would be challenges associated with the digital way towards economic development in countries such as China.

In general, technological determinists argue that communication technology is fundamental to society; the sequence of invention and application of communication technology influences social change; and communication revolutions lead to social revolutions (see McQuail, 2000).

As for the societal effects, it is true that some people find in communication technologies 'new ways to commit crime, initiate romance or make a fast buck – age-old human tendencies that are all too often blamed on the technologies themselves' (Standage, 1998 p. 2). Indeed, the rise of the network society has brought with it new challenges for law-enforcement. New types of cyber crimes such as terrorism, money laundering and computer hacking are poised to by-pass the scrutiny of conventional legal authorities at the national state level. The potentially destructive nature of computers and the Internet, for instance, was recently highlighted by Vladimir Zhirinovsky, the nationalist politician in Russia:

> The era of detective stories and James Bond has long been over. Now there is a different era – the era of computers and the Internet. And we can bring the entire West to its knees with our Russian computer specialists. Let us put viruses into their secret programs like we did recently, and they will not be able to do anything.[16]

Meanwhile, optimists are convinced of the long-term revolutionary role that digital technologies could play. 'While it [the digital age] might be evolutionary, in the sense that all changes and benefits will not appear overnight, it will be revolutionary' (Kranzberg, 1985, p. 52, quoted in Castells, 1996, p. 29).

Governance of New Technologies

The advancement of new information and communications technologies (ICTs), which is necessary for achieving fast communications, is coupled with the question of who controls the process of technical change and whether this process is controllable.

On 3rd April 2000, US District Judge Thomas Penfield Jackson released his 'conclusions of the law', which ruled that the world's largest software house Microsoft violated antitrust law[17] in maintaining its monopoly power by anti-competitive means and attempted to monopolise the Web browser market. On the technical side, Judge Jackson's ruling would potentially tip the balance between the two rival Web browsers: Microsoft's Internet Explorer and Netscape Communication's (now owned by America Online) Navigator/Communicator. In order to be able to 'surf' the World Wide Web, Internet users would normally have to use one of the two competing Web browsers. Therefore, the competition between the two browsers is essentially a fight for controlling the 'gateway' to the online world. In the courtroom, however, the 'Plaintiff' was the United States of America (represented by the Department of Justice) and 19 states and the 'Defendant' was Microsoft Corporation. To a certain extent, this is a highly politicised case – the power of the Federal and sate authorities against a single commercial organisation, i.e., Microsoft. One of the important implications of this case is the question of who should control the digital age: the state authorities or the commercial organisations. Whilst the commercial organisations (e.g. Microsoft and Netscape) are fighting against each other for controlling new communications technologies and communications networks,[18] the state authorities and individual citizens are also trying to define their role.

A classical Marxian view about the relationship between technology and the society is primarily that the development of technologies is determined by a 'social formation' or a range of 'social needs' (Marx, 1976). To Marx, technology is a commodity, which is of use value to satisfy various social needs. Schumpeter (1942) sees technical change and innovation as a force of 'creative destruction', which will eventually demise the social institutions of the capitalist society.

As far as the governance of technical change is concerned, the state is often viewed as an important player. In the history of telecommunications and broadcasting, a prominent role has been assumed by the states and that is mainly content regulation and ensuring universal service. Proponents of an expanded role for government argue that just as government has sponsored, managed, and funded the development of the economic infrastructure (e.g., roads and schools), so in this post-industrial information age, government should support the communications infrastructure (Gasman, 1994). Some place the role of the state at the centre of the relationship between technology and the society:

> What must be retained for the understanding of the relationship between technology and society is that the role of the state, by either stalling, unleashing, or leading technological innovation, is a decisive factor in the overall process, as it expresses and organizes the social and cultural forces that dominate in a given space and time. To a large extent, technology expresses the ability of a society to propel itself into technological mastery through the institutions of society, including the state (Castells, 1996, p. 13).

In some domains of the ICT sector, the state has evidently 'extended' its power since the 1980s. State subsidies, for instance, have been used widely to promote the so-called strategic technologies including certain aspects of new ICTs in many industrialised countries. Among others, the European Commission proposed a European strategy for the electronics industry that would have included EU-funded programmes to develop semiconductor processing equipment and an advanced European communications network. This has led to the beginning of a new wave of inter-European collaboration *via* research and development (R&D) programmes such as ESPRIT, RACE, BRITE and EUREKA (Alic, 1990). More recently, the EU has designated a substantial proportion of its Fifth Framework Programme budget to support the development and usage of user-friendly information society technologies.[19] In the US, the Clinton administration proposed a budget of $17 billion to support the development of a national information superhighway (Dai, 1996).

Mosco (1996) differentiates between 'state regulation' and 'market regulation' and claims that the weakening of one form of regulation might lead to the increase of the opposite:

> Political economy takes the entire social field, including the pattern of industry activity, as a form of regulation. For example, a social field primarily influenced by industry decisions, rather than by state intervention, can be characterized as a form of *market regulation*, as opposed to *state regulation*, which takes place when government plays the prominent role. [...] Eliminating government regulation is not deregulation but, most likely, expanding market regulation (p. 201).

The outcomes of both 'state regulation' and 'market regulation' over technical change will be examined in this book. In addition, driven in part by the digital communications revolution the process of globalisation provides a new opportunity for multinational companies, such as those in the automotive sector, to form strategic alliances across national borders and collectively manipulate the course of technical change and innovation. Global and international alliances among multinational firms have become an important factor to the governance of new technologies. However, an associated challenge posed by these corporate alliances is the fact that the conventional forms of state authorities have been by-passed but international regimes are either lacking or insufficient to cope with the changed international environment. In other words, the rise of global capitalism has not been met with strengthened international coordination in terms of regulation.

New communications networks, such as the Internet, are global systems but they are either subject to regulation at the national government level in some countries or under no regulation whatsoever in others. Given the global process of information flow facilitated by the Internet technology, the Chinese government has recently set up the Internet Information Management Bureau (IIMB) under the direct control by the State Council Information Office. The primary mission of the new IIMB is to regulate news provision on the Internet.[20]

Many new technologies, such as digital TV and DVD (Digital Versatile Disc), are global technologies and controlled by different groups of global corporate alliances (e.g. the Digital Video Broadcasting Group and the DVD Forum respectively). Allied corporate organisations are in many cases dictating the global agenda for innovation and the national government in individual countries is not well equipped to cope with this process.[21]

Now that governments and regulators tried and failed to control the new medium of the 19th Century (i.e., the worldwide network of cable telegraphy, Standage, 1998), are the world's national governments of the 21st Century today better positioned and better equipped to cope with the digital revolution? It remains to be seen.

The Design of the Book

Despite the publication of many volumes over the last few years dealing with the socio-economic impact of new information and communications technologies, there are still many gaps in the literature. This is in part due to the constantly changing process of technological innovation on the one hand and fast evolving social process (e.g. organisational changes, government policy changes and regulatory changes) in response to the new technical environment on the other. It is widely recognised that, in the information age, there is a critical need to demystify the political economy of communications (Sussman, 1997). The purpose of this book is to investigate the interplay between the ongoing changes in digital technologies and governance. From mainly a political economist perspective, this book will, firstly, discuss what opportunities the global digital revolution has brought with it for new modes of governance. Secondly, it will address the issue of who governs the process of digital revolution and how the process of technical change is managed. Accordingly, the book is organised into two Parts: Part I on the impact of the digital revolution on governance and Part II on the governance of the digital revolution itself.

In order to achieve the above objectives, discussions presented in the book are largely based on empirical research centred on two sets of case studies. The first set of cases includes the European Union and China, which is part of the western industrialised countries and developing countries respectively. By studying the experiences of the EU and China it will be revealed whether the digital revolution can have a profound impact on the current power structure and policymaking in these countries. Meanwhile, through these cases it will be shown to what extent the key political actors in both the industrialised world and the developing countries are aware of the potential of technical change and whether they are being actively engaged in manipulating the new technology revolution to the advantage of their economic and political governance.

More specifically, within Part I, Chapter 2 discusses about the extent to which the digital revolution has affected the polity and power structure inside the European Union since the early 1990s, when the EU began to mobilise the development of the European information society. This chapter is focused on the relationship between the EU's information society programme and the much-debated process of European integration (in terms of 'deepening' and 'widening' of the Union). Further to this discussion, Chapter 3 investigates whether the European politics is already being characterised by 'networked governance' in the information age. Major policy networks established under the EU's information society programme are analysed.

In contrast with the European experience, Chapter 4 extents the horizon of the book to the developing nations. The case study about China in Chapter 4 reveals the great enthusiasm of the Chinese government in devising new industrial policies to govern national economic development in the digital age. Altogether, these three chapters, i.e., Chapters 2, 3 & 4, provide new evidence for our understanding about the pertinence of the digital revolution to governance at a global level – encompassing the experiences of both the industrialised countries and developing countries.

The second set of cases in Part II of the book covers three important areas of the digital revolution: the Internet, digital TV and Digital Versatile Disc dealt with in three chapters, i.e., Chapters 5, 6 & 7 respectively. By analysing the ways these technologies were manipulated, the case studies will shed some light on our understanding of how the innovation process and new technologies are manipulated and what consequences this process might produce.

Among others, major players contributing to the governance of the digital revolution examined in this book include government forces (as manifested in policies and regulations), international business organisations (e.g. multinational firms and the alliances among them) and individual political activists (e.g. pro-democracy and human rights campaigners and their organisations).

With a focus on the Internet, Chapter 5 will show the different, and also confrontational, ways the Chinese government and dissident groups use the global communications network for their political purposes. It seems that, in a developing country such as China, the potential of innovative technologies (e.g. the Internet) as a means of advancing economic development is often compromised by the ruling regime's concern over losing political control. Although the Chinese case is unique in many ways, the fight for controlling the digital information highway does demonstrate two opposing views at the global level with regard to the Internet technology: the two voices in favour of and against state regulation.

Moving into the case of new TV technologies (including High Definition TV and digital TV systems), Chapter 6 questions the effectiveness of government regulation in promoting innovation *vis-à-vis* market forces.

Instead of simply rejecting the government intervention approach, Chapter 7 analyses the outcomes of manipulating the course of innovation by allied forces of commercial organisations at the global level in the absence of any government regulation. The empirical basis of the discussion presented in Chapter 7 is the global standardisation for DVD, which is another domain of the current digital revolution.

This book comes to an end in Chapter 8, in which some concluding remarks are offered regarding the politics of the digital revolution.

Notes

1. Shakespeare, W., *A Midsummer Night's Dream*, II.I.
2. Digitisation, according to *The Oxford Interactive Encyclopedia* (developed by The Learning Company, Inc., 1997), is the production of information recorded as a succession of discrete units, rather than as continuously varying (analog) parameters. Digital systems most often record information in binary code, using only two states: one and zero.
3. Department of Trade and Industry (1998a), *Our Competitive Future: Create a Knowledge Driven Economy*, 16 December.
4. *The New York Times*, 19 April 2000.
5. John Varley, Barclays' director of retail banking, cited in the *Financial Times*, 12 April 2000. Note that Barclays currently has 1.2m telephone banking customers and 800,000 online accounts – up from 20,000 a year ago.
6. In order to save memory space, computer engineers in the 1970s and early 1980s developed computer programmes using only two digits, instead of the full four digits, to describe a year. For instance, '79' was used rather than '1979'. It was widely believed that the change of millennium, i.e., from 1999 to 2000, would likely cause major problems throughout the world due to the failure of computers in recognising the year '00'. To many computers, the year '00' could be 2000 or 1900.
7. The concept 'cyberspace' was first used by William Gibson in his novel *Neuromancer* (1984, Gollancz, London). In *Neuromancer*, 'cyberspace' is a 'dataspace', a vast 'world in the wires' known as 'the matrix', where transnational companies trade in information in a visual, Cartesian and electronic space (Kitchin, R., 1998, p. 2). Kitchin (1998) argues that 'cyberspace' can generally be divided into three domains, i.e., the Internet, intranets and virtual reality. Perhaps extranet should be included as well.
8. *Far Eastern Economic Review*, 20 April 2000, Vol. 163 No. 16, http://www.feer.com/tw.html.
9. *The Guardian*, 6 April 2000.
10. Leonard (1999) suggests that the EU should be understood as a 'network Europe' rather than an out-of-date hierarchical structure or an ineffective free trade area. He argues that, 'Networks don't figure prominently in political theory, but we all benefit from them in our everyday lives – in friendships, clubs, churches, trade unions, political parties or the Internet. These networks are not planned by a central authority

11. – they arise from the interactions of decentralised actors. The rules and order that govern them depend on reciprocal relationships, shared values and common identity rather than a rigid hierarchy' (1999, p. 21).
11. *From Bricks to Clicks: Big Business Goes Online*, *The Guardian* supplement, April 2000.
12. *The Times*, 28 April 2000. Among others, BA planned to increase procurement orders from its goods and services suppliers handled over the Internet from 25% at the moment to 80% by March 2002.
13. See *Financial Times*, 19 April 2000.
14. The term 'governance', according to *The Oxford Interactive Encyclopedia* (developed by The Learning Company, Inc., 1997), refers to 1) the action, manner, or fact of governing; Controlling or regulating influence; the state of being governed; 2) the function or power of governing; authority to govern; 3) conduct of life or business.
15. See Chapter 4 for more detailed discussion.
16. Quoted in *Washington Post*, 9 May 2000. The recent computer virus attack by the 'ILOVEYOU' bug has indeed crippled millions of computers throughout the world. This suggests that Vladimir Zhirinovsky's remarks might not be entirely groundless propaganda stuff.
17. Namely, the Sherman Antitrust Act.
18. The auction of radio spectrum for the next generation of mobile phones, the so-called 3G communications, in Britain is a typical example. The British auction finally raised £22.5 billion on 27 April 2000, several times the amount originally expected by the British government. It is not difficult to understand why the bidders – exclusively commercial companies – wanted to secure a victory in the bidding process at whatever price: holding a licence in the 3G communications sector over the next 20 years would likely lead to a competitive advantage. The right to build the next generation of communications network is widely believed strategically important for a communications company in the network society. The winning bidders for the five 3G licences are Vodafone Airtouch, BTCellnet, one2one (now owned by Deutsche Telekom), Orange and TIW (Telesystem International Wireless, a Canadian mobile phone operator, with major financial backing from Hutchison Whampoa headed by Li Ka-Shing). Britain is the first European country to auction off its airwaves.
19. For more details regarding the EU's technology policy on the information society, see Chapter 2.
20. See *The New York Times*, 21 April 2000. Popular Chinese portals such as Sina.com, Sohu.com and Netease.com were banned by the Chinese government in early 2000 from running foreign news on their sites.
21. A large number of transatlantic strategic alliances and mergers have taken place involving American and European companies in the telecommunications sector. In most cases these alliances and mergers were subject to the scrutiny of the Federal government in the US and the European Commission in Europe. However, the approval process on the two sides of the Atlantic is independent of each other. In addition, the major concern of both the US government and the European Commission is the potentially anti-competitive impact of these alliances. As for the global technological alliances, it is often 'market regulation' taking effect and 'state regulation' is very much marginalised, if any. The European Commission has, indeed, called for strengthened international coordination over the Internet but there is hardly any progress so far.

PART I
THE DIGITAL REVOLUTION AND GOVERNANCE

2 'eEurope' and European Governance

Introduction

The information society is an outcome of the rapid development in new information and communications technologies (ICTs). Based on digital techniques new ICTs are bringing about a new industrial revolution throughout the world, which is no less significant and far-reaching in any sense than the other industrial revolutions of the past. New ICTs, as promised, will enable us to access, process and communicate digitised information unconstrained by space, time and volume in an interactive way. In addition to their impact on many other social and societal changes, new ICTs are widely regarded as a strategic technological domain contributing to long-term economic growth and national competitiveness.

The information society, as an idea, is not entirely new. It has its roots in the literature of 'postindusrialism' which was popular in social science studies of the 1960s and 1970s and heralded the end of the industrial capitalism era and the arrival of a 'service' or 'leisure' society (Lyon, 1995). Some writers describe the information society as the era of societal development which is dominated by an 'informational mode' of production' (Castells, 1989) or 'digital economy' (Tapscott, 1996) or 'informatisation' of the socio-economic process (Dordic and Wang, 1993). Due to the fact that the ICT revolution has dramatically increased the reliance of all types of social organisations on the intermediation of new information and communications networks and, therefore, the lapse of conventional sense of time and space, the information society can be called a 'network society' (Castells, 1996). A key aspect of the ICT revolution is the pervasive nature of digitisation – a technical process of turning all types of source information in analogue form into computer readable codes, i.e., different combinations of '1s' and '0s' (binary code). The outcome of digitisation is the so-called 'convergence' – previously separated sectoral domains such as media, information and communication are now integrated into a single technological and industrial sector (Baldwin, McVoy and Steinfield, 1996). The emergence of the network society driven by digitisation/informatisation and convergence poses unprecedented challenge to the traditional way of governance. On the other hand, it also promises opportunities for exploring and developing new modes of governance.

What seems new, and insufficiently studied and analysed, is the wakening up of government in industrialised and developing countries to the ICT revolution and the information society since the early 1990s. Increasingly, the information society has become an important aspect of government policy making in a large number of countries. Consequently, a strong link between the information society and governance has been established and this deserves more attention from the academic community than it is given at the moment. Following the lead by the Clinton/Gore administration in launching the National Information Infrastructure (NII) programme in the US, the European Union (EU) has adopted a range of new policies dedicated to promoting the development of the information society in Europe since the early 1990s. Compared to any other major technological programme sponsored by the EU in the past, the scale and scope of the current European policies towards creating an information society in Europe is unprecedented.

In parallel with the policies at the EU level, most EU Member States have adopted similar policy measures to promote the development of the information society within their own countries. Moreover, the information society has also been identified as a new opportunity as well as a challenge by many local government authorities at the regional and municipality levels in Europe. It can be said that, to a great extent, the process of information society development is facilitated by a bold 'policy push' approach. The paramount objective behind this 'policy push' approach is to achieve in part the ultimate European ideal of integration; and that is to build an ever closer community in Europe.

There are many complicated and important issues related to the information society currently under public debate. This chapter aims to investigate the 'policy push' approach adopted in Europe and examine the extent to which such policies have contributed to strengthening the process of European integration. In order to achieve this, the chapter firstly discusses the global context and reviews the policy process associated with the development of the information society in Europe. Secondly, the chapter looks into the European initiative to develop a 'Common Information Area'. Thirdly, a large part of this chapter is devoted to the discussion about the relationship between the information society and European governance. Finally, implications for European integration will be drawn upon the development of a 'virtual Europe' or 'government online'. More specifically, such important questions will be asked as: In what global context did the European 'policy push' approach for the information society come into force? Why is the information society a European issue? What is the European solution and how effective is it? Does the development of the information society herald a new era of policymaking at the European level, and what implications can be drawn upon this process for the study of European integration? How realistic and significant is it for the central and east European countries to become a part of the 'Common Information Area', if they wish to join the European Union club?

It is claimed that the 'information society is a means to achieve so many of the Union's objectives. We have to get it right, and get it right now'.[1] For instance, among others, 'Europe's main handicaps are the fragmentation of the various markets and the lack of interoperable links. To overcome them it is necessary to mobilize resources and channel endeavours at European level in a partnership between the public and private sectors'.[2] In short, the EU is determined to embrace the opportunities offered by the information age.

Europe and the Global Information Society

The European vision on the information society was set in a global context of the early 1990s with the assumption that Europe was competing directly with other nations such as the USA and Japan for technological leadership in the information age. The European Commission suggests the pattern of global development in the information age is one similar to that in the industrial age:

> Some aspects of this new society are already being put into place; many people are beginning to reap the benefit. Naturally, these changes will be led by the Triad powers first, but will gradually extend to the rest of the planet.[3]

The American way towards the information society was initially centred on the development of a national information superhighway system, later known as the National Information Infrastructure (NII). Leading politicians in the US claimed that, '[m]ost important, we need a commitment to build the high-speed data highways. Their absence constitutes the largest single barrier to realizing the potential of the information age'.[4] The American vision has, among others, the following core elements:

- The rapid development of new ICTs and the dissemination of electronic information has led to the creation of a new civilisation;
- To realise the full benefit of the information age, a national information superhighway (interconnected high-speed networks to tie together millions of computers;
- It used to be that a nation's transportation infrastructure determined success in international economic competition; today the determining factor is a nation's ability to move information digitally and to increase the value of this information on the new information infrastructure;
- It will be up to the policymakers to determine how best to build a universal and high-speed network;
- Public policy can make a difference in the key areas of the computer revolution; it is policy that can determine whether a nation can reap the benefits of new ICTs;
- However, public policy lags behind technology;
- Government leadership is needed to provide direction and coordination;
- Government investment and leadership will produce the power to leverage more investment from the private sector; without government funding a country would end up with a balkanised system consisting of incompatible parts;[5]
- The US must move first – ahead of other nations.

The 'American vision' seems to have, to a certain extent, influenced the European way of thinking. This influence is evident in, for example, the Delors White paper:

> The government decisions taken in the USA and Japan aim at organizing and speeding up the process, by supporting companies' efforts. The emphasis has been on establishment of the basic infrastructure and support for new applications and technological development'. ... This process [the dawning of

the multimedia age] has already started in the USA, where it is giving birth to unprecedented partnerships and mergers between companies. It will gain ground in Europe. It is forcing the public authorities to review the regulatory framework.[6]

In some key aspects, as shown later in this chapter, the characteristics of the European policies on the information society are comparable to those of the 'American vision'.

It is worth noting that, whilst European technology (and industrial) policy has had a positive impact on the course of European integration (e.g. the decisions on and management of research and development, or R&D, at the European level; the transformation of many 'national champions' into 'European champions', etc.), many aspects of it were not as successful or effective as they had been intended. This has led to a change of policy and strategy at the European level from mainly promoting indigenous high technologies represented by large companies to a much broader approach, i.e., advocating the application of new technologies by all quarters of the society, in particular the small and medium sized enterprises (SMEs). What has remained unchanged is the long-standing European endeavour to promote the so-called 'European competitiveness' – a concept which is sometimes regarded as a 'dangerous obsession' by some economists.[7]

European technology policy before the early 1990s was orientated towards identifying and supporting strategic technologies in the belief that ownership in these technologies would gain competitive advantage for Europe over its trading partners who did not have these technologies. As large companies are more likely to have the technical capacity for being engaged in the process of hi-tech R&D, it was these companies that were the main beneficiaries of European financial support in literally all of the major European technology programmes. The uneven spread of the major indigenous companies in Europe has certainly added frustration to the process of consensus building among the member states in deciding which technologies should be supported and at what scale.[8]

With the publication of the 1993 Delors White Paper, the EU authorities began to emphasise on societal needs as a basic starting point for designing technology policies and the new focus is on fighting unemployment and protecting the environment.[9] The European authorities have now come to the conclusion that SMEs are equally, if not more, important to improving European competitiveness as they provide the majority of jobs within the EU.[10] Accordingly, current EU policy is more geared towards encouraging, facilitating and helping SMEs to use new technologies for expanding and strengthening their businesses so that more jobs can be created. A specific example demonstrating this change of EU policy towards new technologies is the contrast between the Fifth and Fourth Framework Programmes. Whilst the Fourth Framework Programme supports the development of new information and communications technologies with a substantial proportion (26%) of the overall budget (€13.1 billion), the Fifth Framework Programme was changed to foster the development of a 'user-friendly information society' with comparable proportion (24%) of the total budget (€14.9 billion).

A potential benefit of the EU's modified technology policy lies in that the process for consensus building among the Member States could be much less confrontational. This is in part due to the fact that SMEs are located all over Europe and available financial resources at the European level would provide universal benefits, rather than being concentrated on a small number of large companies. Meanwhile, the change of funding priorities, as shown by the modification to the Framework Programme, also suggests that Europe is not just a 'technology community' but an emergent information society offering jobs and opportunities as well. The emphasis on the societal aspects of new information and communications technologies would require competence in a much wider range of policymaking (rather than just technology policy) at the European level in order to govern the process of change throughout Europe. On this ground, it could be argued that the development of a 'user-friendly information society', which is focused on the application and dissemination of new ICTs *via* cross-sector and cross-border cooperation, would be more effective than the previous technology policies in promoting European integration.

'*e*Europe' and the 'Common Information Area'

In December 1999 the European Commission, headed by the new President Romano Prodi, launched a new initiative entitled '*e*Europe – An Information Society for All', in order to accelerate Europe's transition into an information society. Most significant of all, the Commission claims that '*e*Europe is a political initiative', which is 'to ensure the European Union fully benefits for generations to come from the changes the Information Society is bringing'.[11]

The European Commission has set three key objectives for the '*e*Europe' Initiative:

- Bringing every citizen, home and school, every business and administration, into the digital age and online;
- Creating a digitally literate Europe, supported by an entrepreneurial culture ready to finance and develop new ideas;
- Ensuring the whole process is socially inclusive, builds consumer trust and strengthens social cohesion.

Overall, the '*e*Europe' Initiative promotes access to the Internet by all sectors of the society and calls for increased finance to the development of the digital age. It is also evident that the '*e*Europe' Initiative manifests a strong influence on Europe by the recent development in the United States. For instance, the urge for fast Internet for researchers echoes the fast Internet link currently being created in the United States between research organisations; 'cheaper Internet access' reflects the European Commission's recognition of lower cost for Internet access in the United States compared to that in Europe; 'government online' is already well developed in the United States, where congress documents, politicians' speeches, and a wide range of federal government and state government services are accessible electronically *via* the Internet. Meanwhile, venture capitalists' 'entrepreneurial culture' in the United States is far more willing to finance the development of new ideas than anywhere in Europe. One should not be surprised when the media commented that '[t]en years after Senator Al Gore discovered the US's information superhighway, Romano Prodi is desperately trying to accelerate Europe out of the slow lane'.[12]

To be sure, the rapid development of new information and communications technologies including the deployment of high-speed information and communications networks have resulted in the emergence of a global network society.[13] Within the network society, effective governance by any public authority may not be achieved without the availability of an interconnected and interoperable communications network. The challenge to Europe is the fragmentation of the information infrastructure and communications market. This is contradictory with the ultimate goal of the Treaty of the European Union (TEU), which is to create 'an ever closer union among the peoples of Europe, in which decisions are taken as closely as possible to the citizen'.[14] More specifically, the *Maastriccht Treaty* has set the basic legal foundation for the development of the 'Common Information Area'. More specifically, Article 3 (n) and Article 29 (b, c, and d) call for the construction of Trans-European Networks including Trans-European Transportation Networks, Energy Networks and Telecommunications Networks. Meanwhile, Article 3 (m) and Article 130 give the European Commission the necessary competence in coordinating the European-wide efforts to foster 'better exploitation of the industrial potential of policies of innovation, research and technological development'.

Telecommunications networks and services used to be owned and run by the EU Member States. Liberalisation and privatisation in the telecommunications sector since the mid-1980s, and particularly after January 1998, has reduced the degree of national control and built up momentum towards Europeanisation of the communications industry. However, telecommunications services are in each country still largely dominated by the previously state-owned network and service providers and cross-border communication in Europe is far from a single European market at the moment.[15] Compared to its major trading partners such as the US and Japan, Europe is disadvantaged. The European Commission's solution to this problem is to create 'a common information area within the Community', which will enable the Community fully to seize the opportunities offered by the 'irreversible' move towards the information society.[16]

The 'Common Information Area', according to the European Commission,[17] consists of the following elements:

- *Information:* converted and collated in electronic/digital form;
- *Hardware and software:* for processing information;
- *Physical infrastructure:* for disseminating/receiving information;
- Basic telecommunications *services*;
- *Applications:* for improving the structuring of information and user-friendliness;
- *Users:* trained in operation of the applications and aware of the potential of ICTs.

The development of the 'common information area' in Europe, and indeed as in the case of the US or any other country, is also faced with the challenge of adequately financing the programme. According to the

European Commission's own estimate, the establishment of the Trans-European Telecommunications Networks (TEN-Telecom), which is an essential part of the 'Common Information Area', alone would require investment at a total of €150 billion over a ten-year period starting from 1994; about €67 billion would be needed during the first five-year period (1994-99) for the priority projects selected.[18]

Table 2.1   Trans-European Telecommunications Networks: proposals for a priority programme

Information Highways	Target Area for Strategic Projects	Investment Required 1994-99 (billion €s)
Interconnected advanced networks	- Establishment of high-speed communications network - Consolidation of integrated services digital network	20 15
General electronic services	- Electronic access to information - Electronic mail - Electronic images: interactive video services	1 1 10
Telematic applications	- Teleworking - Links between administrations - Teletraining - Telemedicine	3 7 3 7
Total		67

Source: Adapted from the Delors White Paper, European Commission (1993a)

To be sure, financing the establishment of the 'Common Information Area' in Europe is a daunting, if not impossible, task. In the US, it is estimated that over $100 billion of private investment would be needed to build the National Information Infrastructure. Meanwhile, federal investment represents 'an initial, rather than an ongoing, investment' but is a key 'to spark the development that will create the demand for this network as a commercial enterprise'.[19] The European Commission suggests that, similar to the American approach, the investment associated with creating the 'Common Information Area' 'will be covered by private investors' and financial support from the national and Community authorities 'will play a marginal role to provide an incentive, as with other networks'.[20] In the meantime, it is claimed that the Community could provide €5 billion over the entire period of financial support out of its budget for networks, Structural Funds and the research programme. In addition, the European Investment Bank (EIB) loans and European Investment Fund guarantees, etc., would supplement this assistance.[21]

In order to entice private sector investment in the information society related projects, the most popular policy ethos within the EU at the moment is the so-called 'public-private sectors partnerships'. In other words, EU public funding, in most cases, will only be approved if the required level of private sector and/or other local public sector organisations (e.g. higher and further education) contribution (the so-called match funding) is made available.

Towards a European Regulatory Authority?

The 'Common Information Area', as characterised above and anticipated by the European Commission, would help create European services markets and speed up the administrative and decision-making procedures. However, one of the most critical challenges faced by the European authorities is the lack of a single regulatory authority, and the difficult process of creating such a body, for the 'Common Information Area' in Europe. More specifically, two important factors have contributed to the existence of this challenge: technological and political.

First, the wide application of digital techniques – digitisation of various information sources and the communications process as well as the communications equipment and infrastructure – have enabled a process of convergence. In other words, the previously separated sectors, such as computing, broadcasting, telecommunications and publishing, are now coming together to form a large and integrated digital information and communications technology sector. The lapse of the conventional sectoral borders has made many aspects of previously sector-specific legislation obsolete. Technological change and the new market environment would seem to be better regulated by an entirely new framework of legislation. For instance, in Britain, British Telecom is still barred from offering live TV broadcasting. The revolution in digital TV broadcasting has prompted a national debate about which regulatory authority, Oftel or the Independent Television Commission (ITC) or a new 'Communications Commission', should be in charge of the new industry.[22] It is often argued that convergence of telecommunications, audio-visual, publishing and information technology may create new pressures for a European Regulatory Authority and/or new approaches to its role.[23] However, if individual Member States can not decide on which particular authority should be in charge of the digital age, it would be very difficulty for the EU to establish a European regulatory authority in response to the digital convergence.

To be sure, there are reasons for the creation of a European Regulatory Authority and, in particular, the need to promote competitive markets. As far as the creation of an open, competitive and market-driven European information society is concerned, '[d]isparate national regulatory reactions carry a very real threat of fragmentation to the internal market'.[24] However, it is recognised that there are a range of practical issues that need to be resolved in creating a European Regulatory Authority and, among others, any attempt to create a new regulatory body with a policy function or an appellate role would require a Treaty amendment.[25] On the other hand, it would be possible under the present Treaty to create a body with an essentially 'managerial' or 'operational' role. The creation of a regulatory body for telecommunications at the level of the European Union is likely to be an organic process, with regulatory functions added to a new body as the need to do so becomes clearer.[26]

Second, despite the liberalisation and privatisation process involving the telecommunications sector in Europe, and the fact that many telecommunications companies are now operating beyond their national borders, this sector is still largely ruled by the national regulatory authorities (NRAs).[27] The creation of a European level regulatory authority for the European telecommunications industry or the overall ICT sector has never been close to reality. Despite the call that '[a]n authority should be established at European level whose terms of reference will require prompt attention',[28] it remains a politically sensitive issue to recommend, for example, the abolishing of Oftel (Office for Telecommunications) and the

ITC in Britain in order to create a European regulatory authority for the ICT sector across Europe. Therefore, the 'Common Information Area' at the moment, if realistic at all, is being achieved on the condition that there is a lack of a set of 'common rules' and 'common authority' in charge of this area. Until a set of common rules agreed and common regulatory authority is established at the European level, the 'Common Information Area' remains an ideal, rather than a reality:

> European telecommunications face considerable difficulties, notably the incompatibility and non-interoperability of the national telecommunications services' networks. The principal problem is not technological, it is the result of the structure and organisation of the market: the absence of telecommunications operators of a European stature and the non-existence of basic services at European level (electronic mail and file transfer, remote access to databases and interactive image transmission services).[29]

It is worth noting that the European Commission, in its competition policymaking capacity, has been a major player in Europe over the last few years in overseeing the ever-growing number of cross-border mergers and alliances between major telecommunications companies. European Commission approval is a necessity for any of such mergers or alliances including those involving a European company as a partner. Despite the lack of a regulatory authority for the telecommunications sector at the European level, this sector is one of the areas in which the European Commission has been rapidly building up its competencies. For example, During the period February 1995 to February 1998, the European Commission undertook a total of 24 merger decisions involving telecommunications companies.

The large number of merger decisions, as shown in Table 2.2, within a short period of time regarding the telecommunications sector suggests that the European Commission has already been operating as a 'European authority' – a role which might still be less than a fully-fledged regulatory authority. Given the progress towards liberalisation in most telecommunications markets, as argued by some writers, it is reasonable to assume that Member States will be obliged to loosen their hold over the regulatory process but progress is likely to be slow at best'.[30]

The coming of the digital age and, in particular, the fast development of e-commerce (electronic commerce) poses new threats to the effectiveness of regulation and law enforcement at the national government level. Digital goods, such as digital music, computer software and online services are nowadays increasingly traded over the Internet and across national borders. It is suggested that, largely due to the lack of a single European taxation regime, EU states with outdated control systems have failed to cooperate with one another and in collecting VAT (Value Added Tax) and, therefore, created a 'single market for fraud but not for law enforcement'.[31] This kind of new challenge certainly adds more weight to the argument in favour of a solution at the European level.

Given that a common European Regulatory Authority might not be achievable within the current power structure of the EU, Prodi and his 'cabinet', i.e., the European Commission, have set themselves an innovative target:

> The Commission will support the creation of a .eu top-level domain to encourage cross-border electronic commerce within the EU and assist those companies wishing to establish in EU-wide Internet presence.[32]

Top level domains, such as .com, .net, .org, etc., are already being widely used for global and transnational information transactions on the Internet. What would a .eu domain add to the global network? The irony is, whilst a .eu domain might help add an 'EU' face to the Internet, such a top level domain would not solve the problem associated with the lack of an EU level regulatory authority for the digital age. Rather, European national regulatory authorities will continue to exist in parallel with national top level domains such as .uk, .fr., .nl, etc.!

Without the presence of a European Regulatory Authority to oversee the rapidly growing information and communications technology sector, the European Commission needs to steer carefully in the process of policy making. In reality, as discussed above, the Commission is faced with two fundamental dilemmas. First, there is a mismatch between the converging information and communications technology industry and a plethora of sector-specific regulations (e.g. telecommunications directives, cable directives, digital television directive, etc.). Second, in terms of market, the fragmented European markets are faced with challenges from globalisation, which is accelerating fast in scope and intensity. In short, the EU with its current power structure and regulatory environment is not best equipped to cope with the fundamental changes in technologies and market. Undoubtedly, this situation does not help improve efficiency of the policy process and business transactions at the European level and would be ultimately detrimental to the EU's global competitiveness.

Table 2.2 Merger decisions taken by the European Commission concerning the telecommunications sector (February 1995 – February 1998)

Date	Decision Number	Subject
17.2.1995	M.468	Siemens/Italtel
19.7.1995	M.490	Nordic Satellite Distribution
16.8.1995	M.618	Cable&Wireless/Veba
15.9.1995	M.604	Albacaom (BT/BNL)
6.11.1995	M.544	Unisource/Telefonica
22.12.1995	M.595	BT/Viag
29.2.1996	M.689	ADSB/Belgacom
5.3.1996	M.683	Hermes Europe Railtel
18.12.1996	M.802	Telecom Eireann
24.1.1997	M.876	Telia/Ericsson
16.4.1997	M.900	BT/Tele DK/SBB/Migros/UBS
12.5.1997	M.902	Warner Bros/Lusomundo/Sogecable
11.6.1997	M.908	Stet/Mobilekom
20.9.1997	M.975	Albacom/BT/ENI
14.11.1997	M.1046	Ameritech/Tele DK
28.11.1997	M.1069	WorldCom/MCI
6.12.1997	M.975	Albacom/BT/ENI/Mediaset
8.12.1997	M.856	BT/MCI (II)
9.12.1997	M.856	BT/MCI
19.12.1997	M.1027	DT/Beta Research
20.1.1998	M.1055	Cegetel/Vodafone-SFR
24.1.1998	M.1046	Ameritech/Tele DK
30.1.1998	M.993	Bertelsmann/Kirch/Premiere
4.2.1998	M.1027	DT/Beta Research

Source: European Commission.

Given the above discussion, which clearly identifies the lack of and growing need for a European Regulatory Authority at the EU level, the European Commission recently concluded that any attempt to set up such a new authority is unnecessary and counter-productive:

> The Commission considers at this stage that the creation of a European Regulatory Authority would not provide sufficient added value to justify the

likely costs. In addition, it could lead to duplication of responsibilities, resulting in more rather than less regulations. The issues identified that might be better dealt with at EU level can be addressed through adaptation and improvement of existing structures.[33]

The Commission maintains that setting up a new regulatory body at the European level would incur considerable costs such as political, legal, technical, economic and linguistic skills that would be required for it to carry out its tasks effectively across the Community. 'These costs,' says the Commission, 'do not just relate to the administrative costs related to the Agency itself, but the wider costs to the economy as a whole of adding another layer of administration'.[34] Of the various costs associated with setting up a European Regulatory Authority, the most significant and sensitive one could well be the potential political costs. Any proposal to set up such an Authority would certainly invite fierce objection from the National Regulatory Authorities in the Member States. To be sure, if a European Regulatory Authority were to be set up, it would not be economic or effective, unless the NRAs were abolished. But this would have far-reaching implications the whole of the EU power structure and the political shock to be generated from creating the European Regulatory Authority could be a radical one. By avoiding the 'political' costs, the Commission's approach was cautious.[35]

Instead of advocating a European Regulatory Authority, the European Commission has proposed to design a 'new regulatory framework', which will have to cater for both technological and market changes that cannot be predicted with any degree of confidence. In the 1999 Communications Review, the Commission has set three policy objectives for such a 'new regulatory framework':

- To promote an open and competitive European market for communications services;
- To benefit the European citizens (by ensuring affordable and universal access to services at European level; protecting consumers; ensuring data and privacy protection for citizens, etc.);
- To consolidate the internal market in a converging environment (e.g. provision of communications networks and services at European level; no discrimination in the treatment of companies across the EU; effective management of scarce resources, establishment and

development of trans-European networks and the seamless interoperability, etc.).

The proposed 'new regulatory framework' constitutes a substantial simplification and consolidation of current EU legislation. More specifically, the twenty existing legal measures concerning the information and communications sector are reduced to six.

The new European Commission, led by Prodi, apparently has a very different view from that of its predecessor on the issue of the European Regulatory Authority. As a matter of fact, the Bangemann Report, representing the opinion of the European Commission on the information society, has already recommended to the Council of Ministers that a regulatory authority at the European level for the European information infrastructures and services should be established to address:

- the regulation of those operations which, because of their Community-wide nature, need to be addressed at the European level (e.g. licensing, network interconnection, management of shared scare resources and advice to member states regulatory authorities on general issues);
- a single regulatory framework valid for all operators, which would imply lifting unequal conditions for market access.

It would seem to be a logical next step after 1st January 1998, when the EU telecommunications markets were opened up for competition, that a EU level regulatory authority came into being in order to cope with the change. On the contrary, the Bangemann Report recommendations failed to generate the necessary political dynamics within the EU power structure for creating a new EU institution. During the years after the publication of the Bangemann Report, the creation of a European level regulatory authority for the European telecommunications industry or the overall ICT sector proved to be a politically sensitive topic. Needless to say, the Prodi '*eEurope*' Initiative is substantially different from the Bangemann Report – the two are actually conflicting with each other, so far as the European Regulatory Authority issue is concerned.

In calling for further integration among EU Member States, Romano Prodi recognised recently that the challenges posed by globalisation are too large and too complex for any country to tackle single-handed, and the need for a collective European response has never been greater.[36]

Table 2.3 Simplification/consolidation of EU legislation on ICTs

Current Legislation	Simplified and Consolidated Legislation
Article 86 Directives: • Service Directive (90/388/EEC) • Satellite (94/46/EC) • Cable (95/51/EC) • Mobile (96/2/EC) • Full Competition (96/19/EC) • Cable Ownership (99/64/EC)	Liberalisation Directive
Article 95 Directives/Decisions:	
• ONP Framework Directive (90/387/EEC amended by 97/51/EC)	Framework Directive
• Licensing Directive (97/13/EC) • GSM Directive (87/372/EEC) • ERMES Directive (90/544/EC) • DECT Directive (91/287/EEC) • S-PCS Decision (710/97/EC) • UMTS Decision (128/99/EC) • European Emergency Number Decision (91/396/EEC) • International Access Code Decision (92/264/EEC)	Licensing and Authorisation Directive (inc. scarce resources)
• ONP Leased Lines Directive (92/44/EEC amended by 97/51/EC) • TV Standards Directive (95/47/EC) • Interconnection Directive (97/33/EC amended by 98/61/EC)	Access and Interconnection Directive
• Voice Telephony Directive (98/10/EC)	Universal Service Directive
• Telecoms Data Protection Directive (97/66/EC)	Telecoms Data Protection Directive

Source: Adapted from European Commission (1999b), *Towards a New Framework for Electronic Communications Infrastructure and Associated Services: The 1999 Communications Review,* COM(1999) 539 Final, 10 November.

If the EU Member States agree that European integration is to proceed further in the digital age, there would seem to be an evident need for the establishment of a European Regulatory Authority at the EU level. A comparable example is the creation of the 'euro land' and the launch of the euro. Despite the various weaknesses, the launch of the European Central Bank (ECB) is a necessary condition for making the euro and the 'euro land' viable. There needs to be a similar 'watch dog' for the development of the 'Common Information Area' or 'eEurope'. Otherwise, the nature of the European ICT market can not completely dissociate itself from being a collection of piece meal developments within individual Member States. Unfortunately, the political conditions for creating a regulatory authority at EU level are not available for the time being. Until then, the European information society will remain 'virtual', rather than 'real'.

The Information Society and European Governance

The development of the 'Common Information Area' or 'eEurope' to date suggests that the extent to which European governance takes effect is limited. This is in part demonstrated by, among others, the lack of a European level regulatory authority, which is competent enough to cope with the complexity and variety of critical issues raised by the advancement of information and communications technologies and market changes. Despite this, the EU authorities (in particular the European Commission) have also made great effort to take advantage of the information age for the sake of enhancing European governance.

The Policy Process

New ICTs are widely regarded as a strategic technology domain contributing to long-term economic growth and national competitiveness. In response to the National Information Infrastructure programme launched in the US, the EU has adopted a range of important policies dedicated to promoting the development of the information society in Europe since the early 1990s. It is hoped that the creation of an information society would improve the competitiveness of Europe against other industrialised countries such as the US and Japan.

Compared to other major technological programmes sponsored by the EU in the past, the scale and scope of the current European policies towards creating an information society in Europe is unprecedented.

The creation of an information society was identified as a priority area on the EU's policy agenda in the early 1990s and the issue has been pursued with continued political efforts throughout the Union ever since. This is manifested in a variety of policy initiatives implemented at all levels of public authorities in the EU.

As discussed earlier, major policy initiatives at the EU level led to the start of the European programme on the information society. The European Commission made it first important policy move regarding the issue of the information society in 1993 with the publication of the Delors White Paper on *Growth, Competitiveness and Employment*.[37] The Delors White Paper recognises the 'enormous potential' of the information society for new services relating to production, consumption, culture and leisure activities and this 'will create large numbers of new jobs'. Endorsing the vision set within this White Paper, the Bangemann Report of 1994, *Europe and the Global Information Society*, makes the second important push in terms of public policy making towards the information society. The Bangemann Report was presented to the European Council's meeting in Corfu on 24-25 June 1994 and it has become one of the most important official policy documents concerning the information society in Europe. Led by Martin Bangamann, the ex-EU Commissioner for Industry and Technology, the 20 members of the authoring team constituted the so-called High-Level Group on the Information Society (HLGIS).[38] The third important policy document is the European Commission's Action Plan published in 1994 and entitled *The Action Plan: Europe's Way to the Information Society*.[39] The Action Plan outlines the specific measures Europe would need to take in order to promote the development of the information society in Europe.

In the early 1990s the European Commission set the pace for the development of the European information society by publishing the three major pieces of policy documents, i.e., the Delors White Paper, the Bangemann Report and the Action Plan. This move has gradually gained momentum due to the launch of a large number of new or complementary policy documents by the European Commission to follow up the development in the field of information society. With such a large collection of new policies in its hands, the European Commission represents the most influential European public organisation so far as the information society is concerned. In a 'network society', where the traditional hierarchical administrative structure is becoming increasingly challenged, Brussels has become the Centre of the European information society.

Figure 2.1 Selected official documents of the European Commission for promoting the information society

- White Paper on Growth, Competitiveness, and Employment: The Challenges and Ways forward into the 21st Century, COM(93) 700 final, Brussels, 5/12/93. [The Delors White Paper]
- Europe and the Global Information Society: Recommendations to the European Council, Brussels, 26/05/94. [The Bangemann Report]
- The Action Plan: Europe's Way to the Information Society, COM(94) 347 final
- Standardisation and the Global Information Society: The European Approach, COM(96) 359
- Green Paper: Living and Working in the Information Society: People First COM(96) 389, 22.07.96)
- Follow-up to the Green Paper on Copyright and Related Rights in the Information Society COM(96) 586 Final 20/11/96
- Cohesion and the Information Society, COM(97) 7/3
- A European Initiative in Electronic Commerce, COM(97) 157
- The Social and Labour Market Dimension of the Information Society, People First - The Next Steps, COM (97) 397 of 17 July 1997
- Ensuring Security and Trust in Electronic Communication, COM(97) 503
- Action Plan for Promoting Safe Use of the Internet, COM(582) final, 26/11/97
- Convergence of the Telecommunication, Media and Information Technology Sectors (The Green Paper) COM(1997) 623
- Protection of Minors and Human Dignity in Audiovisual and Information Services, SEC(97) 1203
- The Need For Strengthened International Coordination, COM(98) 50
- Proposal for a European Parliament And Council Directive on a Common Framework for Electronic Signatures, COM(1998) 297 final, Brussels, 13.05.1998
- Internet Governance: Management of Internet Names and Addresses, COM(98) 476, final, Brussels, 29.7.98
- Job Opportunities in the Information Society: Exploring the Potential of the Information Revolution, COM(98) 590 final.

Compared to the EU policy process regarding technologies and the industry, the new policies related to the information society at the EU level have met with hardly any resistance from the national governments. It can be said that the information society is a new opportunity for consensus building within the European Union and the European Commission should be credited for its timely efforts in advocating this opportunity.

In parallel with the policies at the EU level, most EU Member States have adopted similar policy measures to promote the development of the information society within their own countries.

It will be misleading to suggest that the European Commission has superseded the national governments in the EU in decision-making regarding the information age. But it is true that the significant and influential policy moves made at the European level since the early 1990s have had tremendous impact on policymaking at the national government level. In other words, the 'policy push' approach is strengthened by a large number of national government initiatives across Europe. For instance, the Danish government has launched its 'Info Society 2000' Programme, under which, a nationwide optical fibre network would be laid down to connect all of the nation's municipalities. France Telecom, on behalf of the French government, has drawn up a new plan to upgrade the current Minitel network to a more capable national information superhighway.

In Britain, the Department of Trade and Industry (DTI) has recently launched an 'Information Society Initiative (ISI)', which was designed to raise awareness, first, among the business community. More specifically, the ISI Programme was to develop a network of 80 Local Support Centres, giving SMEs access to advice on the use of new ICTs and new ways of doing business in the information society. The DTI's recent White Paper,[40] *Our Competitive Future: building the knowledge driven economy*, has an accompanying report on the 'digital economy' which clearly advocates that the new information and communications technologies provide an unprecedented opportunity for building a competitive economy. The DTI also claims that Britain should become the most productive environment in the world for electronic commerce by the beginning of the new Century.[41] The development of the digital economy and the information society, in the view of the British government, represents challenges not only to the business world but also to the government:

> This new world challenges businesses to be innovative and creative, to improve performance continuously, to build new alliances and ventures. But it also challenges government: to create and execute a new approach to industrial policy.[42]

The challenge to government goes further: the new alliances and joint ventures, for example, formed between large companies from different industrial sectors and different parts of the world have made the traditional regulatory and policy approach at the national government level increasingly incompetent, if not entirely irrelevant. The traditional approach is sector-specific and confined to national borders. Would the information society provide a new opportunity and additional arguments for the national governments in Europe to transfer more regulatory power to a European level of governance and then to a global level of governance?

Institutional Mechanisms

In parallel with the process of drafting new policy documents, the European Commission has also been active in facilitating the creation of a number of important agencies and forums with the main task of implementing and disseminating EU policies and strategies concerning the information society since the early 1990s. The earliest move, in terms of institutional development, was made by the publication of the Bangemann Report, which specifically recommends that,

> ...there must be, at the Union level, one Council capable of dealing with the full range of issues associated with the information society. With this in mind, each Member State may wish to nominate a single minister to represent it in a Council of Ministers dedicated to the information society. The Commission should act similarly.[43]

Despite the growing importance of the Bangemann Report in Europe and abroad,[44] its particular recommendation for creating a 'Council of Ministers' for the information society has not achieved the necessary blessing from the Member States. So far, as discussed above, sectoral regulations initiated by Member States still dominate information society related domains across Europe. However, the European Commission itself has acted rather boldly by devising a series of institutional mechanisms to give the information society more European characteristics. In turn, these institutional mechanisms help boost the European Commission's political profile as a European public authority.

One of the institutional changes was the renaming of Directorate-General XIII (DGXIII) in early 1999 as 'Information Society: Telecommunications, Markets, Technologies – Innovation and Exploitation of Research'. Compared to its old name, which was 'Telecommunications, Information Market and Exploitation of Research', the new name has a focus on the 'information society'. Despite the fact that some other Directorates-General also have an interest in policies related to the information society, DGXIII's new name does give it the legitimacy to assume more responsibilities for this area of policymaking and implementation.

It seems that DGXIII is already taking over control over the European information society programme. For instance, within the Fifth Framework Programme, DGXIII has been given the task to manage the Information Society Technologies Programme which provides a single and integrated programme that reflects the convergence of information processing, communications and media. The Information Society Technologies Programme has a budget of €3.6 billion for the period 1998-2002.

In addition to the renaming of DGXIII, a number of new institutional arrangements have been carried out by the European Commission for the promotion of the information society. These include, among others, the following:

- the High Level Group on the Information Society (HLGIS)
- the Information Society Activities Centre (ISAC)
- the Information Society Projects Office (ISPO)
- the High Level Group of Experts on the Social and Societal Aspects of the Information Society
- the Information Society Forum
- the EU-CEEC Information Society Forum
- Joint High Level Committee (JHLC)
- the Euro-Mediterranean Information Society Forum (EUMEDIS).

The HLGIS is also known as 'the Bangemann Group' who authored the Bangemann Report. The ISAC was jointly established by DGIII (Industry) and DGXIII with the task to specifically coordinate information society projects. The ISPO is part of the ISAC and its aim is to promote cooperation and development in the various areas of the information society. The ISPO acts as a link between the European Commission and external organisations interested in the information society.

As proposed by the Commission's *Action Plan: Europe's Way to the Information Society*, the High Level Group of Experts on the Social and Societal Aspects of the Information Society was set up in February 1995. The aim of the Group was to provide the Commission with an overall assessment. The High Level Group of Experts will be mandated to report on the social and societal aspects of the Information Society. The Group has 14 external experts, who were selected and nominated on a personal basis.

The Information Society Forum was set-up as an independent advisory body. The main purpose of the Forum was to '...provide the opportunity for representatives from a variety of different groups, including the social partners, to contribute to open debate and reflection on the challenges of the Information Society including the social and societal aspects as well as to raise the level of public awareness. The Forum will work on the framework for implementing the Information Society. The Forum should also indicate to the Commission the priority projects that need to be implemented...'.[45] The Information Society Forum now has over 180 members.

The EU-CEEC Information Society Forum was another initiative of the former Commissioner Martin Bangemann. Ministers and industrial leaders from the Central and Eastern European Countries (CEECs) and representatives from EU industrial and research organisations were brought together by Martin Bangemann to discuss the implications of the Information Society for the CEECs that had, or were negotiating, Association Agreements with the EU. Consequently, it was agreed by the participants that an EU-CEEC Information Society Forum be established.

In October 1997, the European Commission and the CEECs decided to establish a Joint High Level Committee, comprised of EU and CEEC government representatives, in order to regularly review the implementation of the conclusions and recommendations of the EU-CEEC Information Society Forum. The JHLC reports to a ministerial conference.

The Euro-Mediterranean Information Society (EUMEDIS) Initiative, officially approved by the European Commission in February 1999, was specifically designed to reduce the region's informational and technological gap *vis-à-vis* the neighbouring countries by the development of the Euro-Mediterranean Information Society. EUMEDIS aims at interconnecting the Euro-Mediterranean research communities and launching pilot projects in five priority sectors of intervention:

- Information and communication technologies applied to Education
- Electronic commerce and economic cooperation
- Healthcare networks
- Multimedia access to cultural heritage and tourism

- Information and communication technologies applied in industry and innovation.

The EU-CEEC Information Society Forum (and the Joint High Level Committee) and the Euro-Mediterranean Information Society Initiative represent the EU's new strategy to officially engage the CEECs and the Mediterranean Region by joint efforts in developing the information society. In this respect, the information society has important implication for considering the issues such as European enlargement and security.

'eEurope' and the Democratic Deficit

It is widely believed that there exists a democratic deficit within the EU.[46] This is in part due to that the European Commission is not an elected government body and the large-scale bureaucracy in Brussels lacks transparency. Although the EU Treaty has conferred a number of fundamental freedoms on EU citizens, there are considerable practical difficulties preventing them from exercising those rights. The development of new ICTs offers an opportunity for the European Commission to move one step closer to the European citizens by promoting digitisation of European documents and putting them on line. It can be said with confidence that the European Commission is one of the most advanced public authorities in the world with sophisticated online representation. One could hardly think of any aspect/part of the European Commission (and the rest of the EU) which is not connected to its official websites. 'Virtual Europe' – digitisation of European official documents and the electronic representation of all European Union institutions facilitated by new information and communications networks such as the Internet – is perhaps the most evident achievement of the European information society process.

The availability of the vast amount of public information on the Internet has indeed helped improving citizens' access in all member countries to information regarding European legislation, public policies and services available on websites such as *EUROPA*,[47] one of the European Union's most comprehensive official sites.

The success in the European integration process will not be achieved if European citizens are not well informed of issues related to the functioning of the EU and its policies. As noted by the European Commission, an adequate access to information of and on the European Union can largely benefit the European integration process. The Commission believes it is important to bring the EU closer to the citizens by making it more transparent and closer to everyday life through the EU's commitment to allowing the greatest possible access to information on its activities.[48] Although it differs from country to country, the vast majority of European citizens would like to be better informed than they are at the moment about the EU. Recent survey suggests that, among those asked from the 15 Member States, on average 68% of European citizens need or would like more information on the EU.[49] For the time being, the majority of EU citizens (67%) are most likely to consult the television when they look for information about the EU and, on average, newspapers and magazines are still one of the preferred sources of information for 40% of EU citizens.[50] With the rapid growth and popular use of the Internet, European citizens from work, home and public places will increasingly access digital information on the European Union, wherever networked computers are available.

The vigorous promotion of public sector information online at the EU level has also prompted policy responses at the national government level within some Member States. For instance, in an effort to promote the development of the digital economy, the British government has proposed that, by 2008, all government services will be made available electronically. France has been lagging long behind most other EU countries and the United States in terms of Internet penetration. For the time being, a meagre 7% of the French population are connected to the Internet, compared with 15% in Britain and 23% in the USA.[51] In order to catch up with countries with a more advanced digital economy, the French government unveiled a set of new measures and policy goals in the beginning of 1999. These include, among others, doubling funding to modernise the national administration's use of the technology to FFr130 (euro 19.8 million), and committed to making all government forms available online before 2000, from about 50% today.[52]

The development of 'Virtual Europe' has digitally stitched different parts of Europe together, although it is still actually divided by national borders.

The progress of digitisation of European public information seems impressive. However, there is still a long way to go before the 'Virtual Europe' becomes a user-friendly virtual environment, in which citizens from different parts of Europe can live like European citizens without encountering real difficulties associated with physical geography. The European Commission itself acknowledges the challenges ahead:

> We have done our utmost to make it as user friendly as possible. This is an enormous task because of the many areas of the European Union's work, and

the vast amount of information which we make available to the European Citizens.⁵³

It is perhaps too early to predict the impact of the 'virtual Europe' development, which is still at its nascent stage, on the course of European integration and the effectiveness of European governance. However, history could shed some light on our understanding of this issue. In the late 19th and early 20th Centuries, the British government launched a strategic initiative to develop an 'all red' cable telegraphic communications network, which was to build an international cable network linking all parts of the British empire without ever touching upon any foreign soil. This British-owned international cable network was expected to provide an efficient means of communications between the centre of the Empire in London and the colonies spreading across the globe. Possessing over 60% of the world's telegraphic cables, the British dominance of world cable communications remained unchanged before the First World War.⁵⁴ There is no doubt that the existence of the 'all red' global cable network provided Britain with a strategic means to maintain the necessary administration within the Empire. However, the importance of this communications network is no substitute of real politics and the impact of the former should not be exaggerated:

> It remains to be discovered whether the creation of this secure submarine cable network actually furthered the political unity and coherence of the empire as well. At first sight, the fact that an exchange of views between London and the self-governing colonies could take place within a day seemed to offer a solution to the British government's problem of wishing to present a united imperial front in world affairs... and no doubt the advocates of imperial federation welcomed the cable as a means of drawing the empire closer together to meet the challenges of the twentieth century. But while the process of consultation was made much swifter, there is little evidence to suggest that differences of opinion between British and colonial politicians were in any way eased, let alone removed, by the use of the telegraph (Kennedy, 1979, p. 93).

The use of new information and communications technologies, such as the Internet, to create an online 'virtual Europe' would certainly help facilitate and speed up the administration process between Brussels and the rest of the European Union. The electronic representation, i.e. a 'virtual Europe', and the development of a 'Common Information Area' would, as believed, contribute to the creation of an 'ever closer Union' among the peoples of Europe. Therefore, the European Commission urged that '[a] great deal of effort must be put into securing widespread public acceptance and actual use of the new technology' and '[p]reparing Europeans for the advent of the information society is a priority task'.[55] However, the information society is not a panacea for the problem of fragmentation faced by the European Union. It is not the intention of this chapter to draw a comparison between the EU and the 19th Century British Empire. However, given that the 'all red' imperial cable network has failed to prevent the British Empire, on which the sun never set, from collapsing, would the 'virtual Europe' or 'Common Information Area' project provide a forever lasting bond for the European nations in the information age?

EU Governance or Global Governance?

The EU strongly endorses the vision that the emerging information society is a global phenomenon and the European information society is, therefore, an integral part of a global process.[56] The global dimension of the information society seems to strengthen the argument in favour of governance at the EU level, rather than the national government level.

Over the last few years, the European Commission has undertaken a number of initiatives to make the European Union a 'united force' on the international arena. For instance, among others, the European Commission represented the EU as a whole to launch the 'Global Information Society' initiative with the G7 countries plus South Africa in Brussels in February 1995. The European Commission represented the EU to participate in the negotiations on the WTO Telecommunications Agreement and Information Technology Products Agreement. The EU has brought the Central and East European Countries, which sighed the Association Agreement, and the Mediterranean countries onto the bandwagon of the information society development. In addition, the EU has become an important bargaining power *vis-à-vis* the US over the way that the Internet as a global network should be managed. With regard to electronic commerce, the EU has demonstrated a substantially different approach from that of the US. The former advocates increased data security and privacy protection *via* legislation (at EU level) whilst the latter is in favour of voluntary protection of data security and privacy (i.e., self-regulation by the industry). The on-going debate between the EU and the US will have tremendous impact on the future of electronic commerce at the global level.

In recognising the nature of the emergent digital marketplace and the information society being global, the European Commission argues for the need for strengthened international coordination. More specifically, an International Charter on the global information society should be agreed and signed by the international community. According to the European Commission, an International Charter would:

- be a multi-lateral understanding on a method of coordination to remove obstacles for the global electronic marketplace;
- be legally non-binding;
- recognise the work of existing international organisations;
- promote the participation of private sector and relevant social groups;
- contribute to more regulatory transparency.[57]

The EU approach toward the process of globalisation in relation with the information society apparently leads to two important points, which are potentially contradictory with each other. On the one hand, the international community should reach 'a forward-looking understanding on how best to develop common approaches to problems and their solutions, i.e. to develop a sustained method of coordination in which public and private sector interests are adequately represented'.[58] On the other hand, '[w]hat is not required is to establish an international supervisory authority or a set of binding rules', i.e., this International Charter should be 'legally non-binding'.[59]

The Information Society and EU Enlargement

'The trend of international affairs is that long-term separation leads to unification and long-term unification leads to separation'.[60] The European Union's eastward enlargement prompted by the end of the Cold War is approaching at a time when West European economies, and societies at large, are subject to a rapid change arising in part from the development of new information and communications technologies. It is believed that this enlargement will increase overall EU interest in ICTs with positive repercussions on related policies and possibilities offered by ICTs are likely to seem even more significant in the CEECs than they do within the EU (European Commission, 1997d). Being aware of this positive co-relation between enlargement and ICTs, the EU authorities and governments in the CEECs have keen interests to promote the development of the information society. However, the public authorities from both sides of Europe are faced with the challenge of reducing the gap, both technical and economic, between the CEECs and the EU countries so that the perceived benefits of the information society can be made available to all Europeans.

EU Membership: The Telecommunications Perspective

One of the major consequences prompted by the end of the Cold War, in terms of international relations, was the dissolution of the former Warsaw Pact and a growing number of the organisation's members becoming attracted to the western part of Europe. Since the early 1990s, ten former socialist countries from Central and Eastern Europe have signed the Europe Agreements with the European Union and applied for EU membership. The Europe Agreements introduced bilateral cooperation between the applicant countries and the EU, which will lead to advanced integration in a large number of fields such as trade agreements, competition, approximation o laws, standardisation, etc. (European Commission, 1997e). More specifically, the Agreements include, among others, a) programmes promoting economic, financial and cultural cooperation between the EU and the CEECs in order to help the latter during their transition to a market economy; b) requirement that competition rules be established in order to facilitate this transition; c) programmes promoting the alignment of national laws within the CEECs with EU legislation. The Europe Agreements remain the most important legal documents, which contractually combine the applicant countries together with the Union during the pre-accession period. The political significance of the Europe Agreements lies in the progressive establishment of a free trade area between the central and east European countries and the European Union and the explicit recognition that the ultimate aim of the CEECs' accession to the European Union (Cullen International, 1997).

As far as the information society is concerned, it is expected that the Europe Agreement provides for cooperation aimed at enhancing standards and practices towards EU levels in telecommunications policies, standardisation, regulatory approaches and the modernisation of infrastructure (European Commission, 1997a). The focus of the bilateral cooperation under the Europe Agreement is on the approximation of regulation, networks and services and further steps ensuring gradual sectoral liberalisation within the applicant countries. The proposed eastward enlargement of the Union serves well the key objectives of the EU's telecommunications policy, which are:

> ... the elimination of obstacles to the effective operation of the Single Market in telecommunications equipment, services and networks, the opening of foreign markets to EU companies and the achievement of universally available modern services for EU residents and businesses (European Commission, 1997c).

Table 2.4 Dates of the Europe Agreements and EU membership applications

Country	Date of Signing	Date of Entering into Force	Membership Application
Bulgaria	Mar. 1993	Feb. 1995	n.a.
Czech Rep.*	Oct. 1993	Feb. 1995	Jan. 1996
Estonia	Jun. 1995	Feb. 1998	Nov. 1995
Hungary	Dec. 1991	n.a.	Mar. 1994
Latvia	1995	n.a.	Oct. 1995
Lithuania	Jun. 1995	n.a.	Dec. 1995
Poland	Dec. 1991	Feb. 1994	Apr. 1994
Romania	Feb. 1993	Feb. 1995	Jun. 1995
Slovakia*	Oct. 1993	Feb. 1995	Jun. 1995
Slovenia	Sept. 1993	Jun. 1997	Jun. 1997

Notes: *There had been a Europe Agreement between the EU and the former Czechoslovakia signed in December 1991. The separation of the latter into the Czech Republic and the Slovakia has led to the re-negotiation of the Agreement.

The fall of the Berlin Wall and the collapse of the socialist systems in Central and Eastern Europe has provided an opportunity for most of the former Soviet satellite countries to adopt a new approach, i.e., a market-oriented strategy, towards their telecommunications sector.

First of all, the 'switch off' by certain applicant countries from the network of the former Soviet Union, which previously routed all of the international calls generated from and destined to these countries,[61] means these countries would need to develop their new and independent communications infrastructure.

Second, full or partial privatisation of the former state-owned operators is an important feature of telecommunications policies in the CEECs since the early 1990s. For instance, the Czech Republic has decided to undertake partial privatisation of the state-owned telecommunications company (SPT) by the end of the year 2000.

In Hungary, MATAV, the former state monopoly, is already majority owned by the private sector (with only 23% of capital currently owned by the state). Lattelekom, the former state monopoly in Latvia, has become a limited company since 1994 and foreign companies now own 49% of its capital. In Bulgaria, the state-owned Bulgarian Telecommunications Company (BTC) has been given exclusive rights over access to telecommunications network until 1 January 2005 and over the provision of voice telephony until 1 January 2003. The government of Lithuania has planned to privatise the state operator, Lithuania Telecom, by the year 2000. The Romanian government announced in 1997 that the state-owned monopoly, Rom Telecom, would be partially privatised and the company's exclusive rights for the operation of fixed network and the provision of voice telephony would by abolished by 1 January 2000. The Slovak government is also considering options for privatising the state monopoly Slovenske Telecom.

Third, the telecommunications reform programmes, such as privatisation of the state-owned operators and the liberalisation process in service provision has led to the penetration of foreign companies into the CEEC markets. Telecommunications companies from the EU are certainly among the winners in the newly opened markets.

In preparing their bid for joining the EU, the candidate countries need to adapt themselves immediately or gradually to EU telecommunications laws and regulations by means of new telecommunications legislation. Up until now, the set up of an independent telecommunications regulatory authority and separation of regulation from network operation has been achieved in some applicant countries.

On the technical side, modernisation is badly needed in most applicant countries. Although this is already taking place in these countries in terms of upgrading the obsolete electro-mechanical equipment and manual switches to new generations of equipment, the process of modernisation will be costly and a long-term endeavour.[62] The penetration of EU (and other western) firms (as strategic partners) might help provide the badly needed digital equipment and new technologies such as the GSM standard for mobile telephony, but the 'help' is not unconditional.

The Digital Gap

On the one hand, the EU's proposed eastward enlargement would seem to increase the Union's position in Europe. This is suggested by an increase of 33% of geographical area and 28% of population represented by the 10 applicant countries from the CEECs. On the other hand, however, the fundamental economic gap between the applicant countries and the EU Member States is also significant. For instance, the total of GDP (Gross Domestic Product) in the 10 CEEC applicant countries (at €234 billion) accounts only 4% of GDP in the EU (at a total of €6441.5 billion) at current market prices in the year 1995. As for GDP per head in the same year, the average of the 10 CEEC applicant countries (at €2220) accounts only 13% of the EU average (at €17260).

Table 2.5   The economic gap – basic data: 1995

	Area (1000 sq. km)	Population (millions)	GDP (€ billion)	GDP Per head (€)
Hungary	93	10.2	33.4	3340
Poland	313	38.6	90.2	2360
Romania	238	22.7	27.3	1200
Slovak Rep.	49	5.4	13.3	2470
Latvia	65	2.5	3.4	1370
Estonia	45	1.5	2.8	1850
Lithuania	65	3.7	3.5	930
Bulgaria	111	8.4	9.9	1180
Czech Rep.	79	10.3	36.1	3490
Slovenia	20	2.0	14.2	7240
CEEC-10	**1078**	**105.3**	**234**	**2220**
% of EU-15	33	28	4	13
EU-15	3236	371.6	6441.5	17260

Source: Adapted from European Commission (1997d), *Agenda 2000*.

The wide gap between the 10 CEEC applicant countries and the EU in term of GDP suggests that eastward enlargement 'carries a risk that supports for a broad social policy would become weaker in the Union as a whole, especially if adaptation of acceding countries to the *acquis*[63] were inadequate' (European Commission, 1997d).

Despite the ongoing economic reform and increased freedom of communication resulting from the liberalisation process, most economic sectors in the CEECs were largely insulated from the influence of new ICTs until quite recently. In particular, the public information sectors were closely controlled and grossly under-developed and the very long period of economic decline created a vicious circle in which low demand and lack of infrastructure reinforced each other (European Commission, 1997d).

The implication of the fundamental economic gap between the two sides of Europe might not be confined solely to the area of social policy; rather, many other domains of the Union's policy could be challenged significantly. Among others, the development of the information society would certainly not be an even process unless the fundamental gap is bridged. The much lower GDP in the 10 CEEC applicant countries, compared to that of the 15 EU countries, would not adequately equip the former to invest in their information society infrastructure and services at a level, which could be afforded by the latter.

The 'communications gap' between the two sides of Europe remains huge. According to *CommunicationsWeek International*, in the year 1996, teledensity (number of fixed telephone lines per 100 population) was 44.02% for Western Europe (the EU and Scandinavian countries) and only 15.94% for the CEECs (including Russia). Mobile phone penetration rate amongst the local population reached 3.88% in West European countries, compared to a meagre 0.13% for the CEECs in the same year. The cable TV sector shows similar pattern: cable TV connection rate was 7.86% for Western Europe and 0.99 for the CEECs in 1996. As for the number of Internet hosts in 1996, Western Europe exceeded 1.5 million whilst the CEECs had only 67,000.

In addition to the difference in ownership, the level of technological development also varies within the communications sector. As shown in Table 2.6, whilst all telephone lines had a direct international dialling capacity in Western Europe, only about three quarters of telephones had this capacity in the CEECs in 1996; whilst local exchange digitisation reached 65.2% in Western Europe, this was only 17.4% in the CEECs. In other words, the majority of the local exchange equipment installed in the telecommunications networks in the CEECs was analogue of an analogue nature.

Although the European Commission recognises that enlargement will benefit the EU's telecommunications sector as a whole by providing a larger market for products and services, and by the possibility of acceding countries to act as 'disseminators' for further extension of the market, it is also fully conscious of the *status quo* of the ICT sector in the CEECs:

> CEEC telecommunications networks have suffered from decades of general neglect, under-investment, insufficient maintenance and lack of modernisation. They thus lag considerably behind the EU levels. Public operators are under pressure to rapidly upgrade and extend their networks, to improve the quality of telephony and to introduce new services. However, up to now, actual investment falls substantially short of estimated needs (European Commission, 1997d).

Table 2.6   The communications gap: The CEECs and Western Europe*

Type of Communication	W. Europe	The CEECs
Teledensity	44.02%	15.94%
Mobile phone penetration	3.88%	0.13%
Lines with international dialling	100%	75.79%
Local exchange digitisation	65.20%	17.40%**
Payphones	1,420,865	428,660
Private circuits	3,759,930	50,859
Cable TV connections	7.86%	0.99%**
Internet host	1,555,000	67,000

Notes: *The CEECs include countries from Central and Eastern Europe as well as Russia; and Western Europe includes the EU and the Scandinavian countries; **Average for countries from the CEECs excluding Russia.
Source: Adapted from *CommunicationsWeek International* (1996).

The relatively lower level of ICT infrastructure deployment in the CEECs has resulted in a substantial difference between demand and supply. In terms of telecommunications, as shown in Table 2.7, the average waiting time for a telephone line in the 10 applicant countries for EU membership is normally a substantially long period. In the five countries including Estonia, Latvia, Lithuania, Poland and Romania the average waiting time is between 2.9 years to 4 years. For citizens in these countries, the potential benefits offered by the information society could take a long time to reach them. In reality, many of these people are still waiting in a long queue for getting a telephone line, which is the very basic necessity for other types of information society services such as the Internet.

The Internet, arguably, represents one of the most important elements of the information society. Therefore, the level of access to Internet reflects a country's current level of participation in the global information society. Figures in Table 2.8 suggest that, whilst the number of computers connected to the Internet per 1000 inhabitants in both the EU-15 countries and the 10 CEEC applicant countries has been steadily growing since the early 1990s, the annual rate in the former is substantially higher than that in the latter. In the years 1997 and 1998, the average rate of computers connected to the Internet per 1000 inhabitants for the EU was about four times that of the 10 CEEC applicant countries (i.e. 16.8 *versus* 4.4 and 24.5 *versus* 5.7 respectively).

Table 2.7   Average waiting time for a telephone line in the CEECs

Country	Average Waiting Time for a Telephone
Bulgaria	Over 1 year in 1996*
Czech Rep.	1.9 years in 1996
Estonia	3.8 years at the end of 1996
Hungary	0.4 years by the end of 1996
Latvia	3.5 years by the end of 1996
Lithuania	3.5 years by the end of 1996
Poland	2.9 years in 1996
Romania	4 years (maximum 5 years)
Slovakia	10.2 months in 1997
Slovenia	1 year**

Notes: *In 1996, out of 480,000 applications for a telephone number, 358,000 had been waiting for more than two years; **As stipulated by a government decree, the maximum waiting time if network is available must not exceed 30 days.
Source: Figures are from Cullen International (1997).

Although some Central and East European countries (e.g. Slovenia, Estonia and Hungary), where higher connection rate is observed, have already overtaken certain EU countries (Greece, Portugal, Italy, Spain and France) by 1997 in terms of Internet connectivity, it would certainly take a long period of time before the gap between the EU-15 average and the CEEC-10 average is closed, if at all possible.

Within the 10 CEEC applicant countries, a large proportion of decision-makers and opinion-formers already use the Internet as an important source of information.

Table 2.8 Computers (hosts) connected to the Internet per 1000 inhabitants

	1992	1993	1994	1995	1996	1997	9/1998
Austria	1	2	3	7	11	14	19
Belgium	0	1	2	3	7	11	18
Denmark	1	2	4	10	21	33	55
Finland	3	7	14	41	56	63	89
France	0	1	1	3	4	6	8
Germany	1	1	2	6	9	14	17
Greece	0	0	0	1	2	3	4
Ireland	0	1	2	4	8	11	14
Italy	0	0	1	1	3	3	6
Luxembourg	0	1	1	5	9	12	17
Netherlands	2	3	6	11	18	26	38
Portugal	0	0	1	1	2	4	5
Spain	0	0	1	1	3	5	7
Sweden	3	5	9	17	27	29	46
Great Britain	1	2	4	8	12	18	24
EU-15 Average	*0.8*	*1.7*	*3.4*	*7.9*	*12.8*	*16.8*	*24.5*
Bulgaria	0	0	0	0	0	1	1
Czech Republic	n/a	0	1	2	4	6	7
Estonia	0	0	1	2	5	10	14
Hungary	0	0	1	2	3	7	9
Latvia	0	0	0	1	2	3	5
Lithuania	0	0	0	0	0	1	2
Poland	0	0	0	1	1	2	3
Romania	0	0	0	0	0	1	1
Slovakia	n/a	0	0	1	2	3	4
Slovenia	0	0	1	3	7	10	11
CEEC-10 Average	*n/a*	*0*	*0.4*	*1.2*	*2.4*	*4.4*	*5.7*

Source: Based on European Telework Development (1999).

According to a recent survey by the European Commission, 45% of decision-makers and opinion-formers questioned have indicated that the Internet plays an important role in their search for information about the European Union.[64] However, among the general public in the 10 CEEC candidate countries only 3% on average believe the Internet is an important source of information about the EU.[65] This lack of awareness about the potential importance of the Internet among the general public in the CEEC countries reflects the relatively low level of Internet connectivity in these countries.

Decision-makers and opinion-formers are normally those well-educated with easy access to computers and the Internet. To a certain extent, this group of the society are among the social elite. If the public authorities in both the EU and the applicant countries believe the Internet is an important part of the information society, public policies should be directed towards emphasising on raising the level of computer ownership and Internet access by the general public, rather than just the social elite, in Central and Eastern Europe.

The European Commission attaches great importance to the development of the Trans-European Networks, in which the construction of a pan-European telecommunications infrastructure (i.e. TEN-Telecom) is an integral part:

> The continued development of the Trans-European Networks (TENs) will serve to enhance both sustainable development and the internal cohesion of the Union by tying regions closer together. ... TENs also have a particular important role to play in creating new links with the Central and Eastern European candidate countries. It is precisely the trans-European nature of the benefits from these projects which justifies continued substantial contributions at the Union level towards their realisation (European Commission, 1997b).

Given the inadequate provision of up-to-date communications infrastructures in the CEECs and the lack of necessary investment, enlargement will increase the degree of challenge associated with the development of the 'Common Information Area' in Europe. To be sure, the larger the Union's map the more investment would be needed. On the other hand, a pan-European 'Common Information Area', as proposed in the Delors White Paper, would be a prerequisite for making the Europe a 'common market' in the information age, in which the CEECs are an integral part.

Impact of EU Policy: The Information Society Projects

The policy measures formulated and implemented at the European, national and local government levels have resulted in the creation of a large number of collaborative projects (involving partners from both the pubic and private sectors) in relation with the information society. In order to promote the European information society programme, 'the Commission proposes to accelerate the administrative procedures, act as a catalyst, to use the existing financial instruments and to supplement them through recourse to saving...'.[66]

Table 2.9   Information society project starting date

Starting Date	Pre-1994	1994	1995	1996	1997	1998
New Projects		70	281	663	514	237
Total Projects	79	149	430	1039	1607	1844

Source: Adapted from ESIS Database – Statistical Overview, January 1999.

According to the ESIS (European Survey of the Information Society),[67] a total of 1,943 information society projects in Europe had responded to its statistical survey by January 1999. The starting dates indicate that the European policies on the information society have played an important role in prompting the launch of the projects: there were only 79 projects before 1994 when the Bangemann Report was published; the total number of projects increased to 1,844 by the end of 1998.

As discussed before, both the Delors White Paper and the Bangemann Report suggested that the private sector should be mainly responsible for financing development of the information society in Europe. However, the ESIS survey[68] shows that, out of the 75% of total projects calculated, projects funded by private investment account for a meagre 12%. In contrast, 43% and 65% of projects have benefited respectively from European Commission and national/regional/local government funding.

The leading role of the public sector, rather than the private sector as proposed, in promoting the development of the information society is also demonstrated by the role of public sector organisations as the coordinator in the large number of projects. More specifically, according to the ESIS survey, a total of 57% of project coordinators are from the public sector (government bodies at different levels account for 28%; research and educational organisations 29%).[69]

Conclusion

The IS represents a new approach at the EU level in policy making; it is a significant shift from the mainstream technology policies of the past. In other words, the IS gives more emphasis on meeting the needs of the European society at all levels, rather than just that of the European industry. To be sure, previous technology policy measures on the ICT sector and the current policies towards the information society are both centred on improving European competitiveness in a global context. However, previous technology policy had met with great difficulties in obtaining consensus among the Member States whilst new information society promotional measures have experienced a much smoother process. It can be said that there are no significant political difficulties or objections associated with development of the European information society in general. This less contentious nature of policy making for the development of the information society has enabled Brussels to become *the* Centre of '*e*Europe'. As the information society is still at an infant stage of its development, the full picture of such a society and its long-term implications for the political map of Europe may take some years to become clear.

The development of the European information society has been driven primarily by a discernible top-down policy push approach. This approach was prompted and led by the European Commission, whose voice was then echoed by the national governments of the Member States. The European Commission and the national governments of the Member States seemed convinced that the information society provides an unprecedented opportunity for the 'deepening' and 'widening' of the European integration process.

The 'digital way' towards European integration is indiscernible. Digital communication facilitated by a common and integrated European information infrastructure helps in a very significant way disseminate European policy across Europe at increasingly lower cost with increased efficiency. In the meantime, as the new digital communications infrastructure is being used to connect all parts of Europe together, the Europeans are in a much better position to communicate with each other without being constrained by distance.

In particular, the great amount of information related to the various EU institutions available nowadays at the European citizens' finger tip would certainly help improve their access to and understanding about EU pulbic policies. Optimists may claim that the 'digital way', although quiet and indiscernible, is becoming an effective dimension towards European integration. In the digital information age, the distance between the EU and its citizens would seem to disappear. 'We are on the verge of a revolution that is just as profound as the change in the economy that came with the industrial revolution. Soon electronic networks will allow people to transcend the barriers of time and distance and take advantage of global markets and business opportunities not even imaginable today, opening up a new world of economic possibility and progress'.[70]

To be sure, the European information society is an integral part of the emergent global information society (GIS). The smooth development of the GIS, due to its nature of being transnational and borderless, will require a high level of international collaboration between governments from all countries. This gives a new opportunity for building new policy and regulatory competencies into EU level public authorities, in particular the European Commission. In this respect, the EU has already made progress: the European Commission represented the EU to launch the 'Global Information Society' initiative with the G7 countries in Brussels; the European Commission represented the EU and participated in the negotiations for the WTO Telecommunications Agreement and Information Technology Products Agreement since the mid-1990s; the EU has brought the Central and East European Countries, which signed the Association Agreements, and the Mediterranean countries onto the bandwagon of information society development.

However, the 'eEurope' alone may not be sufficient to bridge the widely perceived 'democratic deficit' within the EU, which is deeply embedded in the European power structure.

In a digital age, time and geographical distance is lapsing and sectoral and national borders can not be guarded as tightly as they used to be. This seems to be a perfect opportunity for the EU to prepare itself for becoming an 'ever closer Union' and a public authority with considerable international governance competence. In reality, however, the nature of EU polity does not provide sufficient room for a 'European Regulatory

Authority', for instance, to be established. The Member States and their National Regulatory Authorities are not prepared to hand over their sovereignty and regulatory power entirely over to Brussels. Despite the recommendation made in the Bangemann Report to create a regulatory authority for the ICT sector and the information society at the EU level, the European Commission under the Prodi leadership adamantly rejected this idea five years later. Prodi and his European Commission suggested the costs for establishing a European Regulatory Authority would be too high for the European economy to bear. It is not unreasonable to speculate that the political costs for creating a EU level regulatory authority would be too high for the Prodi Commission to bear. As a milder alternative, the European Commission has now proposed to simplify and consolidate the current 20 pierces of EU regulation on the ICT sector into only 6 Directives. This proposal constitutes the most distinctive feature of the 'new regulatory framework' suggested in the European Commission's 1999 Communications Review. If the EU wishes to take the full advantage of the information society to 'deepen' European integration, the European authorities would need to recognise that a 'new regulatory framework' proposed by the current European Commission might not be as effective as a 'European Regulatory Authority' could have been.

As for the issue of EU's eastward enlargement, there exists a tremendous gap between the EU countries and the CEECs, as far as the development of the ICT sector is concerned. New ICTs, such as the Internet and telecommunications, might help bridge the communication and information exchange between the two sides of Europe, but the level of ownership in equipment and, therefore, opportunities for accessing information for the citizens in the EU and those in the CEECs differ significantly. The fall of the Berlin Wall was the beginning of disappearance of political barriers between Eastern and Western Europe. Ten years on, the economic barriers continue to divide the European Continent. Until the economic barriers are removed, the 'digital gap' will not be closed and the benefit of the European information society could well be very limited, as far as the CEECs are concerned.

Notes

[1] Bangemann, M. *et al* (1994), *Europe and the Global Information Society: Recommendations to the European Council*, Brussels, 26 May. 'The Bangemann Report' thereafter.

2   European Commission (1993a) *White Paper on Growth, Competitiveness, and Employment: The Challenges and Ways forward into the 21st Century*, COM(93) 700 final, Brussels, 5 December. Thanks to the leading role played by Jacques Delors, the former European Commission President, in drafting and launching this White Paper, the White Paper is widely known as 'The Delors White Paper'.
3   The Delors White Paper, European Commission (1993a).
4   Gore, A. (1991), 'Infrastructure for the Global Village', *Scientific American*, September, p. 111.
5   It is estimated that private investment needed to connect optical fibre to every home, office, factory, school, library and hospital at an estimated total of $100 billion (Gore, 1991).
6   The Delors White Paper, European Commission (1993a).
7   For example, Krugman, P. (1994), 'Competitiveness: A Dangerous Obsession', *Foreign Affairs*, March/April, pp. 28-44.
8   A typical case was the long-lasting disagreement between the British government and some other governments (e.g. the French and Dutch) in deciding the European Action Plan proposed by the European Commission for subsidising HD-MAC, the failed European HDTV (High Definition TV). Both the French and the Dutch governments wanted to approve the proposed €850 million but the British government strongly objected to any further financial subsidy to this perceived European 'strategic' technology. The reason for this was in part due to the fact that the two leading multinational companies, Thomson Multimedia and Philips Electronics, leading the HD-MAC project are respectively French and Dutch. Britain, on the contrary, had no major commercial interest in this European technology. Having blocked the European decision on financing HD-MAC for a long time, the British government eventually accepted a compromised deal with its counterparts – the Action Plan was reduced to €228 million and approved. For more detailed discussion on the European technology policy for HDTV, see Dai, Cawson and Holmes (1996).
9   Peterson, J. and Sharp, M. (1998), *Technology Policy in the European Union*, Macmillan, London, p. 221.
10 The 18 million or so SMEs (companies with less than 250 employees) collectively provide about two thirds of jobs within the EU.
11 European Commission (1999a), *eEurope: An Information Society for All*, Communication on a Commission Initiative for the Special European Council of Lisbon (23 and 24 March 2000), Brussels, 8 December. Under the 'eEurope' Initiative the Commission has proposed 10 priority areas of action: 1) European youth into the digital age (bring internet and multimedia tools to schools and adapt education to the digital age); 2) Cheaper Internet access (increase competition to reduce prices and boost consumer choice); 3) Accelerating e-commerce (speed up implementation of the legal framework and expand use of e-procurement); 4) Fast Internet for researchers and students (ensure high speed access to Internet thereby facilitating co-operative learning and working); 5) Smart cards for electronic access (facilitate the establishment of European-wide infrastructure to maximise uptake); 6) Risk capital for high-tech SMEs (develop innovative approaches to maximise the availability of risk capital for high-tech SMEs) 7) 'eParticipation' for the disabled (ensure that the development of the information society takes full account of the needs of disabled people); 8) Healthcare online (maximise the use of networking and smart technologies

for health monitoring, information access and healthcare); 9) Intelligent transport (safer, more efficient transport through the use of digital technologies); 10) Government online (ensure that citizens have easy access to government information, services and decision-making procedures online).

12 *Financial Times*, 9 December 1999.
13 See Castells, M. (1996), *The Rise of the Network Society*, Blackwell, Oxford.
14 *The Maastricht Treaty*, Article A.
15 The fragmentation of the information and communications services market and the variety of incompatible standards throughout the world often create problem or inconvenience for people travelling and working across national borders. If you travel with a laptop computer using a modem for remote accessing to the Internet, for example, you need to know in advance what telephone socket is used in the destination country. According to TeleAdapt, there are over 40 different phone plugs around the world and their designs vary enormously. 'The telephone companies in each country are renowned for their own self-imposed rules and regulations. The telephone sockets used were decided many years ago when the telephone systems were being put into place. Nobody thought to talk to any one else and assumed their local design was superior to all others. Nobody seriously thought that in 30 years time people would wander around the planet plugging small lumps of plastic and silicon into the sockets either, therefore there was no problem – until now (http://www.teleadapt.com/)!' The operation of a 'Common Information Area' should at least help avoid problems such as this in Europe.
16 The Delors White Paper, European Commission (1993a).
17 *Ibid.*
18 *Ibid.*
19 Gore (1991), p. 111.
20 The Delors White Paper. This point is also recommended in the Bangemann Report, which states '[t]he creation of the information society should be entrusted to the private sector and to the market forces'.
21 *Ibid.*
22 Up until now, in Britain, Oftel and the ITC are still co-existing and there is no evidence to suggest the emergence of a 'Communications Commission' type of establishment, which would be all-embracing in the converged digital information and communications sector.
23 NERA & Denton Hall (1997). *Issues Associated with the Creation of a European Regulatory Authority for Telecommunications*, A Report for the European Commission (DGXIII), London, March.
24 The Bangemann Report, *op cit.*
25 NERA & Denton Hall, *op cit.*
26 NERA & Denton Hall, *op cit.*
27 At the moment, each of the 15 EU Member States has its own regulatory authorities concerning the telecommunications sector.
28 The Bangemann Report, *op cit*. Largely due to the leading role played by Martin Bangemann, the former European Commissioner responsible for telecommunications and industry, this report is widely known as the 'Bangemann Report'. As recommended in this Report, a regulatory authority at the European level for the European information infrastructures and services would seem necessary. The Report

29 believes there is a clear requirement for the new 'rules of the game' to be outlined as a matter of urgency.
29 The Delors White Paper. European Commission (1993a).
30 Curwen, P. (1995), 'Telecommunications Policy in the European Union: Developing the Information Superhighway', *Journal of Common Market Studies*, Vol. 33, No. 3, p. 355.
31 *Financial Times*, 8 February 2000. At the moment VAT rates in the EU varies between 15% and 25%. In 1999, total VAT loss in the EU was estimated at about 5% (or euro10 billion) of total VAT take through fraud.
32 European Commission (1999a), *eEurope: An Information Society for All*, Communication on a Commission Initiative for the Special European Council of Lisbon (23 and 24 March 2000), Brussels, 8 December.
33 European Commission (1999b), *Towards a New Framework for Electronic Communications Infrastructure and Associated Services: The 1999 Communications Review*, COM(1999) 539 Final, 10 November.
34 *Ibid*.
35 It was reported that Romano Prodi recently promised to go ahead with European integration but pledged not to trample on national sensitivities. See *The Times*, 10 February 2000.
36 *The Times*, 10 February 2000.
37 European Commission (1993a) COM(93) 700 final.
38 Other members of the HLGIS are: Enrico Cabral Da Fonseca, Peter Davis, Cario de Benedetti, Pehr Gyllenhammar, Lothar Hunsel, Pierre Lescure, Pascual Maragall, Gaston Thorn, Candido Velazquez-Gastelu, Peter Bonfield, Etienne Davignon, Jean-Marie Descarpentries, Brian Ennis, Hans-Olaf Henkel, Anders Knutsen, Constantin Makropoulos, Romano Prodi, Jan Timmer and Heinrich von Pierer. It is interesting to note that some of the HLGIS Group are actually former chief executives of large European companies.
39 European Commission (1994), *The Action Plan: Europe's Way to the Information Society*, COM(94) 347 final.
40 Department of Trade and Industry (1998a) *Our Competitive Future: Building the Knowledge Driven Economy*, CM 4176, London, HMSO.
41 For instance, to make 1 million businesses connected to the digital market place by 2002.
42 Blair, T. (1998), 'Forward' to the DTI White Paper *Our Competitive Future*.
43 The Bangemann Report, *op cit*.
44 For example, a global competition scheme, 'The Bangemann Challenge', for the best ICT projects was initiated by the City of Stockholm. Under this scheme, Stockholm challenges cities in the whole world to show their finest information technology projects in the Global Bangemann Challenge. This international IT Award Program started in early 1997 and will end in June 1999. During the two years nearly 700 projects entered the competition. Projects submitted range from high technology to application of computer access to information; from technologically advanced regions like the USA and Scandinavia to communities with relatively limited resources in for instance Colombia and the Australian Outback. For more details, see http://challenge.stockholm.se/.
45 See http://www.ispo.cec.be/infoforum/isf.html.

46 This is confirmed by a recent study report sponsored by the European Commission. See Lebessis, N. and Paterson, J. (1997), *Evolution in Governance: What Lessons for the Commission?* Forward Studies Unit, European Commission, Brussels.
47 The EUROPA website is http://europa.eu.int.
48 European Commission (1998a), *Public Sector Information: A Key Resource for Europe: Green Paper on Public Sector Information in the Information Society*, COM(98) 585.
49 *Eurobarometer*, No. 49, September 1998. This includes 23% of EU citizens really needing to know a lot more and 45% wanting to have some information.
50 *Ibid.*
51 *CommunicationsWeek Inernational*, 15 February 1999.
52 *Ibid.*
53 http://europa.eu.int/geninfo/mailbox/index_en.htm.
54 Kennedy (1979).
55 The Bangemann Report, *op cit*.
56 For instance, the Bangemann Report is entitled *Europe and the Global Information Society*, which puts Europe into a global context.
57 European Commission (1998b), *Globalisation and the Information Society: The Need for Strengthened International Coordination*, COM(98) 50 final, Brussels.
58 *Ibid.*
59 *Ibid.*
60 LUO Guanzhong (1330-1400), *Sanguo Yanyi* [Manoeuvring of the Three Kingdoms].
61 For instance, the national communications networks in Estonia, Latvia and Lithuania, had been part of the former Soviet networks until the beginning of the 1990s.
62 Bearing in mind that other aspects of the CEEC economies need to be modernised as well.
63 Community *acquis* refers to Community rules, standards and all the measures implementing common policies.
64 European Commission (1998d), *Central and Eastern Eurobarometer*, No. 8, May.
65 *Ibid.*
66 The Delors White Paper, *op cit*.
67 ESIS Database – Statistical Overview, January 1999. http://esis.kuntalitto.fi/Statistiques/index.htm.
68 ESIS Database – Statistical Overview, January 1999.
69 For more details, see ESIS Database – Statistical Overview, January 1999.
70 US Vice President Al Gore, quoted in Clinton, W. and Gore, A. (1997), *A Framework for Global Electronic Commerce*, http://www.iitf.nist.gov/eleccomm/ecomm.htm.

3 Networked Governance for a 'Network Society'?[1]

Introduction

Following on the discussions in the previous chapter about the impact of the emergent information society upon the process of European integration, this chapter investigates further into the formation and functioning of networked governance in Europe. In the context of the European information society programme, two transnational policy networks involving a large number of subnational public authorities from many parts of Europe have been chosen as the empirical ground of the analysis. The choice of the policy networks perspective, essentially an actor-based approach, serves the purpose of providing a conceptual framework for the understanding about the interaction between the European institutions, primarily the European Commission, and the alliance of regional and local government authorities.

There are basically two opposing schools of thought dominating the stage of academic debate about the issue of who governs the European Union (EU); from a neorealistic perspective, the 'states' are here to stay and they dominate and will continue to dominate the political fate of Europe; whilst from a neofunctionalist point of view, however, the 'dissemination of power' is the focus and supranational institutions will become central actors, transgressing national boundaries by forging influential transnational policy communities (Kohler-Koch, 1996). The emergence of the vast literature on the role of policy communities/policy networks in recent years is associated with the second school.

Although the idea of policy networks has been particularly prominent in the UK (Ansell, Parsons and Darden, 1997), it is becoming an increasingly important approach endorsed by students of the international EU studies community. Some suggest that the so-called policy community/policy network model has already become the dominant model for analysing the policy process in Western Europe (Richardson, 1996). This is because policy network analysis allows us to go beyond specifying EU policy opportunity structures in abstract terms towards actually understanding who benefits from them (Peterson, 1997).

Applying the theories of policy networks to the analysis of the formation and operation of two major transnational alliances, i.e., the Inter-Regional Information Society Initiative (IRISI) and the TeleCities network, this chapter seeks to address a number of important questions such as: What role do policy networks play in disseminating policy innovations at the European level? To what extent are EU information society policies influenced by the lobbying of pan-European interest groups and how are organised interests fed into the process of EU governance in terms of policy outcome? Doe the arrival of the 'information society provide new political opportunities for both the European institutions, such as the European Commission and the Committee of the Regions, and European regional and local authorities at the subnational level to improve their policymaking profile? Does the operation of the new information society policy networks suggest in any sense a closure between the European Commission and the subnational policy actors at the expense of the national governments within the EU? Finally, Does the development of the information society policy networks provide new argument in favour of 'Europe of the regions' rather than 'Europe of the states'? It is hoped that the search for answers to these questions will contribute to the understanding about the constantly changing and extremely complicated process of European governance in the context of globalisation facilitated to a great extent by new information and communications technologies (ICTs).

Policy Networks in the Network Society

In his widely cited volume, *The Rise of the Network Society*, Castells defines a 'network is a set of interconnected nodes';[2] networks constitute the new social morphology of our societies and the diffusion of networking logic substantially modifies the operation, and outcomes in processes of production, experience, power and culture (1996). In the network society, the 'inclusion/exclusion in networks, and the architecture of relationships between networks, enacted by light-speed operating information technologies, configurate dominant processes and functions in our societies (*Ibid.*, p. 470). In other words, Castells believes the presence or absence in the network and the dynamics of each network *vis-à-vis* other networks are critical sources of power and change in the network society.

It is argued that Europe is fast becoming a 'network Europe' – different parts of Europe is linked together with a high-speed or broadband information infrastructure, which constitute the core of a 'Common Information Area' (Federal Trust, 1995). If the power structure of the global network society is essentially characterised by the functioning of 'networks', as Castells argues, how important are the new 'policy networks' to the governance of a 'network Europe'?

It is suggested that a 'policy network' may be defined as 'a (more or less) structured cluster of public and private actors who are stakeholders in a specific sector of policy and possess resources which allow them to affect policy outcomes' (Peterson 1997, p. 7). Theoretically, 'the workings of policy networks are critical for promoting the diffusion of policy innovations' (Mintrom and Vergari, 1998, p. 128). Proponents of policy network theories argue that there are different types of policy networks operating within the policymaking process. In parallel with 'policy network', other terms are also widely used such as 'policy communities' and 'issue networks'.[3] Some have suggested that, among the variety of different terms, 'policy network' could be used as a generic term (Richardson, 1996).

Despite the wide range of literature and varied theoretical approaches, there is a consensus that 'EU governance is not based on government-like structures, on a strong authoritative basis' and that 'power is exercised by sharing and pooling resources among many divergent actors (often through establishing policy networks)' (Tömmel, 1998, p. 54). Consequently, '[a] considerable amount of EU decision-making now occurs within policy networks' (Peterson, 1997, p. 17). In describing the patterns of multi-level governance in the Eurpeanisation of regional policies, Benz and Eberlein (1999) argue that EU policymaking is achieved by power-sharing between different levels of government and policy networks are formed for collaboration based on variable combinations of government authorities – European, national and subnational. Within the 'triad' (European-national-subnational) of EU policymaking, the overall pattern 'is not that of three levels of actors engaged in policy-network cooperation, but of constantly shifting alliances within the triad. We see incidents of successful national – subnational alliances, followed by successful EU-subnational alliances, within the same region' (Ansell, Parsons and Darden, 1997, p. 350).

The empirical research presented in this chapter has identified large-scale across-border alliances among subnational public authorities, who were then collectively engaged in alliance with the European institutions at the EU level.

Compared to the nature and role of the national government in Western democracies, the European Commission, the Executive of the EU, suffers from a number of weaknesses in terms of the limited power in policymaking. Then why is the Commission still interested in encouraging, financing and opening its door to various policy networks, which are eager to share its already limited power in policymaking? Richardson (1996) offers the following explanation:

> By drawing other policy actors into the policy process, the Commission may be able to build coalition in favour of its own notions of desirable policy change. By assisting the formation of networks of 'relevant' state and non-state actors, or by 'messaging' the way that these networks operate, the Commission can maintain its position as an 'independent' policy-making institution and can increase its leverage with the Council of Ministers and the European Parliament. Information and ideas are important building blocks in the process (p. 15).

Meanwhile, the European Commission expects that these policy networks are able to elaborate – on the basis of exchanging experiences – policy proposals and, on the other hand, the creation of the European-wide policy networks mobilises the regions as potential allies of the Commission in that they are stimulated to claim further funding or an extension of European policies to their advantages (Tömmel, 1998). That is to say, there seems to exist a kind of symbiosis relationship between European institutions, in particular the European Commission, and European-wide transnational policy networks – one can not live, at least as well as they do today, without the other.

The interdependence of European institutions and the inter-regional or transnational policy networks reflects a more general trend of Europeanisation of regional/local development and localisation of EU policies characterised by the multi-layered decision-making framework of EU governance. The motivation behind this trend is that region level authorities are seeking more autonomy and participation in European policy games (from below) and the European Commission is looking for partners and support for territorial and other issues (Benz and Eberlein, 1999).

Europeanisation and the Information Society

The information society is about the rapid development and changes intermediated by the advancement and diffusion of new information and communications technologies, which is transforming many aspects of economic and social life. From an economic and social cohesion point of view, the information society refers to the results of a wide process of structural change, with strong technological, socio-economic and institutional components, which have a pervasive impact across all realms of human activity. As far as its impact on regional development is concerned, the information society has the following potential,[4] as recognised by many European regions:

- It makes globalisation of the economy possible;
- It has wide implications in the spatial organisation and territorial distribution of economic activities;
- It has implications in the competitiveness of regions and in the relative role of regions in the global context.

Optimists believe that one of the characteristics of the digital communications networks is that distance is becoming increasingly irrelevant – business and work collaboration, and the exchange of information can just as easily take place across oceans as within the same city (Bangemann, 1997). As a result, it can be predicted that there will be a steady increase in cross-border communications, including telephone conversation, multimedia communication, collaborative working, and electronic trading, etc. (*Ibid*.) The potential of new ICTs to bridge geographical distance has led quite naturally to a focus on the potential of the information society to contribute to the development of and greater integration of, in particular, peripheral and less-favoured regions in Europe (High Level Group of Experts, 1996).

Thanks to the increasingly sophisticated telecommunications networks (e.g. fixed line networks, mobile networks and satellite networks), the rapid introduction of multi-channel digital TV broadcasting and, more importantly, the phenomenal growth of the Internet, there is a growing need for international coordination in coping with the challenges posed by the information society.[5] Seemingly, the emergent network society provides a new opportunity and powerful argument in favour of enhanced governance at the supranational level. It is argued that,

> The European Union has an important role to play, in accordance with the principle of subsidiarity, where objectives can not be sufficiently achieved by member states because of the scale or effects of changes involved, where states are unable to provide an adequate institutional framework, and because of the implications of information networking for cross-border trade and EU-wide development (Federal Trust, 1995, p. 28).

It is not surprising at all that the European Commission recognises the potential of the network society and is willing to explore the opportunities offered by new ICTs for raising its policymaking profile. The publication of the European Commission's White Paper in December 1993 (or the Delors White Paper), *on Growth, Competitiveness and Employment*, and the Bangemann Report in May 1994, *on Europe and the Global Information Society*, is of great significance in terms of providing a new vision on the way the geography of Europe is shaped in the information age. One of the key proposals presented in the Delors White Paper was the accelerated development of the Trans-European Networks (TENs) including a Trans-European Network of Transport, Trans-European Network of Energy and Trans-European Network of Telecommunications (TEN-Telecom). Although work in the European Commission on the TENs had started before the Maastricht Treaty, it is this Treaty that gave specific legal backing to the concept of Trans-European Networks in Article 129 (b) to (d) and provides therefore a firm legal base for Union action in this field (Federal Trust, 1995, p. v).

As discussed in Chapter 2, the TEN-Telecom proposal was to construct a physical or technological network as the fundamental backbone to connect the separated or fragmented national European markets together and this would, as hoped by the EU authorities, constitute the key element of a pan-European information infrastructure. With a fully liberalised telecommunications infrastructure run on a commercial base in place, 'an IT-rich Europe, united (communicatively, at least), by universal broadband network will be sufficiently endowed in technical and economic terms to compete with the world's best (Federal Trust, 1995, p. 7).'

European integration is not just about a 'technology' Community but also a 'social' and 'economic' (if not yet political in its full sense) community. Therefore, the Bangemann Report has proposed a series of applications, i.e. principal areas of development using new information and communications technologies, in particular the new communications infrastructure.

The launch of the two important policy networks, i.e. IRISI and TeleCities, in Europe happened at a time when '[m]ost nations recognise that building an infrastructure for communicating and facilitating the movement of information throughout the society, is a useful tool for governance as well as a vital part of economic and social development' (Lin, 1997). European cities and regions needed to access the financial resources available at the European level (handled by the European Commission); they also needed to be better informed of European policymaking and learn from the experience of other places in many aspects of local governance in the information age.

Although a 'growing area of entrepreneurial policy response at the local level has been try and gain some leverage over ICT developments' (Gibbs and Tanner, 1997, p. 34), the resources and capacity of public authorities at the subnational level to individually explore the political and economic opportunities offered by the information society are very limited. Instead, transnational alliances with other policy actors of the same or similar status in other parts of Europe could be more beneficial.

On the other hand, '[t]he European Commission also needs these associations not only to obtain technical information, but also in order to use them as an information network for EC problems' (Sidjanski, 1997, p. 7). It is believed that regional and local authorities are better situated and understand the local situation and dynamic at regional level and, in the meantime, they are the focal point of any strategy building and they can provide the continuation in the learning and the experience gained in the new environment (The Policy Studies Institute *et al*, 1997).

Regarding the role of the regions in shaping the European information society policy, the IRISI network envisages the following aspects:

First, the telecommunications revolution is both a threat and an opportunity for regions and the challenge for the regions therefore is to manage the process of adjustment and transformation to the information society so that it reflects both the regional and public interest.

Second, regions are at the heart of the European information society agenda because they are essential to its successful diffusion – the local agenda is of crucial importance to the development of the information society.

Third, regions provide a framework for integrating telematics services and applications and, by adopting a local perspective, regions acquire a sense of the importance of integration.

Fourth, regions offer the opportunity to monitor and evaluate the impact and effectiveness of progress towards the information society.

Finally, regions are important agents of social change – the impact of social innovation and change is manifested at the local level.[6]

In short, the new information society policy networks were launched by the EU and subnational public authorities to take the advantage of new ICTs, which are intrinsically transnational – in spatial terms, they offer the potential to overcome the constrains of national borders and local isolation. This is perhaps one of the strengths of the IRISI and TeleCities networks.

Europe of the Regions: The Regional Information Society Initiative

The European information society policy agenda serves the purpose of achieving, amongst others, economic and social cohesion and the completion of the internal common market. The new Treaty of the European Union (TEU), signed in 1993, provides a solid legal foundation for European cities and regions to become involved in the process of creating a European information society. Referring to the Trans-European Networks, the TEU[7] stipulates:

- To help achieve the objectives referred to in Articles 7a and 130a and to enable citizens of the Union, economic operators and regional and local communities to derive full benefit from the setting up of an area without internal frontiers, the Community shall contribute to the establishment and development of trans-European networks in the areas of transport, telecommunications and energy infrastructures.
- Within the framework of a system of open and competitive markets, action by the Community shall aim at promoting the interconnection and interoperability of national networks as well as access to such networks. It shall take account in particular of the need to link island, landlocked and peripheral regions with the central regions of the Community.

In line with the TEU, the Bangemann Report recommended ten important applications necessary for launching the information society in Europe, one of which is to develop City Information Highways. This is to '[s]et up networks providing households with a network access system and the means of using on-line multimedia and entertainment services on a local, regional, and national and international basis.'[8] A large number of local (city and regional) public authorities throughout Europe have responded positively to the policy initiatives of the European Commission and actively preparing themselves to face the perceived challenges posed by the information society. This has led to the launch of numerous 'digital' or 'virtual' city and 'tele-region' projects.[9] In the meantime, European cities and regions have also formed consortia to join up efforts and resources in developing information society related projects. On the one hand, these consortia are indicative of the local authorities' desire for being engaged in a process of 'collective learning';[10] on the other hand, they have become, to a certain extent, a new platform for the European authorities (particular the European Commission) to disseminate information society policies and strategies.

In response to the Bangemann Report, and under the auspices of the European Commission, six European regions[11] signed a 'Memorandum of Understanding' in November 1994 to jointly launch the Inter-Regional Information Society Initiative (IRISI). The IRISI regional consortium agreed to work together and progress towards the information society. The member regions agreed to share experience with each other in formulating their regional information society strategy. Under their contract with the European Commission, each of the IRISI members has the overall responsibility for the respective region's participation in developing the regional information society strategy. Each IRISI region represents a region-wide partnership of organisations from sectors such as local businesses and industry, local government, education and training bodies, trade unions, co-operative and the voluntary sector, etc. The operation of the IRISI partnership in each region is coordinated by a local IRISI Steering Group, which drives the process of formulating and implementing the regional information society strategy.

The IRISI's priority fields of collaboration were chosen to mirror the ten major applications recommended in the Bangemann Report. Recognising the importance of this inter-regional initiative as a 'best-practice example', especially for less developed regions in Europe, the European Commission was willing to provide the necessary technical assistance and financial support in its practical organisation and implementation of the cooperation among the members.[12]

Three Directorates-General of the European Commission provide financial support to the European inter-regional information society initiative. These include DG-XVI (Regional Policy and Cohesion) in charge of the European Regional Development Fund (ERDF) under Article 10 of the TEU; DG-V (Employment, Industrial Relations and Social Affairs) in charge of the European Social Fund (ESF) under Article 6 of the TEU and DG-XIII (Information Society) in charge of the European Telecommunications Policy budget. Undoubtedly, the inter-regional information society network helps translate the concept of the information society into the process of achieving the goals of the European regional policy, social and employment policy and technology/industrial policy, which are three important policy domains.

At the regional level, each of the six IRISI regions established their own Regional Information Society Steering Group (RISSG) and a Regional Information Society Unit (RISU) with funding from DGXVI. The RISSG and RISU are responsible for forging partnerships, formulating a regional strategy and developing an action plan for the region. The six IRISI regions, with financial and technical support from DGXIII, then established a Network Management Committee (NMC), whose membership consists of representatives from the six RISSGs, DGXIII and DGXVI. The NMC has its Network Bureau in Brussels.[13]

The IRISI network has established a series of thematic inter-regional work groups seeking in-depth discussion and understanding about the key issues related to the information society. These thematic work groups are used for exchanging experience and collective learning between different European regions.

Table 3.1 The European Regional Information Society Initiative: RISI and IRISI

	Region	Initiative (Partnership)	Country	EU Funding (€)	Population (1,000's)
R I S I	Steiermark	TELEKIS	Austria	250,000	1,175
	Liège	FASIL	Belgium	249,990	250
	West Finland Alliance	PARADDIS	Finland	249,800	1,314
	North Karelia	NOKIS	Finland	n.a.	178
	Midi-Pyrenees	TELEPARC	France	n.a.	173
	Limonsin	ACTI-Limousi	France	249,680	723
	Poitou-Charentes	SERISE	France	250,000	1,595
	Bremen	BRISE	Germany	n.a.	684
	Brandenburg	BIS2006	Germany	250,000	2,500
	Schleswig-Holstein	INFOSH	Germany	250,000	2,700
	Attica	ATHINA	Greece	n.a.	3,600
	Epirus	RISE	Greece	250,000	679
	South West of Ireland	STAND	Ireland	n.a.	532
	Shannon	ShIPP	Ireland	250,000	400
	Calabria	ARIANNA	Italy	250,000	2,000
	Murcia	ESSIMUR	Spain	n.a.	1,099
	Extremadura	INFODEX	Spain	250,000	1.094
	Västerbotten	AC-Direkt	Sweden	250,000	260
	Blekinge	IT-Blekinge	Sweden	n.a.	160
	Wales	WIS	UK	n.a.	2,886
	North of England	NiSTRAT	UK	250,000	3,100
	Yorkshire & Humberside	CoMPRIS	UK	250,000	4,950
	Total Population				**32,000**
I R I S I	Nord Pas-de-Calais		France	n.a.	1,200
	Saxony		Germany	n.a.	4,800
	Central Mecedonia		Greece	n.a.	1,700
	Piemonte		Italy	n.a.	4,400
	Valencia		Spain	n.a.	3,800
	North West England		UK	n.a.	7,000
	Total				**25,700**

Source: Adapted from RISI (http://www.risi.lu/Internal/EC/gen-inf/reg-list.htm) and other sources.

The IRISI network, from the European Commission's point of view, operates as a 'test-bed' for its new vision and new policy initiatives on the information society. Clearly, 'IRISI has been successful in raising the Information Society as an issue in the region.'[14] As for the regions, participating in the IRISI process is an important means for securing European funding:

> Now that the Information Society is being mainstreamed and resourced by the European Union – resources allocated to it can be expected to rise dramatically as money moves from physical infrastructure to telematics – IRISI is going to become much more important [to the participating regions].[15]

As a matter of fact, five of the six IRISI regions had received further substantial support from the EU structural funds by April 1997, when the initial phase of the network concluded, in order to 'keep the show on the road'.[16]

In addition to the financial benefit, the operation of IRISI also helps raise the political and policymaking profile of the regions:

> It [IRISI] will give the regions a significant voice in defining just how the Information Society will be interpreted at the local level. Projects have to meet local need.[17]

On the completion of the pre-pilot phase of the regional information society initiative, i.e. IRISI, in 1997, the European Commission selected 22 European regions for funding under the RISI (Regional Information Society Initiative) scheme. The increased membership has turned the regional information society network into a much more influential organisation. Similar to its predecessor IRISI, RISI aims at integrating the concept of the information society into regional development strategies in less developed regions of the European Union. The principal objectives of RISI include:

- Developing consensus and partnership among key regional players[18] around a regional information society strategy defining the challenges and opportunities associated with the information society in a regional context;
- Developing a regional action plan for implementing the information society strategy in order to contribute to regional economic development;

- Creating a common platform for the exchange of experience, know-how and projects among the regions.

The most recent development of the regional information society network was the formation of the eris@ (European Regional Information Society Association) incorporating both the IRISI and RISI members. It was also decided that membership of the newly launched eris@ would be open to all European regions and, most significantly, regions from central and east European countries can now join the network. It seems likely that the eris@ has the potential to become a new factor contributing to both the 'deepening' and 'widening' of European integration in the information age.

Europe of the Cities: The TeleCities Network

The TeleCities has become one of the most important policy networks related to the information society development in Europe. In October 1993, representatives of 13 European cities[19] signed the 'Manchester Declaration' to launch a collaborative initiative entitled TeleCities. By July 1998, this network had been joined by 121 members with its coordinating office in Brussels.

Table 3.2 Membership of the TeleCities network

Type of Membership	Membership (July 1997)	Membership (July 1998)
European local authorities (full members)	81	89
Local authorities from the CEECs	7	9
Provinces (associated members)	3	3
European local authorities (observers)	2	2
Private organisations (observers)	15	18
Total	108	121

Source: Based on the TeleCities Network (1997 and 1998).

It is suggested that, by July 1998, the 89 full members of the TeleCities Network represent 44.5 million inhabitants of the EU (or about 14% of the total EU population) (The TeleCities Network, 1998).

The main objective of the TeleCities network is to promote and develop telematics applications supporting urban regeneration *via* cross-border collaboration in terms of sharing experience and ideas in formulating information society policies and strategies at the municipality level and promoting joint projects between member cities. More specifically, the TeleCities network has identified four priorities of operation:[20]

- Support the development of telematics projects and strategies on a cohesive, trans-European basis;
- Identify projects of common interest where European financial support would give a clear added value element to telematics applications;
- Develop an effective dialogue with relevant European institutions working in the field of new information and communications technologies;
- Participate in the building of the global information society.

The priorities of TeleCities suggest that, first of all, the nature of this network of city governments is 'trans-European' or transnational. In other words, TeleCities has become an important new platform, on which European local governments can directly communicate and collaborate with each other. This 'trans-European' or transnational feature has the potential to reduce the level of barriers associated with physical geography and national borders.

Secondly, TeleCities is important to its member cities in terms of attracting EU funding. As European financial support is often allocated to projects involving partners from more than one European country, the TeleCities network offers a convenient solution to the problem of partner seeking for organisations based in the member cities in proposing telematics projects. EU funding can be said one of the magnetic factors holding the TeleCities members together.

Thirdly, the existence of the TeleCities network has increased the collective 'bargaining' power of the local governments *vis-à-vis* the relevant European institutions in charge of policy making in the field of new information and communications technologies. TeleCities simply adds a new channel of dialogue or a new link between the European local authorities and the various European institutions. At almost every major TeleCities events (e.g. conferences and seminars), officials from the European Commission and members of the European Parliament were often among the invited speakers.

Fourthly, most local authorities, like those TeleCities members, have a strong desire to overcome the constraints of locality, rather than becoming isolated in the process of the global digital revolution. In order to achieve this, members of the TeleCities network wish to participate in the building of the global information society, as outlined by the G7 conference of February 1995 in Brussels.

The TeleCities network has established 9 different thematic Working Groups. It is worth noting that each of these Working Groups consists of representatives from different member cities, who have teamed up to discuss issues related to a particular area of the information society. The Working Group papers and reports are then distributed among all the members of the TeleCities network.

A New Mode of European Governance?

Members of both the TeleCities and the IRISI/RISI networks are either exclusively or mainly subnational public authorities from many parts of Europe. These networks of regional/local authorities, which are policymaking bodies themselves, apparently constitute a new mode of European governance and serve the purpose of strengthening European regionalism in the information age.

Compared to conventional types of policy networks, the existence and operation of the information society policy networks depend crucially upon access and affordability to advanced information and communications technologies and infrastructure. It can be said that the IRISI/RISI and the TeleCities are policy networks formed and operating in a 'network society', in which 'network Europe' is a part.

The most important features of the two policy networks discussed in this chapter, i.e. RISI and TeleCities, include, among others: disseminating European policies and strategies; transnational cooperation; direct interaction with the public authorities at all levels in order to influence European regional policy outcomes (in terms of policy orientation and funding allocation); reliance upon EU funding.

Disseminating European Policies and Strategies

The regions and cities involved in the cross-border policy networks have a consensus that collaboration at the regional level is fast becoming a favoured policy instrument. Apart from the economies of scale and opportunities for mutual that learning transnational collaboration might offer, pan-European policy networks provide policymakers and key actors with useful insights into a range of possible policy alternatives.[21] In the meantime, regions and cities could act as laboratories for the development of the information society applications and services: '[w]hat collaboration at the regional level does provide however is an "a la carte" menu of policy options and tools with which regions can experiment locally.'[22]

Regarding the role of the newly launched European Regional Information Society Association, it was suggested that the formation of the organisation is a vital step in developing a strategic approach to the information society and one of its aims is:

> To provide a forum to discuss policy relevant to regional development and the Information Society. We are co-operating with the EC [European Commission] on the Policy Responses requested at the Regional/National/European [level] as we enter the new structural fund programme period.[23]

Table 3.3   Information society policy dissemination *via* new policy networks

The Bangemann Report	IRISI/RISI/eris@	TeleCities
Ten Applications suggested: • Teleworking • Distance learning • A network for universities and research centres • Telematic services for SMEs • Road traffic management • Air traffic control • Healthcare networks • Electronic tendering • Trans-European public administration networks • City information highways	*Working Groups*: • Education & training • Healthcare • Public administration • Rural areas • SMEs • Social affairs	*Thematic Working Groups*: • Teledemocracy • Employment and teleworking • Economic development and SMEs • Quality of life for disabled people • Public administration and city information highways • Education and training • City healthcare • Environment • Technical standards

It can be said that new policy networks have become an effective conduit for disseminating European policies and strategies on the development of the information society.

Table 3.3 compares the six Working Groups of the IRISI/RISI/eris@ network and the nine Thematic Working Groups of the TeleCities network with the ten major applications recommended in the Bangemann Report, one of the key European Commission policy documents launching the European Information Society Programme. It is evident that both the IRISI/RISI/eris@ and the TeleCities networks have organised their Working Groups or priority areas in a way reflecting the recommendations of the Bangemann Report.

Transnational Cooperation

The new geography of the information society offers potentially significant opportunities for European cities and regions, especially those 'peripheral' areas in terms of regeneration. On the one hand, more and more cities and regions are becoming aware of the need for drawing up new strategies in order to adapt the regional economic base to the challenges of the new ICT revolution. This would require new ways of collaboration between the 'key regional players' or key stakeholders within the city or region involving both the public sector and private sector organisations. On the other hand, cities and regions are encouraged to cooperate with their counterparts in other parts of Europe. The European Commission's High Level Group of Experts (HLGE) on the information society sees the inter-regional groups, such as the TeleCities and the IRISI/RISI, as import vehicles for transnational cooperation and the sharing of experience and, therefore, recommends:

> It should be a central policy aim to encourage the cooperation of regions around Europe so that cooperative learning between cities and regions about the IS [Information Society] can take place. These networks should have some justifiable potential for synergies between them for instance by virtue, for example, of similar industrial histories. ICT networks should be developed to encourage the interchange and building-up of experience. Therefore, a major function of these networks should be to help the transfer of experiences to other regions (HLGE, 1996, pp. 46-47).

With the increased availability of new ICTs at an ever declining cost, such as the Internet, video-conferencing and telecommunications, etc., the TeleCities and IRISI/RISI/eris@ networks are attracting a growing number of members from all over Europe (both the EU and the CEECs) to join the transnational clubs of collaboration. In the commercial world, '[c]ompany HQ, in remote Massachusetts or Osaka, care little for where their workers are located as long as they are joined corporately by satellite and fibre-optic links in order to communicate efficiently and to down-load extensive computerised files from one location to another (Federal Trust, 1995, p. 16).' A similar trend is certainly gathering momentum within the public sector.

The legacy of experimental information society policy networks, such as the IRISI, is highly praised by the European Commission and other European regions are encouraged to join the bandwagon:

> For regions to develop effectively, they must have access to the networks of the Information Society and undertake actions relating to awareness raising, training and support for new SMEs. Regions need to seize the opportunities associated with the Information Society. The IRISI regions have demonstrated that they can and should play a prime role in the development of the European Information Society.[24]

Multilevel and Collective Lobbying

The European Commission, particularly DGXVI, DGXIII and DGV, is closely involved in the establishment and operation of the IRISI/RISI/eris@ and TeleCities networks throughout the process. In the case of IRISI, for instance, the European Commission is represented in the Network Management Committee. On the one hand, the European Commission is obliged to make sure that the new policy networks would work – they ought to deliver those promised deliverables to the expectation of the EU funding. But on the other hand the close involvement of the European Commission has provided the convenience for these policy networks to lobby the relevant parts of the Commission for continued and increased financial support. As a matter of fact, the information society policy networks are active in lobbying not only the European Commission but also other European institutions including the Council of Ministers, the European Parliament and the Committee of the Regions. They lobby not only the local and regional authorities but also their respective national governments, which in turn would have influence on all of the European institutions.

Figure 3.1 is a new model produced by the European Regional Information Society Association (eris@), which indicates the main channels of political lobbying used by the RISI members individually and collectively. In order to achieve their objectives, the RISI network exercises its direct lobbying at all levels of policymaking within the entire framework of EU governance: the local and regional level; the national government level and the EU level. During the last round of Structural Funds negotiation, for instance, the RISI network was particularly active. In an attempt to achieve 'a more prominent and coherent place for Information Society developments within the Structural Funds framework', the eris@ specifically suggested to its members that it would be necessary to do the following:[25]

- To act very reasonably quickly;
- To be very clear and precise about the changes that are proposed and the arguments and justifications for their adoption;
- To mobilise the support of the regional authority in seeking to influence their national government to bring pressure to bear and to make direct representations to the Commission;
- For RISI projects to make direct approaches themselves to their relevant national ministries and to the Commission;
- RISI projects in the same Member State might consider taking collective action and making joint approaches;
- For RISI Regions to mobilise other non-RISI regions in their country, encouraging them to address the information society in a strategic fashion and to lend their support in efforts to mainstream the information society as a vehicle for regional recovery and development;
- For RISI projects to consider a collective approach through their new Association [i.e., eris@] in making representations to the Commission, the European Parliament and to the Committee of the Regions.

The eris@ also specifically suggested that once Member States have submitted their proposed programmes to the European Commission, RISI projects should enter a dialogue with the appropriate desk officers in the relevant Geographical Units of DGV and DGXVI with a view to presenting their information society priorities and the justification for them, thereby seek to persuade the desk officers of the importance of including information society measures in the regional Structural Funds programme.[26]

The RISI network has certainly been successful in winning important friends inside the European Commission. At a recent Annual Conference of the RISI regions in Lübeck, the Director of DGXVI, Graham Meadows, offered himself as the 'godfather in Brussels' of the RISI regions.[27]

Figure 3.1   Information society policy networks and EU regional policymaking

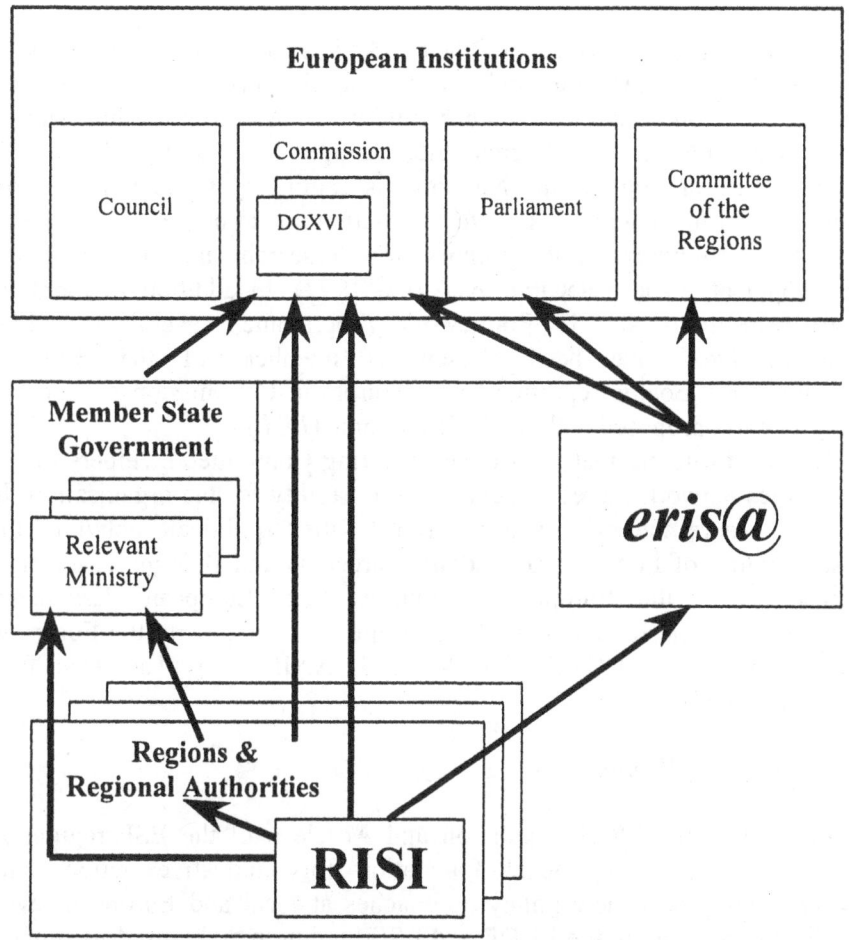

Source: Adapted from the European Regional Information Society Association (1998), *Newsletter*, Issue No. 4, Special Edition, October-November.

Members of the TeleCities Networks share the view of those of the eris@ and are convinced of the strategic importance of lobbying (or having dialogue with) the European institutions, in particular the European Commission:

Cities are the engines of regional economic development. Consequently, they play an important role in the realisation of the Information Society. ... TeleCities also recommends to strengthen the dialogue between cities and the

European Commission. This will enable the members of the TeleCities organisation to continue to respond to the needs and aspirations of citizens and enterprises (The TeleCities Network, 1996).

To be sure, the TeleCities Network has been active in making 'contribution' to European policy ever since its inception. For instance, having been consulted in September 1996 by the European Commission in the preparation of the Digital Sites action line of the Telematics Applications Programne, the Network 'is continuing its lobbying to the European Parliament and others, for this action line to be further developed within 5th Framework Programme for Research and Technological Development' (The TeleCities Network, 1997). In addition to lobbying with respect to the 5th Framework Programme, several TeleCities representatives have been chosen as members of the Strategic Requirements Boards reporting to the European Commission on specific priority areas proposed within this Programme (*Ibid.*).

It is worth noting that each of the Steering Committee members of the TeleCities network shares a specific responsibility for the organisation. In part to ensure the effectiveness of TeleCities' political lobbying, the responsibility of Lewisham (London), Barcelona and Bologna is to make contacts with the European institutions (e.g. European Parliament, Committee of the Regions) and hold political meetings with the European Commission (e.g., DGXIII, III, V, XVI, XXII, etc.) (The TeleCities Network, 1997).

The Role of EU Funding

Article 10 of the ERDF regulation and Article 6 of the ESF regulation provide the necessary legal foundation for innovative actions and experimenting with new policy approaches at local and European level. Under EU regulation, the ERDF and ESF funding may be used to support innovative actions in regional development through pilot schemes, which encourage the pooling of experience and the development of inter-regional cooperation.

One of the priority areas for pilot actions qualified for ERDF and ESF assistance during the 1995-1999 period was the translation of the information society concept into regional development policies, in particular those of the Less Favoured Regions (LFR), in the EU through stimulating, experimenting, evaluation and diffusion of best practice.

European regions involved in the RISI activities believe that '[a]ccess to EU Structural Funds is ... likely to play an important, catalytic role in helping to finance the implementation of RISI strategies.'[28] The Chairman of the eris@ Management Committee stated that the objective, from a Regional information Society Initiative (RISI) perspective, 'is to embed the Information Society into the regional development policies and achieve the best possible outcome in terms of financial assistance for the Information Society.'[29]

It is unclear at the time of writing to what extent the information society concept has been 'embedded' into the regional development policies. However, the RISI network and its various projects have certainly achieved remarkable, if not 'the best', policy outcome in terms of securing EU financial assistance since the mid-1990s. More specifically, the RISI initiative has been allocated €20 million and €15 million of the ERDF and the ESF funding respectively.[30]

Table 3.4   Multi-regional information society projects (RISI 2)

Regional (including lead region)	Project Acronym	Sector	ERDF Funding (€)
Madeira, Burgenland, Lappi, Valle d'Aosta, Västerbotten, Hampshire	TOURISM	Tourism	1,744,806
Vorarlberg, Dytikí Elláda, Andalucía, Rhône Alpes, Northern Ireland	RMP	Rural markets	2,125,619
Nordrhein-Westfalen, + Niedersachsen, Wallonie, Vlaanderen, Extremadura, Lorraine, Gelderland, Västernorrland, Northern Ireland	IDAN	Internationalisation of SMEs	1,560,000
Kríti, Epeiros, Islas Baleares, Tampere, Sardegna	TEMeTeN	Health	2,335,069
Galicia, Norte	OUEA	Cooperation between municipalities	1,045,779
Tarn, Andalucía, Haute-Garonne, Etelä-Savo, Dublin and Longford, Scotland	ENTER-SKILLSNET	SMEs in rural areas	1,585,840
North West + Galway, West-Vlaanderen, Aalborg, Zeeland, The Wirral	CRISM	SMEs and public services	1,111,000
Total ERDF contribution to the 7 projects (€)			11,508,113

Source: Information from Inforegio (1999),
http://www.inforegio.org/wbpro/prord/art10/info/info3_en.htm.

Table 3.5 Selected TeleCities information society projects with EU funding

Partners*	Project Acronym	Starting Date and Duration	Total Budget (€)	EU Funding (€)
Den Haag, Newcastle, Leeds, Livorno, Roma, Helsinki	EQUALITY	1.1.96 (2-year)	4,313,500	1,870,000
Antwerp, Nice, Nürnberg, Rotterdam, Stockholm, Amarou-ssion, Joensuu, Strasbourg, Wien	INFOSOND	1.1.96 (2-year)	4,984,000	2,000,000
Den Haag, Amaroussion, Antwerp, Barcelona, Institute Municipal d'Informatica, Berlin, Bologna, Lewisham, Salerno, Helsinki, Liège, Manchester, Nice, Ronneby, Stockholm, Vienna, Nord Pas de Calais, Piemonte	INFOCITIES	Dec. 97 (2-year)	293,000,000	5,000,000
Olivetti,** Antwerp, Nice, Roma	MAGICA	1.1.96 (2-year)	3,450,000	1,650,000
Bologna, Antwerp, Barcelona, Lewisham, Augsburg, Thessaloniki	PH-NET	Apr. 96 (27-month)	1,500,000	750.000
Barcelona, Gothenburg, Cologne, Lewisham, Toulouse, Leipzig, Torino, Las Palmas, Bologna	DALI	1.12.95 (18-month)	4,418,900	2,000,000
Bologna, Lewisham, Ronneby	DIALOGUE	Jan. 98 (1-year)	990,000	475,000
Newcastle University,** Newcastle, Helsinki, Turin, Thessaloniki, Zeeland	DISTINCT	Feb. 98 (2-year)	10,800,000	4,000,000
Barcelona, Green-wich, Southwark, Lewisham, Bologna, Göteborg, Cologne	GALA	Jan. 98	10,800,000	n.a.***

Notes: *The first partner is the coordinator for each project; **Partners other than local or regional authorities in projects are not indicated, unless they are project coordinators; ***EU funding is in the range of 30-40% of the total budget (e.g. EU funding at 35% of the total budget would be €3,810,000).
Sources: Information is from the TeleCities Network (1997) and (1998).

In addition to financing the 6 IRISI and 22 RISI initiatives, the European Commission has selected 22 RISI projects for financial support following a call for proposals launched in September 1995. Among these projects, 9 were designed for transnational cooperation between organisations from over 40 EU regions – with 7 projects funded by the ERDF and 2 by the ESF.

Table 3.4 shows that each of the 7 multi-regional information society projects has received substantial ERDF funding. It was believed that, overall, very few information society initiatives would have got off the ground without the substantial input (in terms of leadership, funds and resources) from the public sector.[31]

Similar to the Regional Information Society Projects, most of the TeleCities projects have attracted substantial European finance. Table 3.5 gives some details about a series of large-scale TeleCities projects in part funded by the EU. The main players within these information society projects are public authorities from European cities. Among other projects, the INFOCITIES project alone has received €5 million, which is a substantial amount of public funding.

Despite the high level of EU funding towards the development of the regional information society initiatives and projects, not all of the regional players were happy about the level of public finance allocated to the RISI network:

> We cannot progress very far on the very very small amount of funding that currently we have available. We're talking here about an initiative, a subject matter which is probably the most exciting development of the 1990s and possibly of our lifetime. We're talking about a method of communication which is going to determine how business is done in the future and yet we are playing with buttons.[32]

Sharing the view of the RISI Network, members of the TeleCities network were not entirely happy with the current level of EU funding to their information society projects:

> Although TeleCities appreciate the support given to a number of projects, the cities were anticipating greater support to their initiatives and a higher level of cross-sectoral funding: only a few projects accepted for funding, and even then with dramatically reduced budgets. We believe that additional funds are required from the EC [European Commission] to meet the demand from urban areas.[33]

Conclusion

The two cases presented in this chapter, the IRISI/RISI/eris@ network and the TeleCities network, suggest that, along with the arrival of the information society, a large number of European regions and cities directly interacted with the European institutions (in particular the European Commission) and sometimes bypassed their respective national government. The resultant outcome of this process of interaction is two-fold. First, the European Commission managed to compensate its relatively weaker position *vis-à-vis* the central governments of the Member States by directly mobilising the policy actors at the subnational government levels, i.e., European regions and cities. It was found in this chapter that EU Structural Funds (and information society related funding opportunities) appeared to be the 'carrots' used by the European Commission at its discretion. Through acting in this way, 'the Commission 'invented' both new modes of formulating and implementing structural policies and new modes of directing the behaviour of lower-level tiers without itself having far-reaching powers and competence at its disposal (Tömmel, 1998, p. 57)'. Whilst representatives of the two major information society policy networks argued that too small a proportion of the European funding had been directed towards the regions and cities, this study found substantial amount of public funding has already been poured into projects under the auspices of these policy networks.

Second, the formation of the inter-regional and transnational policy networks provides new opportunities for the public authorities at the subnational levels (e.g. regional and local) to be engaged in the mainstream European policymaking process by collective bargaining. The two policy networks have both been actively involved in different ways in lobbying the European institutions (e.g. the European Commission and the European Parliament) so that the policy outcomes would turn out to the advantage of the lobbying bodies. Both the IRISI/RISI/eris@ network and the TeleCities network have devised their strategic and organisational mechanisms to facilitate the process of their political lobbying. Meanwhile, the European institutions provided easy access for the information society policy networks' lobbying efforts.

The two dimensions mentioned above, one top-down and another bottom-up, seem to suggest that a new mode of European governance – networked governance or governance by policy networks – has been established, so far as the information society policy process is concerned. This new mode of governance appears to have tipped the balance of the public debate to the advantage of a 'Europe of the regions'.

Since the early 1990s, when the European Commission set the agenda for developing a 'European information society' or a 'network Europe' (Federal Trust, 1995) or a 'Common Information Area' (European Commission, 1993a), other levels of the European public policy actors (e.g. national government level and subnational government levels) have shown, generally speaking, positive response. The European Commission has, indeed, become the 'star' among all of the policy actors involved in promoting the European information society agenda. The launch of the IRISI/RISI/eris@ network and the TeleCities network are both specific responses at the inter-regional and transnational level by the lower tiers of public authorities. It can be said that to a certain extent the two policy networks have become the champions of the European information society policy process. This chapter shows that the arrival of the information society has provided a new political opportunity for both the European institutions, principally the European Commission, and the European regional and local authorities at the subnational levels to effectively raise their policymaking profile within the national and European polity context.

The theories of policy networks proved to be a useful conceptual tool for this chapter. Both the IRISI/RISI/eris@ and the TeleCities are new but very complicated policy networks, which should be taken into account by the study of European governance in the information age or 'the network society' (Castells, 1996). There are a number of important features associated with the two networks compared to other types of European policy networks. First of all, the two networks represent a large number of public authorities at the subnational levels. Members of the networks are normally public policy actors, *albeit* at the local level or regional revel. This character differentiates them from many other policy networks, such as those sector or commercial consortia. Secondly, the two networks are truly transnational in both its membership and scope of operation. Thirdly, members of the two policy networks are mostly 'policy communities' (regional or municipality information society partnerships). Fourthly, the two policy networks consists of a number of 'issue networks' – the Thematic Working Groups and each of these is inter-regional or transnational in its own right. In short, the study of the IRISI/RISI/eris@ and the TeleCities networks provides very interesting and important cases for furthering our understanding about the policy network theories.

Despite the significance of the IRISI/RISI/eris@ network and the TeleCities to the understanding of European governance in the 'network society', it would be misguided to suggest that these two are the only policy networks driving forward the European information society process and that policy networks are the only mode of European governance in the information age. Rather, there are other forms of transnational collaboration which also, if not equally, contribute to the development of the European information society and different modes of governance that have an impact upon the process of European regional integration in the information age.

In addition, it is worth pointing out that the 'network society' has a strong and growing dimension of development, which is characterised by globalisation. Part of the effect of the process of globalisation is that Europe, including its ICT infrastructure, social institutions and the entire polity, is becoming an integral part of the global information society. That is to say, the consideration about any information society policy networks in Europe, such as the IRISI and TeleCities, must be put into an international context. Therefore, any debate about the development of European regional governance in the information age should not be confined exclusively to the geography of the Europe.

The next chapter will look the development of the information society outside Europe with a particular reference to the Chinese experience in governing economic development in the digital age.

Notes

1. An earlier draft of this chapter was presented at the CSGR 3rd Annual Conference on *After the Global Crisis: What Next for Regionalism?* University of Warwick, 16-17 September 1999.
2. Instead of giving a clear and generic definition, Castells (1996) suggests that '[a] node is the point at which a curve interacts itself. What a node is, concretely speaking, depends on the kind of concrete networks of which we speak. They are stock exchange markets, and their ancillary advanced services centres, in the global financial flows. They are national councils of ministers and European Commissioners in the political network that governs the European Union.' (p. 470).
3. The term 'policy community' suggests a very close and stable relationship between policy actors – similar to the relationship between the members of a community; whilst an 'issue network' is defined as a shared-knowledge group having to do with some aspect (or some problem) of public policy. For more detailed discussion about different types of policy networks, see Richardson (1996).
4. See http://www.risi.lu/Internal/EC/gen-inf/concept1.htm for more details.
5. For example, among other international cooperation initiatives, the European Commission recently proposed that an 'International Charter' should be multi-laterally agreed by members of the international community in order to strengthen international cooperation in addressing the issues related to the global information society. See European Commission (1998).
6. See report of the *IRISI Conference on Strategies to Build the Information Society in the Regions*, Torino, Italy, 5-7 October 1995. http://eirs.epri.org/irisi/discussion/torino_report.html.
7. The Maastricht Treaty, Article 129b.
8. The Bangemann Report. The other nine applications are: Teleworking; Distance Learning; University and Research Networks; Telematic Services for SMEs; Road Traffic Management; Air Traffic control; Health Care Networks; Electronic Tendering; Trans-European Public Administration Network.
9. One of the pioneering projects is the Digital City or DDS (*De Digitale Stad*) project, which was launched in 1994 in Amsterdam with financial sponsorship from the Amsterdam City Council and the Dutch Economic Ministry.

10 The term 'collective learning' is described as an important feature of policy networks in Lebessis and Paterson (1997).
11 The six regions are: the Free State of Sachsen (Germany), the Community of Valencia (Spain), the region of Nord-Pas de Calais (France), the region of Central Macedonia (Greece), the region of Piemonte (Italy) an the North West England Region (UK).
12 See http://www_irisi.polito.it/irisi/present.html.
13 For more information see Hughes, G. (1996), 'Progress Report on the Achievements of the IRISI'. http://eris.epri.org/irisi/discussion/paper4.html.
14 The N. W. England IRISI News, 14 April 1997. http://www.irisi.org.uk/news.htm.
15 Ibid.
16 Ibid.
17 Gareth Hughes, IRISI Secretary General, cited in the N. W. England IRISI News, 14 April 1997. It is worth noting that most local and regional authorities have created a designated 'European Office' or, at least a 'European Officer' in charge of European issues including EU funding application. In addition, many some local authorities have also established their own 'Brussels Office', in order to effectively lobby the European Commission on key issues related to the region. For instance, in February 1996 the North West Brussels Office was launched by the North West of England regional authority with Neil Kinnock, the former European Commissioner for transportation, as the principal speaker. The mission of the North West Brussels Office is to lobby and dialogue with the European Commission and other European institutions on important issues such as rail issues, the European Structural Funds, InterReg (the European inter-regional spatial planning programme), the information society (including IRISI) and, overall, the region's European profile. For more details see http://www.u-net.com/northwest/main_top/milest~1/miles0.htm.
18 The European Commission defines 'key regional players' as 'all major players involved in the regional economy who have a direct involvement or may be directly affected by the development of the information society.' The most important ones, among others, include: the regional and local governments; industrial and employer's associations; trade unions; chambers of commerce; financial institutions; regional development agencies; telecommunication operators and information service providers; media and content providers; education and training institutions; higher education, research and development institutions; relevant users groups and the voluntary sector. http://www.risi.lu/Internal/EC/gen-inf/concept2.htm.
19 The 13 cities are Amsterdam, Barcelona, Birmingham, Bologna, Den Haag, Hull, Koln, Leeds, Lille, Manchester, Nantes, Nice and Norttingham.
20 Summarised by Dave Carter, Principal Economic Development Officer of Manchester City Council and former President of TeleCities, in his speech at the *European Digital Cities 1st Conference: The Challenges of the Future*, 8-9 May 1996, Copenhagen.
21 Report of the *IRISI Conference on Strategies to Build the Information Society in the Regions*, Torino, Italy, 5-7 October 1995. http://eirs.epri.org/irisi/discussion/torino_report.html.
22 Ibid.
23 Speech by Patrick Sullivan, Chairman of the eris@ Management Committee, at the *European Information Society Conference* (EISCO), 23 October 1998.
24 Speech by Michael Carpentier, General Director DGXIII, at the *IRISI Conference on Strategies to Build the Information Society in the Regions*, Torino, Italy, 5-7 October 1995.

25. The European Regional Information Society Association (1998), *Newsletter*, Issue No. 4, Special Edition, October-November.
26. *Ibid.*
27. 'The Godfather in Brussels: We want you to go on.' http://www.tsh.de/initiative/english/frandfa.htm. It is interesting to compare this with the view that '[n]etworks of actors – as opposed to "the Commission" or "the Council" – have become guardians of the policy agenda at the sub-systemic level [or the meso-level] of EU governance, over which political controls are often weak or attenuated' (Peterson, 1997, p. 7). So, who is the 'guardian' or 'godfather' to whom?!
28. The European Regional Information Society Association (1998), *Newsletter*, Issue No. 4, Special Edition, October-November.
29. Introduction to the Special Edition of the European Regional Information Society Association (1998), *op cit.*
30. Note that contribution from EU finance to each RISI project is up to 50% of the total project cost.
31. Speech by the Chairman of the Interim Management Committee of the eris@ (European Regional Information Society Association), at the *European Information Society Conference* (EISCO), 23 October 1998.
32. Speech by Geoffrey Piper, the North West of England Region, at the *IRISI Conference on Strategies to Build the Information Society in the Regions*, Torino, Italy, 5-7 October 1995.
33. The TeleCities Network (1996), *European Cities and the Information Society: Declaration to the European Commission*, Declaration of Antwerp, 27 February.

4 New Industrial Policy for the Digital Age: Informatisation and Development

Introduction

In a recent study report, the European Information Society Promotion Office (ISPO) suggested that, 'Even if technologies are more and more global, the information society will not be global and its particular European aspects should remain' (The ISPO, 1997, p. 12.) In equal terms, it might be argued that China should also retain certain 'Chinese characteristics' when building its own digital or information economy. In other words, the political challenge is 'not to reject the evolution because it is technology-led, but rather to accompany it in order to maximise the benefits and minimise the risks' (*Ibid.*).

Although the development and implications of new information and communications technologies in the western industrialised countries have been widely recognised as an important area deserving systematic research, there is insufficient investigation into the impact of these new technologies on the developing nations, such as China. This is largely due to the fact that most accounts of globalisation in the information age have tended to examine the phenomenon from the perspective of a few advanced countries (Madon, 1997).

Whilst western industrialised economies are endeavouring to recreate their leadership in the emergent global information economy (in a way similar to what they have done in the traditional industrial age), many developing countries have embarked upon new technology policies in order to 'leapfrog' or catch up with their western counterparts. Among others, China appears to be an interesting case for the understanding of how a developing nation is determined to take the new opportunities created by new ICTs for economic development but also accompanied by various institutional and political uncertainties.

This chapter discusses the main aspects of the Chinese Informatisation of the National Economy Programme and the accompanying industrial policies to ensure the success of such a programme. The core element of the informatisation programme is the construction of an information superhighway centred on a nationwide high-speed fibre optic cable grid. Running in parallel is the launch of the 'Three Golden Projects' (Golden Bridge, Golden Card and Golden Customs) – now a generic term for a series of 'Golden' Projects involving a large range of industrial sectors in China.

Whilst the 'information superhighway' programme gives more emphasis on the importance of the new information and communications infrastructure, the 'Three Golden Projects' were intended to promote the applications of new ICTs among throughout the country.

The second task of this chapter is to investigate the highly complex (and somewhat confusing) institutional reform and telecommunications restructuring process. In addition, the political and regulatory challenges faced by the present Chinese government in pushing forward the informatisation programme are explored.

Overall, this chapter intends to address such important issues as why and how is the Chinese government responding to the new challenges posed by the information age led by the West? Is China ready to transit from industrialisation to informatisation in terms of national economic development? What are the main barriers to the development of a new information infrastructure and information economy? How to assess China's new industrial and technology policy towards the information age? What role do foreign ICT firms play in the process of informatisation of the Chinese economy and what opportunities does the latter offer foreign firms? After all, what can be learned from the experiences of other countries to improve policy making in China, and what implications can we draw upon the Chinese informatisation programme?

Economic Development: Industrialisation or Informatisation?

Information and communications technologies, throughout the world, are generating a new industrial revolution already as significant and far-reaching as those of the past (Bangemann *et al*, 1994). It is argued and largely accepted that, for the majority of the developing nations, the industrial revolution was a lost opportunity and there is little reason why they should stand by and watch another one by (Dordick and Wang, 1993), p. 25). The sense of urgency for leapfrogging and catching up with western industrialised countries is further enhanced by the threat of the 'double gap (*Ibid.*)' – with the second gap being created by the on-going digital information revolution. To be sure, growth and economic development has been an uneven process and resulted in a division between the rich 'North' and the poor 'South'. Would this division continue to exist and characterise the world economy in the emergent information age?

The 1990s have witnessed the beginning of an emergent information age, in which new information and communications technologies have become one of the most important drivers in economic development throughout the world. Among others, as discussed in previous chapters, the Clinton administration has launched a far-reaching programme to build nationwide information superhighway or, as known later, the National Information Infrastructure. The European Union has implemented new policies to promote the development of the European Information Society. The British government has introduced an Information Society Initiative to help the industry and the general public raise awareness of the challenges and benefits of new information and communications technologies. The Danish government has proposed an 'Info 2000' programme to provide optic fibre links between all of the municipalities in Denmark.

In South East Asia, the Singaporean government has been promoting its 'Intelligent Island' programme (or Singapore One) aimed at developing an information economy; and the Malaysian Government has planned an ambitious 'Multimedia Super Corridor' programme in order to position the country in the forefront of the on-going digital revolution. In a way similar to these countries, the Chinese government launched a high profile programme on the Informatisation[1] of the National Economy – using new ICTs to boost economic development in the early 1990s.

The Chinese government, led by the late paramount leader Deng Xiaoping, has been advocating the development of 'socialism with Chinese characteristics'. This has resulted in a series of Chinese Communist Party (CCP) policies on economic reform and opening up the country to overseas investment over the last two decades. The phrase 'Chinese characteristics' allows for the development of a 'socialist' market economy without abandoning the traditional dogmatic Marxism-Leninism and Mao Zedong Thoughts.

In retrospect, China's economic reform and 'open-door' policies represent a nationwide effort[2] to catch up with a 'lost opportunity' associated with the industrial revolution.

Since the 1990s, the Chinese government has been faced with a new task, and that is to build a digital economy facilitated in part by the vast amount of Chinese characters – those pictorial and square symbols used in the Chinese language. The Chinese characters are complicated and, perhaps, incomprehensive to many of those living in the English speaking world. But what seems more complicated is the new economic and industrial policy launched by the Chinese government and the regulatory structure related to the development of a digital economy in China.

If the industrial revolution were a missed opportunity for the developing countries, would they be left behind the industrialised countries forever in economic development? Do they have to complete the course of industrialisation before moving into the information age? Can the developing countries leap-frog industrialisation and embark upon informatisation? The Chinese strategy for economic development in the information age provides some clues for answering these questions.

New information and communications technologies, according to Alvin Toffler, one of the leading futurists, are bringing about a new mode of production and consumption and, broadly, an entirely new civilisation. In his 'Three-Wave' theory, Toffler categorised the development of human civilisation into three consecutive 'Waves' of change. Specifically, the 'First Wave', known as the agricultural revolution, took thousands of years to complete. The 'Second Wave', known as the industrial revolution, took three hundred years to become prevailing in many parts of the world. The 'Third Wave' brings with it a genuinely new way of life based on, among others, a novel institution called the electronic cottage (Toffler, 1981, p. 24). The 'Third Wave' is sometimes called the 'Information Age', 'Electronic Era, 'Global Village', 'Post-industrial Society', 'Scientific-technological Revolution' or 'Super-industrial Society' (*Ibid.*, p. 23). According to Toffler, the 'Third Wave' first arrived in the US during the decade beginning about 1955 with the widespread introduction of computers and, today, many countries are feeling the simultaneous impact of two, even three, quite different waves of change, all moving at different rates of speed and with different degree of forces behind them (*Ibid.*, p. 28).

To a certain extent, Toffler's claim that 'all the high-technology nations are reeling from the collision between the Third Wave and the obsolete, encrusted economies and institutions of the Second' (*Ibid.*, p. 18) is true in that these countries are leading the digital revolution. But, on the other hand, the 'high-technology nations' list (e.g., Britain, France, Sweden, Germany, and Japan) could have been extended to include some developing countries (e.g. Singapore, Malaysia, China, etc.) as well. The widespread of new ICTs and the rapid development of the global information society (the 'Third Wave', in Toffler's term) makes hardly any exception for any nation not to be influenced by this revolution. Many developing countries are at the moment experiencing the same collision between, mainly, the 'Second Wave' and the 'Third Wave'.

In some cases two 'Waves' might not necessarily 'collide' when they met. The on-going 'Informatisation of the National Economy' programme in China is intended, as the Chinese government wishes, to 'melt' or 'blend' the two processes — industrialisation and informatisation in order to achieve rapid economic growth. In other words, informatisation (the 'Third Wave') does not necessarily bring industrialisation (the 'Second Wave') to an end; rather, informatisation is identified as a new means to achieve industrialisation. As far as the Chinese paradigm of economic development is concerned, the two 'Waves' appear to be in harmony, at least as expected by the country's policy makers, rather than in 'collision'.

The launch of the Informatisation of the National Economy Programme suggests that the Chinese government is convinced that the information age heralds a new era of economic development for China. In other words, there exists an important link between industrialisation and informatisation or these are the two sides of the same coin. The importance of new information and communications technologies to the current and future economic development is fully recognised by Chinese government officials:

> The telecommunications and information industry is very important to economic development and social life. China's economic growth and development in science and technology since the 1980s have created favourable conditions for great progress in information technology. Our government has already given priority to the telecommunications and information industries. The development of China's telecommunications and information industries will not only need government support, but also the assistance of foreign countries. We hope to introduce more advanced technology and capital from abroad to develop and utilise information resources more rapidly and effectively in the development of China's informatisation.[3]

Some commentators claim China's informatisation programme is the country's 'second Great Leap Forward' — this time into the information age.[4] The first Great Leap Forward was initiated by Mao to speed up the process of industrialisation and the establishment of a communist society. Mao told his fellow countrymen to catch up with the Britain in 10 years and overtake the US in 20 years.

As far as industrialisation is concerned, Mao failed to achieve his ambition during his lifetime. Now that the whole world is moving into a digital information age, whither China? Would the 'second Great Leap Forward', i.e., informatisation, enable China to catch up with or even overtake its western industrialised counterparts?

Chinese Technology Policy for the Digital Age

China in the Hi-Tech Race

The 1980s witnessed a fierce competition among western industrialised countries for the so-called hi-tech or 'strategic' industries. Among others, the Reagon administration launched the Strategic Defence Initiative (SDI, otherwise known as the 'Star War') in the USA. In response to the challenge of the SDI, Europe, led by the former French President Mitterrand, launched the Eureka Programme. Japan had no wish to lag behind the US and Europe and launched the 'Fifth Generation Computer' Programme. There might be many purposes behind the launch of these large-scale research programmes in these countries; but improving national competitiveness by utilising and commercialising the research results derived from these programmes was on top of each government's agenda. It is against this international context the '863' Programme was launched in China.

The title of the '863' Programme was coined simply on the basis of the date March 1986,[5] when the State Council formally approved the joint proposal submitted by a group of well known Chinese scientists to set up a national hi-tech research programme. The major objective of the '863' Programme was to promote excellence of scientific research and build up a national capacity of hi-tech R&D to catch up and compete with western industrialised countries. State research funds were allocated to promote R&D activities in the following strategic areas under the '863' Programme:

- information technology (e.g. telecommunications, opto-electronics, artificial intelligence and information processing)
- electronics technology
- laser technology
- space technology
- biotechnology

It is evident that the strategic areas targeted by the '863' Programme are exclusively leading edge technology sectors, which are also drawing the attention of governments and industries from the industrialised countries. As a matter of fact, the '863' Programme has become the *de facto* official Chinese hi-tech programme comparable to the SDI, Eureka and the Fifth Generation Computer in the industrialised countries.

Judged by its results, the '863' Programme was highly successful. For instance, in the area of information technology, Chinese scientists have achieved remarkable success in speech recognition by computer (with Chinese language); a prototype of Synchronous Digital Hierarchy (SDH) technology with 565 Mbps (Megabits per second) capacity was developed among others. Thanks in part to the promotion and support of the '863' Programme, China has built up an internationally competitive industry of satellite launching technologies. It can be said that the '863' hi-tech development programme has provided a sound starting point for China to launch its Informatisation of the National Economy Programme. The particular relevance of the '863' Programme is manifested in the fact that a large part of the programme was devoted to information technology and other closely related hi-tech areas (e.g. electronics technology, laser technology and space technology).[6]

It is worth mentioning that, prior to the '863' Programme, Zhou Enlai, the late Premier, launched the 'Four Modernisations' Programme in the 1970s in order to boost the country's economy – modernisation of industries, modernisation of the agriculture sector, modernisation of national defence and modernisation of science and technology research. Two decades later, in the 1990s, the Chinese government re-interpreted the 'Four Modernisations': each of the 'Four Modernisations' is intrinsically linked with informatisation; and informatisation is a shortcut to achieving the goals of the 'Four Modernisations' (Ma, 1996, p. 20).[7] This re-interpretation was in part prompted by the development and challenges of the new information infrastructure and information society initiatives launched by western industrialised countries.

It can be said that, to a great extent, the 'Four Modernisations' Programme heralded the beginning of the end of the 'Cultural Revolution' and is a bold manifestation of China's effort in promoting industrialisation during the post-Mao period (i.e., after 1976). In comparison, the '863' Programme suggests a growing awareness of the importance of science and technology, in particular information and communications technologies, to achieving industrialisation and modernisation during the Deng legacy, i.e. the 1980s.

Apparently, the Informatisation of the National Economy Programme since the early 1990s signals a dual track strategy for economic development: industrialisation or modernisation in parallel with informatisation. If modernisation were an effort made to catch a missed opportunity of industrialisation, informatisation would potentially enable China to jump onto the bandwagon of the global digital revolution. To a certain extent, informatisation is an important feature of the post-Deng era, as far as China's economic development and technology policymaking is concerned.

Development of the Chinese Telecommunications Industry

China's first telegraph line was installed in Taiwan in 1877, four decades after the invention of the Morse code and one year after the birth of the Bell telephone system. Although telephony and the wide use of fax machines (as well as increased use of electronic mails) have already replaced telegraphic services in the West, they are still being widely used in the rural and remote areas in China. Fast development of communications technologies did not start until the early 1980s.

Table 4.1   Government investment in telecommunications, Rmb[8] billion

Year/Period	Total Investment, Rmb billion
1949-83	6
1993	38
1994	83
1995	98

Source: CIIED (1996).

In 1949, when the Communist Party took power, the total number of telephone line capacity was meagre 310,000 lines for the whole country. During the period over the next three decades, i.e. 1949 to the early 1980s, total telephone exchange capacity reached 3 million lines. However, telephone lines during this period were almost exclusively used by the Communist Party, government agencies and the PLA (People's Liberation Army). In other words, telephony service prior to the late 1980s had hardly anything to do with the every day life of the ordinary people.

The 1980s and 1990s have seen rapid increase in both the amount of telecommunications investment by the government and the total capacity of telephone exchanges, with the import of the first digital exchange (Fujitsu

F-150) by Fuzhou City, a provincial capital in southern China, in 1981. By the end of 1997, the total exchange capacity of China's telephone network exceeded 100 million lines.

Table 4.2 National telephone exchange capacity

Year/Period	Annual Average increase of lines (,000)
1980-85	230
1986-88	600
1990	1,570
1991	2,140
1992	4,345
1993	10,000
1994	19,000
1995	23,000

Source: CIIED (1996).

Table 4.3 Growth of telecommunications: 1980-1998*

	1980	1998	Increase (times)	Annual Growth
Fixed line users (,000)	2,140	87,350	40.8	22.9%
Telephone sets (,000)	4,170	131,430	31.5	21.1%
Teledensity (%)**	0.43	10.53	24.5	19.4%
Exchange capacity (,000)	4,432	134,900	30.4	20.9%
Autoexchange rate (%): local	30	100	3.3	6.9%
Autoexchange rate (%): long-distance	10.7	100	9.3	13.2%
Long-distance telephone lines (,000)	22	1631	74.1	27%
Kilometres of long-distance cables (,000)***	8	182.6	22.8	19%
Telegraphs (,000)	146,629	53,507	-2.7	-5.7
Fax pages (,000)	54	7,899	147.1	31.95%

Notes: *This table excludes mobile, paging and data services. **This is the number of telephone sets per 100 people. ***Including electric and fibre optic cables.
Source: Adapted from Ministry of Science and Technology (1999).

Figures from the Ministry of Science and Technology show that, during the period 1980 to 1998, key indicators of the telecommunications sector have changed substantially. Among others, this includes 40.8 times of increase (or 22.9% annual growth) in fixed-line users, 30.4 times of increase (or 20.9% annual growth) in telephone exchange capacity and 74.1 times increase (or 27% of annual growth) in the total number of long-distance telephone lines. Meanwhile, telegraphic service and use of fax show have shown different pattern of change. During the period 1980 to 1998, the total of telegraphic messages declined by 2.7 times (or -5.7% annual growth rate). In contrast, the total number of fax pages increased by 147.1 times (or 31.95% of annual growth rate).

Despite the rapid increase of government investment and rapid growth in the telecommunications sector, China's role in the global communications revolution, remains similar to that of many other developing countries – adopting, further developing, and promoting the mass use of systems invented outside the country (or technology follower). This applies to technologies such as telegraph transmission, telephone services, radio and TV broadcasting and major computer technologies including the Internet. However, this does not deny the growing importance and great potential of the Chinese ICT industry and the Chinese market.

Significantly differing from the western industrialised countries, the major domains of the Chinese ICT sector are still at their infant stage of development (in terms of current level of service provision and the future potential of the market). In telecommunications, despite the rapid growth since the early 1990s, national telephone penetration rate in 1997 remained as low as 7.4% (with 24% in the cities).[9] This is significantly lower than that of the western industrialised countries. On the other hand, the low rate of teledensity represents an opportunity for further development.

Table 4.4 China in the world league table: telephone lines and position

	1985	1990	1995	1996	1997
Telephone lines (million)	3.12	6.85	40.7	54.95	70.31
World position	17th	15th	4th	3rd	2nd

Source: Adapted from Ministry of Information Industry (MII), August 1999, http://www.mii.gov.cn/dx50/dx00.htm.

New Industrial Policy for the Digital Age 103

Despite the low rate of teledensity, there has been a steady growth in the total number of telephone lines. China's position in the world league table, for instance, has improved rapidly. In 1985, China ranked the 17th with 3.12 million lines. This changed to the 15th in 1990 (with 6.85 million lines), 4th in 1995 (with 40.7 million lines), 3rd in 1996 (with 54.95 million lines) and 2nd in 1997 (with 70.31 million lines) – second only to the US.

Table 4.5   Selected foreign firms in the Chinese ICT sector

N.American Firms	European Firms	Japanese Firms	S.E. Asian Firms
IBM	Philips	Matsushita	Samsung
Hewlett Packard	Siemens	Toshiba	Goldstar
Bell Atlantic	SEM	Hitachi	SingTel
Motorola	BOC	Fujitsu	Telstra
HughesNetwork	Ericsson	Sony	Leader Universal
General Electric	Cable & Wireless	Sharp	News Crop.
Ameritech	Nokia	Sanyo	
AT&T	British Telecom	Kenwood	
Northern Telecom	Deutsche Telekom	JVC	
Microsoft	France Telecom	NEC	
NYNEX	Itatel		
Sprint	GPT		
Bell South	GEC Plessey		
Qualcomm			
3M			
Compress Labs			

The core element of the basic Chinese telecommunications infrastructure is the nationwide public network owned by the former Ministry of Posts and Telecommunications (MPT).[10] This is complemented by 30 or so large-scale private networks operating across the nation (e.g. the military network and networks owned and operated by different ministries). In addition, there are more than 3,000 locally based private networks including those owned by large state enterprises (e.g. the Daqing Oilfield in Northeast China). Generally speaking, no private network is not allowed to provide public services.[11] Further, the Chinese government has also been building up a nationwide fibre optic network, which will be discussed later in this chapter.

The low level of teledensity and the inability of the former MPT to satisfy the ever increasing demand for more and better communications services by business and residential customers had prompted the Chinese government to establish a second network, Liantong (otherwise known as China Unicom, short for China United Telecommunications). Launched on 19 July 1994, Liantong is officially attached to the State Economic and Trade Commission. The new Liantong network was created through combining the private networks of three government ministries, i.e., Ministry of the Electronics Industry (MEI), Ministry of Electric Power (MEP) and Ministry of the Railways (MOR). The new carrier has been granted the right to provide long-distance and local telephony services in areas where demand for telephone services is high and the MPT could not meet this demand.

Although the establishment of Liantong has, in theory, ended telecommunications service monopoly by the former MPT, the Chinese telecommunications market has not been fully liberalised. On the contrary, with hardly any compromise, foreign operators or investors are not allowed to enter the telecommunications service market.[12] It is likely that the present duopoly, in a similar way the British telecommunications market developed during the period the mid-1980s up to the time when foreign companies arrived, will dominate the Chinese market for a long time to come.[13]

Largely due to the potential of the Chinese market, many foreign ICT companies, including network operators, hardware/equipment suppliers and system software houses and contents providers have now identified China as an important part of their global strategic manoeuvring. Among many others, AT&T (telecommunications), IBM (computer), Motorola (mobile phone), Philips (consumer electronics), Ericsson (mobile phone), Nokia (mobile phone), Microsoft (software house) and News Corp. (media contents provider), etc., representing a variety of domains of the ICT sector have already established a strong foothold in China. In 1994, the number of firms with foreign involvement (e.g. joint ventures, fully foreign-owned and cooperative agreements) in the electronics sector alone reached 8,000, with a total investment at $7 billion.

The Chinese Information Superhighway

China is known as the world's largest 'kingdom of bikes' – literally every adult owns a bike and uses it as the primary transportation means to work among the world's largest population. This corresponds to the fact that China still does not have a nationwide motor superhighway system comparable to that in the western industrialised countries. It can be said that the motor way system is one of the most important symbols and achievements of industrialisation. There is no doubt that a sophisticated motor way system will be built (actually, is under construction) but the cost of achieving this is prohibitively high. In this respect, China is left far behind in the world league table. Precisely because of this, the information

Table 4.6   China's information superhighway: The 22 fibre trunk links (1991-95)

Fibre Optic Cable Links	Traversing Provinces	Length	Complete Date
Beijing-Chengde-Tongliao-Baicheng-Qiqihar	Hebei, Inner Mongolia Jilin, Heilongjiang	2,600 km	1995
Beijing-Hohhot-Yinchuan-Lanzhou	Hebei, Inner Mongolia Ningxia, Gansu	1,990 km	1995
Beijing-Shenyang-Harbin	Hebei, Liaoning, Heilongjiang	2,100 km	1995
Beijing-Tianjin-Jinan-Nanjing	Hebei, Shangdong, Jiangsu	950 km	1993
Beijing-Tianjin-Tangshan	Hebei	245 km	1994
Beijing-Wuhan-Guangzhou	Hebei, Henan, Hubei, Hunan, Guangdong	2,945 km	1994
Beijing-Taiyuan-Xian	Hebei, Shanxi, Shaaxi	1,720 km	1995
Chengdu-Chongqing-Guiyang-Changsha-Nanchang-Hangzhou	Sichuan, Guizhou, Hunan, Jiangxi, Zhejiang	4,500 km	1995
Chengdu-Guiyang-Hangzhou-Fuzhou	Fujian, Zhejiang, Jiangxi, Hunan, Guizhou, Sichuan	4,354 km	1995
Chengdu-Kunming	Sichuan, Yunnan	1,200 km	1993
Chengdu-Xian-Zhengzhou-Xuzhou	Sichuan, Shaaxi, Henan, Anhui, Jiangsu	1,700 km	1995
Chongqing-Wuhan	Sichuan, Hubei	790 km	1994
Fuzhou-Shanghai	Fujiang, Zhejiang	1,160 km	1993
Fuzhou-Guangzhou	Fujiang, Guangdong	1,336 km	1993
Guangzhou-Haikou	Guangdong, Hainan	858 km	1993
Guangzhou-Nanning	Guangdong, Guangxi	804 km	1993
Harbin-Changchun-Shenyang	Heilongjiang, Jilin, Liaoning	550Km	1995
Kunming-Nanning	Yunnan, Guangxi	1,200 km	1995
Nanjing-Wuhan	Jiangsu, Anhui, Hubei	980 km	1993
Nanjing-Shanghai	Jiangsu	280 km	1993
Shanghai-Wuhu	Jiangsu, Anhui	300 km	1994
Xian-Lanzhou-Urumqi-Xining	Shaaxi, Ningxia, Gansu, Qinghai, Xinjiang	3,150 km	1995

Source: Adapted from Xu and Armstrong (1995).

age provides a golden opportunity for China to leapfrog and catch up with its counterparts including in the industrialised countries.

It is a widely held notion that industrialisation might not be the only way for economic development in China; on the contrary, informatisation could well be an alternative or complementary, if not more important, path. For the latter, a high capacity and futuristic communications infrastructure is a prerequisite.

China's new technology policy towards the information age is characterised by an ambitious programme to construct a national grid of fibre optic cables to serve as the backbones for the emergent information economy. In the late 1980s, the government decided to switch from coaxial cable to fibre optic cable deployment for long-distance communications.

By the end of the 1990s, China had already completed the deployment of a nationwide fibre optic cable network connecting all of the major cities, provincial capitals and most medium-sized cities (at county, and in some areas sub-county, government level) adopting exclusively SDH (Synchronous Digital Hierarchy) technology for the primary lines.[14]

The scale and capacity of China's national grid of communication can be said of world class and futuristic. It is claimed that, in terms of the scale and capacity of the national telecommunications network, China is now second only to the United States in the world (Yang, 1998).

Table 4.7   The national grid of fibre optic cable links

The Eight 'Horizontals'	The Eight 'Verticals'
Tianjin-Huhhot-Lanzhou	Mudanjiang-Shanghai-Guangzhou
Qingdao-Shijiazhuang-Yinchuan	Qiqihaer-Beijing-Sanya
Shanghai-Nanjing-Xi'an	Huhhot-Taiyuan-Beihai
Lianyungang-Urumuqi-Yining	Lianyungang-Urumuqi-Yining
Shanghai-Wuhan-Chongqing	Beijing-Jiujiang-Guangzhou
Hangzhou-Changsha-Chengdu	Huhhot-Xi'an-Kunming
Guangzhou-Nanning-Kunming	Lanzhou-Xining-Lhasa
Shanghai-Guangzhou-Kunming	Lanzhou-Guiyang-Nanning

Source: Adapted from Ministry of Information Industry (1999).

During the 'Eighth Five-Year Plan' period (1991-95), 22 fibre optic cable lines were constructed with a total length of over 86,000 km (equivalent to 75% of the total length of long-distance telephone lines). This network has been extended by adding to it another 16 long-distance fibre optic cable lines as stipulated by the government under the 'Ninth Five-Year Plan' (1996-2000).

By the end of the 1990s, the deployment of a large number of long-distance fibre optic cables has resulted in the emergence of an integrated 'national grid' of information superhighway capable of transmitting multimedia communication at a high speed. The 'backbone' of this national grid consists of the so-called eight 'Horizontals' and eight 'Verticals'. The national fibre optic cable grid stretches from the east to the west and from the north to the south 'stitching' together all parts of the country.

It is worth noting that, in addition to the national long-distance fibre optic cables, supplementary fibre optic links have also been under construction within each major city throughout China. For example, the total length of fibre optic cable links in Shanghai alone already exceeded 2,000 km in 1995 (Xu and Armstrong, 1995).[15] The national grid of long-distance fibre optic cables does provide links between major cities but it is by no means sufficient to meet the ever-increasing demand of telecommunications traffic. Therefore, the local PTAs (Posts and Telecommunications Administrations, local branches of the former MPT) are faced with a big challenge, which is to provide supplementary fibre optic links at the municipality and/or town levels in the future.

Table 4.8   China's information superhighway: International links

Fibre Optic Links	Length	Capacity	Cost	Complete Date
Shanghai-Kagoshima (China-Japan)	1,250 km	7,560 circuits or 560 Mbps	$64.6 mn	1993
Qingdao-Tae On (China-Korea)	570 km	15,000 circuits	n.a.	n.a.
Guangzhou-Hong Hong (Mainland-Hong Kong)	90 km	2 cables	n.a	n.a
China-Korea-Japan-US	26,000 km	n.a.	$1.2 bn	1999

Links between the newly emergent Chinese information infrastructure and other parts of the world are also being established with a number of international fibre optic cables. For instance, fibre optic submarine cables are already available between China and countries including Japan and South Korea. The Euro-Asia land cable provides direct link between China and Europe. In March 1997, a large-scale project with an overall investment of $1.2 billion was launched in Beijing to construct an international submarine cable line across the Pacific Ocean linking China, the US, Japan and South Korea. This Pacific Ocean information superhighway, with a total length of 26,000 km, was planned for completion by an international consortium by 1999. The consortium members included China Telecom, AT&T, NTT, Korea Telecom, MCI, KDD, SBC, Sprint, Hong Kong Telecom (subsidiary of Cable & Wireless) and Singapore Telecom.[16] The existence of these international fibre optic cables will, in part, ensure that the Chinese national information infrastructure will be an integral part of the emergent global information infrastructure (GII).

The fast growing satellite and digital microwave communications networks also extend the capacity of the Chinese information superhighway. Whilst actively participating in the international satellite launching market (using the Long March rockets, for instance) since the early 1990s, China has successfully developed a domestic satellite communications sector.

The Chinese satellite communications industry consists of mainly 19 earth stations located in 19 major cities.[17] These earth stations are linked with each other *via* the Dongfanghong-3 satellite with Beijing as the central hub. The major function of the satellite communications network is to cover the remote areas (e.g., Xinjiang, Tibet and Inner Mongolia).

Mobile telephone is another fast growth area of the Chinese telecommunications industry. The world's leading mobile phone equipment manufacturers, such as Ericsson, Nokia and Motorola, have already identified China as their strategic market place and have built up strong presence there.[18] It is not surprising at all that, despite the very low level of telephone line connections, one can nowadays use a mobile phone to call anywhere in the world, where the GSM (Global Standard for Mobile communications) standard is adopted.[19]

Building upon the huge capacity of the emerging national information infrastructure, the Chinese National Telecommunications Working Conference (CNTWC) proposed, in summer 1995, that eight major networks should be established by the Chinese telecommunications industry within the next three years:

- A national public phone network covering all cities above the level of county and sections of economically developed towns will be established. The network will have digital programme-controlled exchanges and digital transmission.

- A nationwide liaison network and automatic roaming system for public mobile phone networks will be established. This will enlarge the coverage of the GSM communications networks.
- A national public grouping exchange data network covering cities and towns above the level of counties and parts of economically developed towns; a public digital data network covering nationwide cities above the level of a region as well as sections of economically developed counties will be developed.
- The establishment of elementary narrow zone integrated digital business networks and the completion of a liaison public telephones network and public grouping exchange data network is the target of the fourth proposed network.
- An intelligent network that serving the entire country will be set up.
- An information network of direct liaison and quasi-direct liaison combinations with few time limitations representing a complete nationwide digital synchronous hierarchy network will be built.
- An advanced international communications network using submarine cables and satellite communication means with diversified international business applications will be built.
- ISDN (Integrated Services Digital Network) experimental bureau and testing networks on the basis of ATM (Asynchronous Transfer Mode) exchanges and SDH optical cable communications will be established.

What seems important is the potential impact of Hong Kong on the development of the Chinese ICT sector, in particular telecommunications. The return of its sovereignty to China in July 1997 has certainly made Hong Kong a potentially much more important player than it was in the Mainland Chinese market. In fact, as a part of its overall industrial policy for the information age, China is moving to push the Special Administrative Region (SAR) government to reinvent the former British colony as a regional information technology hub for not only China but also the rest of South East Asia.

Hong Kong Telecom, the major supplier of telecommunications services in Hong Kong, was recently granted the right by the SAR government as the *de facto* monopoly for Video-on-Demand (VoD) services in the territory. In preparing its VoD trial, Hong Kong Telecom has invested HK$1 billion ($129.4 million) over the last few years to undertake a free trial involving 300 homes, which was expected to extend to 300,000 homes by year 2000.[20] The VoD trial was supported by Hong Kong Telecom's hi-tech infrastructure: fibre to the building with ATM switches and ADSL

(Asymmetric Digital Subscriber Line) distribution system in apartment blocks. In addition to this, Hutchinson Telecommunications announced in November 1997 the availability of ATM-switched broadband services throughout Hong Kong.[21] If Hong Kong becomes a regional ICT hub, Mainland China would certainly benefit from the technical knowhow of the major ICT companies based in the territory. The Mainland market, on the other hand, will also be strategic to the ICT companies based in Hong Kong.

In order to make informed decisions, the Chinese government closely monitors the development of the new information infrastructure. For instance, in part to provide in-depth policy analysis and advice, the CASS (Chinese Academy of Social Sciences), the government think-tank, set up a specialised research organisation, entitled Centre for the Chinese Information Infrastructure and Economic Development (CIIED) in 1994. The major research objectives of the CIIED include:

- the impact of the information superhighway on economic development
- the relationship between the information infrastructure and industrialisation
- the measurement factors and calculation of informatisation and economic development
- the system and policy issues with regard to the Three Golden Projects.

The overall task of the CIIED is to analyse the relationship between informatisation and industrialisation in the context of economic development in China. This is manifested in the title of the Centre's internal journal called *Informatisation & Economic Development*.

If a national information superhighway is as significant to the information revolution as the motor superhighway to the last industrial revolution, it might not be an exaggeration to conclude that China is already in the fast lane towards becoming one of the leading information economies in the 21st Century.

The Golden Projects

In parallel with the construction of the national grid of fibre optic cable links, the Chinese government has also been vigorously promoting the application of new ICTs within a variety of industrial and business sectors. The most recent and, perhaps, the most widely publicised policy measure was the launch of the 'Three Golden Projects' – Golden Bridge, Golden

Customs and Golden Card in the early 1990s. The 'Three Golden Projects' have rapidly become another crux of the country's ambitious Informatisation of the National Economy programme.

The Golden Bridge Project The primary objective of the Golden Bridge Project (otherwise known as the National Public Economic Information Communications Network) was to develop an infrastructure for the informatisation of the national economy. This infrastructure was proposed to be a hybrid network architecture consisting of satellite and optical fibre networks, which have interoperability between them. The Golden Bridge network would initially transmit information at the speed of 2Mb/s. In addition to interconnecting with various private networks and the MPT's CHINAPAC, DDN and PSTN (Public Switched Telephone Network), the Golden Bridge network was to be linked to international gateways. Most significant of all, the Golden Bridge Project would also provide network support for other 'Golden' projects. Meanwhile, the Golden Bridge network would support value-added services such as e-mail, EDI (Electronic Data Interchange), multimedia, video conferencing, electronic bulletin board, online database services and video-on-demand, etc. Zhu Rongji,[22] the then Vice Premier initiated the Golden Bridge Project in March 1993.

Thanks to the launch of the Golden Bridge Project an economic statistic information network connecting Beijing, Shanghai, Tianjin and Guangzhou became operational in August 1995. This information network is based on the Shanghai Municipal Statistic Bureau's internal computer network and transmitted *via* the current public telephony system. Services include the provision of information categories ranging from general information, industrial sectors, foreign trade, investments, public finance, price fluctuation and daily consumption available only to the four municipal governments. This economic information network will be extended to connect the four cities with other major cities in China and abroad.

The Golden Customs Project The Golden Customs Project (otherwise known as the Foreign Trade Private Information Networks Interconnection) was launched to construct an effective administration network for foreign trade. The first phase of the Project was to establish interconnections between the private networks of the large number of organisations involved in foreign trade. More specifically, the Golden Customs Project was tasked to develop four application systems for export tax return, foreign exchange settlement abroad, quota and licence administrations and statistics collection for import/export services respectively. The second phase of the

Golden Customs Project was to transform the private networks of foreign trade administrations and make them comply with the X400 standards, promote EDI and paperless trade. The Golden Customs Project was initiated by Li Fengqing, one of the then Vice Premiers, in June 1993.

The Golden Card Project The Golden Card Project (also known as the Electronic Currency or National Credit Card System) was jointly launched by the former Ministry of Electronic Industry and the People's Bank of China to promote the usage of credit and cash cards amongst 200 million people by the year 2000. Trial services were initially provided in 12 coastal cities, such as Shanghai and Shenzhen. By the end of 1994 the number of credit cards in China exceeded 8.4 million, more than doubling that of the previous year. President Jiang Zemin personally initiated the Golden Card Project in June 1993.

The Golden Card Project has been most successful in Shanghai, the largest municipality in China. In August 1995, five major banks, the Industrial Bank, Agricultural Bank, Bank of China, Construction Bank and Communications Bank, finished inter-linking their Automatic Teller Machines (ATMs) throughout the city. Customers can now withdraw cash from any of the ATMs built by the five banks.

Other Golden Projects The year 1993 witnessed the launch of the 'Three Golden Projects', which involved China's politicians at the highest level. This has prompted a 'Golden' rush in the rest of the 1990s – the launch of many other 'Golden Projects', which appear to have brought every major sector in the country on to the information superhighway. In addition to the 'Three Golden Projects', several other 'Golden Projects', such as Golden Tax, Golden Agriculture, Golden Enterprise, Golden Education, Golden Sea, Golden Health and Golden Tobacco have been added to the 'Golden' project series.

The Golden Projects, together with the national grid of information superhighway, are the major elements of China's informatisation programme.

Selectivity and Priorities

China, as a developing country, may not be able to afford spreading its very limited public funds evenly across various domains of the ICT sector. On the contrary, the Chinese government has adopted a highly selective technology policy to target a few well-defined 'priority' areas. For instance, the government has planned to establish a national research centre on telecommunications technologies. This research centre will be jointly financed by the state, industrial groups, higher education institutions, research organisations and users. The major objective of this centre is to promote joint research and development (R&D) activities pertinent to key technologies and products such as high and medium capacity digital switches (including ATM systems, SDH systems), ISDN networks, computer networks (including the Internet), multimedia systems and fax machines, etc. Among others, the state promised to provide up to Rmb800 million yuan (about $96 million) to support R&D activities in the telecommunications sector alone during the period 1996-2000.

In connection with the planned R&D activities, the Chinese government has decided to promote and develop three industrial sectors with economies of scale during the period 1996-2000. These are:

- the digital switch equipment manufacturing sector;
- the mobile communications equipment manufacturing sector;
- integrated cable TV information networks.

Corresponding to the above three priority sectors, three strategic products will also be targeted:

- high capacity fibre optic communications systems equipment;
- standard satellite communications stations;
- digital microwave systems equipment.

During the Ninth Five-Year Plan period, i.e., 1996-2000, the Chinese government has proposed to select 10 domestic firms, each with an annual revenue of above Rmb500 million yuan ($60 million), for receiving state financial support in the ICT sector.[23] In addition, four strategic technology areas, i.e. fibre optic cable communications, ATM, multimedia systems, and mobile communications, will receive an investment at the total of Rmb6 billion yuan ($723 million) by the state during the same period.

Technology Transfer and Foreign Investment

Despite various promotional efforts and supporting measures, the overall technology base of domestic firms in the Chinese ICT sector remains much less competitive than that of the industrialised countries. Therefore, an important element of the Chinese industrial policy for the information age is to encourage technology transfer and direct investment by foreign firms.

This policy has a number of features. First, domestic firms are urged to cooperate among themselves in dealing with foreign companies and in buying foreign products.

Second, import of foreign products should be complemented by technology transfer. This means importing a particular product is more likely to be approved by the government if there is an element of technology transfer combined with the deal. In general, the guiding principle for foreign trade is that market access is tied up with technology transfer, i.e., trade and technology should not be separated.

Third, the decision of importing important/strategic (e.g. hi-tech) products should be jointly made between the users and the concerned domestic industrial sector. Important deals would need central approval by government ministries and departments. In principle, the government would not approve applications for importing products such as digital switches, fax machines and mobile communications products.[24]

Finally, in the telecommunications equipment area, foreign firms are encouraged to invest in manufacturing cellular mobile communications equipment, high capacity fibre optic cables, ATM switching equipment.

Although foreign direct investments are generally encouraged (in terms of investment and technology transfer), they are not normally allowed in the following two areas as far as telecommunications are concerned:

Firstly, digital switches other than those of ATM. Chinese domestic firms are already capable of designing and manufacturing this category of equipment. In addition, foreign companies such as AT&T, NEC, Bell Labs, and Northern Telecom are also manufacturing digital switches in joint ventures with Chinese partners.[25]

Secondly, telecommunications network and service provision. Prior to the separation of China Telecom from the former MPT, the MPT stipulated:

> Foreign organisations and individuals outside China and foreign-owned firms, Sino-foreign joint ventures and Sino-foreign cooperative ventures based in China are not allowed to operate or participating in operating telecommunications services in China.[26]

In the wake of the separation of China Telecom from the MPT and the launch of Liantong (or China Unicom) in 1994, the second telecommunications service provider, the MPT continued to bar foreign investment in the Chinese telecommunications networks and service provision:

> Foreign organisations and individuals outside China and foreign-owned firms,

Sino-foreign joint ventures and Sino-foreign cooperative ventures based in China are not allowed to operate or participating in operating open telecommunications services in China. These mentioned are not allowed to hold stakes by any means in open telecommunications services either.[27]

Needless to say, the Chinese telecommunications services industry is still under tight control by the central government *via* the new Ministry of Information Industry. Telecommunications services are regarded as a strategic industry and closely related to national security. Therefore, the strategic manoeuvring by the telecommunications firms in terms of strategic alliances and mergers currently taking place in many parts of the world does not have any direct link with or impact upon the Chinese telecommunications industry for the time being. Ironically, China Telecom alone, plus Liantong, the newly established second domestic telephony operator, can not provide all the services required by the development of an information economy at the moment in part due to the shortage of investment capital. In the 1990s, China Telecom has imposed high connection fees for new residential customers and the connection fee was an important source of capital supporting the state-owed company's expansion.

The above telecommunications policy banning foreign investment is, however, poised to change. The bilateral trade agreement signed between China and the US in November 1999 has secured the American support for China's WTO membership but, in return, China would have to open its domestic market (including the telecommunications) for foreign competition.[28] This contravenes the Chinese government's previous stance that opening the telecommunications market could be a condition of entering the WTO (Kynge, 1998).[29]

A number of developing countries such as India, Brazil, Chile and most East European countries have already implemented new policies to attract foreign investment to help develop their telecommunications services. In many cases these developing countries have chosen to privatise their former national telecommunications monopolies with a large proportion of stakes offered to foreign companies. To be sure, the choice between meeting cash requirement by drawing foreign capital and being free from strategic and national security concerns is difficult to make. This is apparently a dilemma widely recognised within the circle of Chinese policymakers. As a matter of fact, the Chinese government has sought to raise money in the international capital market for China's telecommunications industry, whilst barring foreign involvement in management and operation. The floatation of China Telecom (Hong Kong) on the Hong Kong Stock Market in 1997, which raised HK$26 billion, was viewed as a bold manifestation of this strategy.

Despite the tight control by the Chinese government, a few foreign operators have managed to insert a foothold into the Chinese telecommunications market. Among others, Cable & Wireless (C&W) and Global One were the front-runners. C&W, *via* its former subsidiary Hong Kong Telecom, has jointly deployed a long-distance fibre optic cable with the MPT providing a direct link between Beijing and Hong Kong. Once this link becomes operational, C&W is unlikely to be excluded from participating in the Chinese telecommunications business. In addition to this, C&W offered a 5.5% stake in Hong Kong Telecom to China Telecom, the operational arm of the MPT. C&W's stake used to secure its future expansion in the mainland market was by all means strategic. However, this appeared to be a rather expensive price, given the fact that Hong Kong Telecom used to be its former parent company's major cash cow (about 80% of C&W's profit was generated by Hong Kong Telecom).

Global One, previously a joint venture between Deutsche Telekom, France Télécom and Sprint of the US, is another active player in the Chinese telecommunications market.[30] Bypassing the regulatory hurdles, Global One has managed to secure major contracts with some provincial governments to jointly develop telecommunications services with local MPT partners.

Coping with Change: Institutional Reform

Despite the fact that China's information superhighway has been joined up with the global information infrastructure, many aspects of the country's communications policy are at odds with the new global communications environment. Chiefly among others, within the telecommunications sector, there does not exist an independent regulatory body; the long-waited telecommunications law has not been enacted; there are still many uncertainties regarding foreign direct investment.

Following years of international diplomacy and consensus building, the WTO has recently become an important organisation, which has radically changed the shape of the global ICT sector. Significant milestones of this change at the international level include the successful completion of the recent WTO agreements on information technology products and liberalisation of telecommunications. Although Hong Kong is among the signatories of the last two WTO deals on IT and telecommunications, Mainland China is not yet a WTO member. It is widely speculated that

China stands a good chance to join the WTO during the course of the year 2000. Undoubtedly, by joining the WTO China would be put under the scrutiny of the organisation's trade rules. However, the WTO membership might not be a panacea to all the problems facing the overall Chinese ICT sector, and telecommunications in particular.

Monopoly, Duopoly and Institutional Convergence

China Telecom was separated from the MPT in 1994 and became a registered company in the following year. However, this has not changed the fact that the MPT, now the Ministry of Information Industry, on behalf of the state, remains the sole owner of China Telecom. Unlike many other countries where independent regulators exist, the MII is also the regulator of the Chinese telecommunications industry and it is fully responsible for issuing operating licences related to all types of telecommunications services in the country. Although Liantong was set up as the second operator in 1994, its role was defined and remains complementary, rather than competitive, to that of China Telecom. China Telecom is the exclusive provider of international telephony and major supplier of domestic long-distance and local services. The former MPT owned the national public network, which does not consist of any private networks owned by other ministries and state enterprises. In addition, it is estimated that China Telecom accounts 98% share of the burgeoning cellular market.[31] Consequently, Liantong and other private networks remain minor players and it is unlikely that any of them is in a position to challenge the mighty China Telecom at present time.

Headquartered in Beijing, Liantong was jointly established by the Ministry of Electronics Industry (MEI), Ministry of Electrical Power (MEP), Ministry of Railways (MOR) and 13 other stakeholders, who were exclusively state-owned organisations, with a registered capital of Rmb1 billion yuan ($120 million). Liantong's mission, as stipulated by the State Council, was to provide complementary services to areas where China Telecom could not reach, building upon the capacity of the private networks owned by the MOR and the MEP. In addition to this, Liantong was also allowed to provide wireless, mobile and value-added services throughout the country.

Within the Chinese political hierarchy, ministries such as the MEI, MEP and MOR enjoy equivalent power to that of the former MPT under the same roof of the State Council (the Chinese cabinet). This has led to constant power struggle and bargaining between the MPT and the three other ministries who owned Liantong. Despite the fact that the MPT had been assigned the responsibility to regulate telecommunications, conflicts between the MPT and other ministries related to telecommunications and other domains of the ICT sector would have to be arbitrated, if not resolved, by the involvement of the State Council itself. As a matter of fact, some high rank officials such as Li Lanqing and Zou Jiahua were often personally involved in the bargaining process by assuming a 'coordinating' role.

The turf fighting and bureaucratic conflicts became more complicated when other players outside the remit of the State Council, such as the PLA, are involved. The PLA, in addition to its own private network, has been developing cellular mobile services in 35 Chinese cities *via* its subsidiary China Electronics Systems Engineering Company. Given the fact that the PLA reports directly to the Chinese Communist Party's Central Military rather than the State Council, whether or not the MPT had the power to regulate the national telecommunications industry including the PLA's private networks remains a question (Yang, 1998). The government had indeed ordered the PLA to sell off its telecommunications networks, and to quit from any commercial operation, by 1998, but this order has been largely ignored. It was reported that, against this order, the PLA has recently decided to build new mobile operations in three more provinces *via* a new company, called Century Mobile Communications, which is joined by several large hi-tech firms of the country.[32] It is believe that the PLA's ambition is to maintain control over its own mobile phone networks and establish the country's third public mobile phone operator.[33]

The National People's Congress (NPC), China's top legislature, recently decided to restructure the government in an attempt to reduce bureaucracy and turf fighting inside the huge government organ. As a result of this restructuring, the number of government ministries was reduced from 40 to 29. Among other affected ministries, the MPT, MEI and the information and network administrative sectors of the Ministry of Broadcasting, Film and Television (MBFT), China Aerospace Industry Corporation, and China Aviation Industry were merged to form a new super-ministry, i.e., the Ministry of Information Industry (MII). Equipped with unprecedented policymaking power and regulatory responsibilities for the overall information age, the mission of the MII is, as recently stated by Wu Jichuan, the new head of the MII and former Minister of MPT, 'to promote economic growth through invigorating such sectors as information products, telecommunications and software'.[34]

To a certain extent the creation of the MII incorporating a number of previously battling ministries and other state organisations signals the emergence of a new regulatory structure in response to the convergence between new information and communications technologies in China. On the surface level the MII is on the way to effectively harnessing the regulatory challenges associated with digital information revolution and convergence.

However, the formation of the MII can not be said a major step towards solving the problems faced by the Chinese ICT sector. Firstly, the military communications networks were still outside the MII's power domain and the PLA continues to be involved in public mobile phone network operation.

Secondly, prior to the creation of the MII, China Telecom was owned by the MPT and Liantong was jointly owned by three other ministries. It had been expected that the difference in ownership might eventually create a duopoly between the two carriers and competition could be nurtured. After the State Council restructuring, the MII has become the new owner of both China Telecom and Liantong. The new ownership structure does not seem to encourage competition between China Telecom and Liantong.[35]

Thirdly, having replaced the MPT, the MII became the new body responsible for policymaking, regulation with ownership in the two public telecommunications carriers. Apparently, the creation of the MII represents at most an 'institutional convergence', rather than an effective response to the challenges brought about by the technological convergence.

The Long March towards the Rule of Law

It is a widely held view that, in order to ensure healthy and fair competition in the digital age, there is a need for new rules taking into account the nature of new ICTs and characteristics of the information economy at national as well as international levels.

Up until now, many countries, including China, have failed to come up with an acceptable solution. The long-awaited Chinese telecommunications law is still in the drafting process and there could be a long way to the eventual promulgation. China's telecommunications law, after a decade of discussions, has now evolved into its ninth draft by the time of writing and there is no sign of it being passed in the near future.[36]

The former MPT was initially given the task by the Chinese government to draft the telecommunications law. As the owner of China Telecom, the absolute monopoly operator, it was unlikely that the former MPT would be willing to deliver a fair and convincing legislation, which promotes telecommunications liberalisation. There was potentially an issue of conflict of interests in this area. Without taking the ownership of China Telecom away from the MPT, this concern would remain valid. Scholars from the Chinese Academy of Social Sciences share this concern:

> Despite that the General Bureau of National Posts and China Telecom were separated from the Ministry of Posts and Telecommunications in 1994 and have become independent accounting enterprise ever since, decisions on resources, salaries and investment within the two enterprises are still made by the central departments of the MPT. ... The combination of administration and enterprise management within the MPT and its branches has led to that legitimacy of the Ministry is being questioned by the telecoms firms operating outside the MPT system and created difficulties.[37]

The creation of the MII, unfortunately, has not speeded up the process of telecommunications legislation. In order to make the rule of law prevailing, it seems crucial that the Chinese government take bold decision to end the combined role of the MII as both the telecommunications regulator and owner of telecommunications companies at the earliest opportunity. Experience of establishing an independent telecommunications regulator in industrialised countries (notably the US and the UK) and developing countries alike (e.g. South Africa) would seem to provide useful references to the Chinese policymakers.

National Coordination

The launch of the national informatisation programme has involved a large number of government ministries and state commissions. In parallel with the regulatory role of the former MPT in telecommunications, there were other powerful state agencies that also had regulatory power. For instance, the State Commission for Wireless Administration (SCWA) was in charge of technical standardisation, policymaking and regulations over the national wireless communication sector. In parallel, the former Ministry of Electronics Industry was tasked to make policies, strategic planning and draft regulations for the national electronics industry. Meanwhile, the State Information Centre (SIC), set up in 1987 as a branch of the State Planning Commission (SPC), was in charge of the information dissemination and information services sector across the country. In short, there were a plethora of state regulatory and administrative departments involved in the ICT sector and the new information economy in China. To nobody's surprise, these government agencies do not necessarily consult each other for planning and regulatory matters.

In an attempt to avoid macro-level confusions in policymaking and regulation, the Chinese government set up the Joint Conference for the Informatisation of the National Economy (JCINE), headed by the former

Vice Premier Zou Jiahua, in 1994. At launch, the JCINE consisted of representatives from a total of 24 government ministries and state commissions. The large number of government ministries and commissions represented at the JCINE further indicates the complexity of the Chinese bureaucracy pertinent to the ICT sector.

Table 4.9   Administrative authorities of selected 'Golden Projects'

Golden Bridge	Ministry of Electronic Industry
Golden Customs	Ministry of Electronic Industry; Ministry of Foreign Trade & Economic Cooperation
Golden Card	Ministry of Electronic Industry; The People's Bank of China[38]
Golden Tax	Ministry of Electronic Industry; State Tax Bureau
Golden Education	State Education Commission; State Science & Technology Commission; Chinese Academy of Sciences

In 1996, the JCINE was replaced by an Information Technology Development Leading Group (ITDLG) under the same leadership. The mission of the ITDLG, similar to that of its predecessor, i.e., the JCINE, was to 'deal with the battling ministries'.[39] Among others, the ITDLG was particularly involved in coordinating the 'Golden Projects' at the national level. This was certainly a response by the new ITDLG to the situation in which individual ministries were solely interested in promoting their own project, which threatened to turn the central government's Informatisation of the National Economy Programme into a collection of unrelated piecemeal efforts.

The plethora of government ministries and commissions involved in the 'Golden Projects' suggest that, in the transition from a centralised industrial economy to a market-oriented and globalised information economy, government bureaucracy will likely become a major factor detrimental to effective governance.

During the Chinese Communist Party's 15th Congress, held in Beijing in Feb. 1998, Zou Jiahua was not re-elected as a member of Politibureau, the top level of China's ultimate political powerhouse. Subsequently, at the Ninth National People's Congress (NPC), Zou stepped down as a Vice-Premier. As a technocrat, Zou was widely viewed a key government official in promoting the informatisation programme, in particular the 'Golden Projects'. Zou's departure from the crown of China's political establishment would undoubtedly add some uncertainty to the country's information age strategy. In a country such as China, the stability and continuity of policies is largely contingent upon the personality and charisma of the individuals who are responsible for policymaking.[40]

Regulating Convergence: Implications of IP Telephony

One of the most important features of the digital revolution is the phenomenon of technological convergence. Using digital techniques, any analogue information (audio, video, printed text or pictures) can be transformed into computer readable binary codes (different combinations of '1s' and '0s'). This is a process of digitisation. Digitisation has led to the coming together of previously unrelated industries, such as computer, consumer electronics, telecommunications and publishing, etc. The result of this process is is the so-called 'convergence'. The main function of the fibre optic cable-based national information superhighway is supposedly to facilitate high-speed transmission of digital data and digital communication, including the Internet.

In the meantime, the process of digital convergence has posed new challenges to regulation. Among others, how should the new information and communications technology be regulated, and by whom? As far as China is concerned, does the 'institutional convergence' represented by the creation of the Ministry of Information Industry sufficiently address the challenges of technological convergence? Are the Chinese authorities loosing control over the digital revolution? One interesting case in this respect is the recent legal dispute over the use of the Internet for making telephone calls, i.e., Internet Telephony or IP (Internet Protocol) Telephony. This legal dispute was widely referred to as 'China's First Network Case'.

To be sure, the convergence between telecommunications and the Internet has caused wide concern and public debate at the international level in terms of regulation. The central point of this debate lies in the controversy whether Internet telephony should be treated in legislation as conventional telecommunications service enabled by public switched telephone network. From the user's point of view, according the European Commission,[41] there are three distinct categories of voice communication making use of the Internet:

- Computer to computer voice service: voice communications transmitted *via* the Internet between two PC users (both users using modems, compatible software, loudspeaker and microphone to communicate).

- Computer/phone voice services: voice communications transmitted *via* the Internet between a PC of one user (with modem, software, loudspeaker and microphone) and another user using a traditional telephone connected to the public switched telephone network.

- Phone-to-phone voice services: voice communications transmitted *via* the Internet, but between two users using telephones connected to the public switched network (part of the communications is transmitted *via* packet means using Internet Protocols instead of fully *via* the national and international public switched networks).

As categorised above, voice communication *via* the Internet, in the European Commission's view, could only be considered voice telephony service if *all* of the following criteria are met: 1) Such communications are the subject of a commercial offer; 2) Such communications are offered to the public; 3) Such communications are to and from public switched network termination points; 4) Such communications involve direct transport and switching of speech in real time. Although certain types of Internet telephony have met one or more of these criteria, no such service currently meets *all* of them. Therefore, the European Commission concluded that Internet Telephony services could not for the time being be considered as conventional voice telephony.[42]

In September 1997, two brothers, Chen Zhui and Chen Yan, started offering IP telephony services to customers at their own electrical goods retailing store in Fuzhou, the capital city of the southern Fujian Province. Initially, the Chens offered 5 minutes of free IP telephone calls to the US to those customers who bought products from the store. As some customers wanted to have longer period of talk, the Chens decided to offer international IP telephone services with a charge substantially cheaper than the China Telecom price.[43] Despite the poor transmission quality of the IP telephone, the very low price was attractive to the customers.

With a view that the Chen's IP telephony service was illegal, Mawei Post and Telecommunications Bureau (MPTB), the local district branch of China Telecom, reported this matter to the local police. On 3 January 1998, in accordance with Article 225 of the Chinese Criminal Law,[44] the local police started investigation into the Chens' IP Telephony case. Consequently, on 7 January 1998, Chen Yan was taken to the local police station for questioning. The police confiscated his IP telephony equipment and fined him Rmb50,000 yuan in total for the alleged crime of 'illegally operating telecommunications services'. In addition, Chen Yan was forced to spend four days of confinement at the local police station.[45]

In May 1998 the Chen brothers sued the local police claiming the latter had abused power and violated their human rights and property rights. They demanded the full refund of the fine; the return of their IP telephony equipment and economic compensation. Mawei District People's Court, the local district court, rejected the case and maintained that the local police's actions and measures against them were lawful. In December 1998, the Chen brothers appealed to the Fuzhou Municipality People's Intermediate Court (FMPIC). In response, on 20 January 1999, the FMPIC finally reached the conclusion that overturned the previous decision by the Mawei District People's Court.

In its decision the FMPIC argued that IP telephony is technically different from conventional voice telephony operated by telecommunications companies – the former is a new type of communication based on the Internet. In other words, IP telephony is a new aspect of the Internet's functionality. The FMPIC decision also confirmed that IP telephony is not a type of long-distance and international telecommunications that is defined by the law and administrative regulations as services exclusively provided by telecommunications companies.

The MII was most disappointed with the decision of the Fuzhou Municipality People's Intermediate Court. An MII official in charge of telecommunications services administration claimed that:

> The court should observe the MII's policy document (MII No. 573, 18 September 1998), which stipulates that China has no plan to open Internet telephony and Internet fax services. The main point [of this policy] is IP telephony services should be managed and regulated solely by state telecommunications organisations [i.e., the MII and China Telecom].[46]

The MII response to the FMPIC court decision was not surprising. Up until now, China Telecom and Liantong, both under the same umbrella of the MII, are the only two companies authorised by the State Council to operate basic telephony services (including local and domestic long-distance calls). China Telecom, with local branches throughout the country, is the only authorised international telephony service provider. Before telecommunications is liberalised in China, IP telephony appears to be an unexpected challenger to China Telecom's monopoly in international telephone calls. Indeed, IP telephony is a new phenomenon and has become a loophole in the State Council's administrative stipulation concerning telecommunications. The MII was determined to close this loophole by

Figure 4.1 Mawei Police's application for approval to investigate the IP telephony case

福州市公安局马尾分局

关于陈彦利用微机互联网经营
国际长途电信业务能否立案侦查的请示

省公安厅刑警总队：

我局于九七年二月二十三日接到福州电信局的报案，在我辖区亭江镇发现电话用户陈彦利用微机互联网通话软件，对外开办国际长途电话业务，按挂发不同国家、地区每分钟收取6元至9元通话费不等，严重扰乱了电信市场秩序，同时也给国家安全带来严重威胁，要求我局立案侦查，依法追究刑事责任。我局受理后，经调查该案内容属实。为此，我局拟根据刑法第二百二十五条对陈彦以非法经营罪立案侦查。当否，请批示。

一九九七年二月二十五日

Source: http://personal.gz168.net/blackwhite/background.htm.

Figure 4.2 Fujian Provincial Public Security Authority's authorisation for investigating the IP telephony case

Source: http://personal.gz168.net/blackwhite/background.htm.

cracking down on any unauthorised operation of IP telephony service:

> In collaboration with other relevant state organisations, the MII will adopt more effective measures to crack down unauthorised illegal operation of telecommunications businesses and will make those responsible for these activities to face the severe consequences.[47]

The harsh position of the MII was based on its own definition of IP telephony, i.e., IP telephony is a type of telecommunications service, rather than a new function of the Internet. But the underlying reason was the MII's fear that IP telephony would lead to the loss of its telecommunications revenue. As China Telecom is a state-owned company (*via* the MII), the MII could defend its position by suggesting that the operation of IP telephony service has disordered the Chinese telecommunications market and led to the heavy loss of national interest.[48] In their report to the police, the Fuzhou Posts and Telecommunications Bureau (China Telecom local branch) went further claiming that the Chen brothers' IP telephony operation had not only disordered the telecommunications market but also posed threat to national security. This claim was confirmed by the Mawei local police in their application to the Provincial Public Security Authority for approval to investigate the Chens' IP telephony case:

> ... Our Station received information ... reported by Fuzhou Posts and Telecommunications Bureau that ... telephone user Chen Yan uses personal computer and Internet software to provide international voice telephony charging Rmb6 yuan to 9 yuan depending on to which country the call is directed. This has severely disturbed the order of the telecommunications market and, in the meantime, posed a serious challenge to national security. Our Station was asked to undertake investigation into this case ... Having confirmed the reliability of the information, we propose to investigate this case on the ground that Chen Yan is suspected of having committed the crime of illegally operating [telecommunications services] as defined by Article 225 of the Criminal Law.[49]

According to an MII official, the MII was aware of the emergence of new services, such as IP telephony, due to the development of new information and communications technologies. However, from MII's point of view, IP telephone is normal telecommunications service and any telecommunications service, including IP telephony, must be accompanied by legislation. Ironically, there does not exist any legislation on IP telephony!

The Chen brothers' IP telephony case has gained wide publicity and debate outside the court. National and local newspapers continuously covered the development of the legal dispute over the case. For the first time, perhaps, the Internet was used by the Chinese citizens to facilitate public debate (*via* e-mails, Web pages, Web bulletin boards, Web discussion forums and chat rooms). The impact and implications of this case on the regulatory process in China was undoubtedly profound.

Regarding the nature of IP telephony, those including some experts from the Internet sector argued that IP telephony is not conventional telecommunications service, whilst the MII and its local branches insisted that there is no differentiation between the two types of commination. Within the legal system, the local police took radical actions against the Chen brothers' IP telephony operation. The police took the view that IP telephony disordered the telecommunications market and posed a threat to national security. This has led to the long-lasting court battle between the Chen brothers and the police.

The court decisions have added further confusion to the IP telephony case. Whilst the Mawei District People's Court (the local district court) ruled that operation of IP telephony was illegal and, therefore, the local police's actions were lawful, the Fuzhou Municipality People's Intermediate Court came to the conclusion suggesting otherwise.

The IP telephony case suggests that, with the lack of clearly defined telecommunications law, 'institutional convergence' (i.e., the establishment of the MII) alone was not sufficient to cope with the challenges posed by technological convergence (e.g. IP telephony). The confusions caused by the IP telephony case would likely contribute to hindering the exploitation of the Internet technology for the sake of economic development. This is contrary to the willingness of the Chinese government that has been advocating the informatisation of the national economy and the construction of the national information superhighway.

Conclusion

The world is now witnessing a fundamental transformation, i.e., a revolutionary shift from an industrial society to the information society. New information and communications technologies increasingly pervade all industrial and societal activities and are accelerating the globalisation of both economies and societies.[50] In other words, new ICTs are, on the one hand, bringing the development of our human civilisation to a new stage. On the other hand, new ICTs are poised to redraw the horizon of the global economy. The leading industrialised countries are responding to the information revolution by launching new policy initiatives in order not to lag behind their competitors. However, the impact of this information revolution is not confined solely to the western industrialised countries; rather, developing countries are also becoming increasingly aware of the challenges of the new ICTs. The case study about China, as presented in this chapter, shows how developing countries attempt to reap the benefit of the digital revolution by means of industrial and technology policy making.

China's new industrial and technology policy for the digital age was manifested, firstly, in the Informatisation of the National Economy Programme. This programme appeared to be far-reaching in a sense that a large-scale and high-capacity national grid of fibre optic cables (the backbone of the information superhighway) has been constructed. Secondly, a series of Golden Projects (Golden Bridge, Golden Customs, Golden Cards, etc.) have been launched in order to promote the use of the information superhighway. Thirdly, government policy allowed for prioritisation and selectivity in terms of the promotion of specific technologies. Finally, the recent institutional reform, in particular the formation of the all-embracing Ministry of Information Industry, has certainly ended the rivalry between a number of previously competing ministries. However, this 'institutional convergence' has not enabled the Chinese government to effectively harness the technological convergence.

Given the very low base of ICT deployment, it seems a sensible strategy to pursue a 'dual-track' economic development strategy, i.e., continued industrialisation and ever increasing informatisation. This apparently provides a golden opportunity for China to make a 'leap-frog' in economic development instead of following every step western industrialised countries have experienced during their industrialisation. Some experts argue:

> The growth model followed by the industrialised countries and largely based on industrialisation does not allow for sustainable growth, particularly if this model is followed by emerging or developing countries.[51]

It is worth bearing in mind that new information and communications technologies are also a double-edged sword. To those nations that were left out of the industrial revolution, 'informatisation is desirable, but it also presents challenges that may very well add to rather than solve their problems. How to turn the information revolution to their advantage and enhance economic growth is a major concern for policymakers in developing countries' (Dordick and Wang, 1993, p. 127). As far as China is concerned, the challenges are many-fold.

First of all, there was a lack of institutional capacity to cope with the rapid development in new technologies and industries. Before the creation of the MII, policies regarding new ICTs were often promoted by various state commissions and government ministries with equivalent policymaking power. These policymaking agencies had their own vested interests, which led to turf fighting. Technological convergence, driven by the progress in digital techniques cries for a new approach of public policy making. The launch of the Joint Conference for Informatisation of the National Economy in 1994 and, subsequently, the Information Technology Development Leading Group in 1996 within the State Council was an effort by the Chinese government to achieve overall coordination across different power domains responsible for the information age. A more recent attempt was the merge of the three big ministries (the Ministry of Posts and Telecommunications, the Ministry of Electronics Industry and the Ministry of Broadcasting, Film and Television) to create a super ministry, i.e., the Ministry of Information Industry. This further demonstrated the desire of the Chinese government to improve the institutional capacity to harness the seemingly ungovernable process of rapid technical change. The establishment of the ITDLG and the creation of the MII form in part the Chinese government's solution to the country's digital age governance issue. Unfortunately, the MII has failed to respond to the challenge of technological convergence in a convincing manner.

Secondly, the success of China's informatisation programme in the long-term will be largely contingent upon the coming of the rule of law. Typically, as far as the digital age is concerned, software development follows hardware development, and policy (as well as law and regulation) lags behind both.[52] To a great extent, it is policy and law that can determine whether a country is capable of reaping the benefits of new technologies. It may be true that, in the western industrialised countries, tomorrow's technologies are manoeuvred by today's business managers under yesterday's law. The same can be said about China – the Mawei District Court, for instance, simply applied the criminal law to the IP telephony case.

Thirdly, unlike in most industrialised countries, universal access is low on the agenda of public policy making in China. The uneven development of the global information society is dictated by the division between countries of 'information-rich' and those of 'information-poor'. The same division is being created within China itself. For instance, telephone penetration rate in the cities had already reached 24% in 1997; but this dropped to only 7.4% when averaged with the rest of the country in the same year. The uneven development process between cities and rural areas during the industrial age in China is being reproduced in the digital age. This can be said a consequence of China's overall economic development policy over the last few decades – the manufacturing industries and cities have been given the priority. Unless there is a fundamental change in this policy, China will remain a country characterised by the division between the haves and the have-nots in a long time to come. Ideally, the overriding objectives of government policies for the information society should be that new ICTs are used to support national economic development in a way equal opportunities are created and all segments of the society, including the underprivileged, the disabled, and the rural residents, can benefit from the process (Thajchayapong et al, 1997).

In order to pursue fast economic growth in the digital age, the Chinese government has not simply rejected new information and communications technologies. Rather, China appears determined to grasp the economic and business potential associated with new ICTs. In other words, when the digital revolution remains an economic matter, the Chinese government would seem to be enthusiastic.

In Part II of this book attention will be shifted to the governance of the digital revolution. The politics of managing the process of technological innovation and controlling access to new ICTs will be analysed.

Notes

[1] The term *informatisation*, according to Dordick and Wang (1993), was first used to denote: a) a process of change leading to an information society; b) a process that does not simply involve progress in telematics, that is, interconnection between computer and telecommunications systems, but also that alters the entire nervous system of social organisation (p. 13).

[2] Deng Xiaoping's economic reform policy was first tested in the rural area with the agricultural sector and his 'open-door' policy started with the launch of the four 'Special Economic Zones' (SEZs, i.e. Shenzhen, Zhuhai, Xiamen and Shantou) along the southern coast in the later 1970s and early 1980s. Jiang Zemin's succession to Deng seems to suggest a continuation of economic reform and 'open-door' policy under the same banner of 'socialism' with Chinese characteristics.

[3] Statement by Li Lanqing, Vice Premier, quoted in Xu and Armstrong (1995).

[4] *Time*, 22 September 1997, p. TD14. China's first Great Leap Forward movement was launched in 1958 by Mao Zedong as a nationwide mass campaign to build a massive iron and steel sector, which was regarded by Mao as a strategic industry. Literally everybody in the country was expected to participate in the mass-making of iron and steel in the late 1950s. Consequently, in addition to the very low quality of iron and steel produced, the mass campaign also led to the radical decline of normal factory production and poor agricultural harvest. This was widely believed the major factor responsible for the nationwide famine occurred in the early 1960s.

5 The date 'March 1986' written in the Chinese language is '86.3.', hence the R&D Programme 863.
6 Actually, the '863' Programme continues to contribute to the current informatisation programme. For instance, one of the on-going '863' projects is focused on research and development for ATM broadband switch equipment.
7 Note that the 'Four Modernisations' Programme has been continued throughout the last two decades and is still going on.
8 'Rmb' stands for Renminbi, the Chinese currency. The basic unit of the Rmb is yuan, which is the Chinese equivalent to dollar in the US or the sterling pound in Britain. The Chinese currency is only partially convertible (under current account), and the current exchange rate is $1=Rmb8.5 yuan as for the end of June 1998. The same exchange rate is used for calculation throughout this chapter.
9 Figures are quoted in Kynge (1998). Compared with the relatively low rate of teledensity in China, the consumer electronics industry shows a significantly different picture: 96% of all urban households and 48.5% of rural households own either a colour or black-and-white TV set in 1997. This corresponds to China's very competitive position in TV manufacturing sector: it is the world's biggest producer of black-and-white TV sets and the third largest supplier of colour TVs, next only to South Korea and the US.
10 MPT has now been incorporated into the Ministry of Information Industry.
11 Note that, as an exception, the PLA has been running commercial mobile phone services from its own network in some parts of the country. The government offered the PLA to halt its commercial operation by 1998 but this ruling has been largely ignored. This point will be further discussed later in this chapter.
12 If China joins the World Trade Organisation (WTO) in year 2000, this will have to change.
13 Note that, after more than 10 years of competition between British Telecom (BT) and Mercury (owned by Cable & Wireless), the two rivals in the duopoly structure before the arrival of cable operators, BT still enjoys about 90% of the local and domestic telephony market in the UK. Bearing this in mind, the Chinese pattern of 'duopoly' might not differ significantly from 'monopoly' (by China Telecom), given the very limited market share of Liantong at the moment.
14 Primary lines are those fibre optic cables linking the major cities and all of the provincial capitals. Some provinces have also decided to adopt SDH technology for their intra-provincial fibre optic cable networks.
15 In comparison, in 1996, Kingston Communications had only 300 km of fibre optic cables in its franchised area in and surrounding the city of Hull in the UK.
16 *People's Daily* (Overseas Edition), 30 March 1997. Note that Hong Kong Telecom has been in the process of being taken over since early 2000 by Pacific Century CyberWorks, an indigenous Internet company in Hong Kong.
17 These are Beijing, Chengdu, Chongqing, Shenyang, Guangzhou, Haikou, Harbin, Urumqi, Hohhot, Qingdao, Shanghai, Xiamen, Xian, Fuzhou, Kunming, Langzhou, Lhasa, Nangning and Wuhan.
18 In May 2000 Nokia announced that it was to develop a major industrial park in Beijing in a joint venture with a local partner focusing on communications technologies and products.
19 China has adopted the European GSM mobile phone standard. More recently the Chinese government has approved the adoption of the American CDMA standard as part of the country's WTO deal with the United States.
20 See *CommunicationsWeek International*, Issue 195, 24 November 1997, p. 3.

21 *Ibid.*
22 Zhu was appointed the Prime Minister, to replace Li Peng, as the recent National People's Congress held in March 1998.
23 Among a total of over 2,000 firms, of which more than 600 are owned by various Ministries, in the telecommunications equipment manufacturing sector alone, choosing 10 large companies to support does indicate the government's determination to kick-start a process of consolidation within this sector. Therefore, the nature of consolidation, if it happens in the future, in the Chinese telecommunications equipment manufacturing industry will be substantially different from that in most of the industrialised countries, where government does not normally promote such a consolidation and concentration process (the market usually assumes this responsibility instead).
24 These are the products which have already been strategically targeted and promoted by the government as discussed above. Import of these products would be potentially detrimental to the development of domestic industries, which are still in their infant stage.
25 Information is from the CASS.
26 MPT (1993), Article 6.
27 MPT (1995), Chapter One, Article 7. Note that a large number of foreign firms have bypassed this stipulation and actually invested in the Chinese telecommunication industry via their joint ventures with local Chinese partners.
28 Until February 1998, over 70 countries/economies had become signatories of the WTO telecommunications treaty, which was designed to liberalise the global telecommunications market. Hong Kong, which is now a part of China, is one of the signatories.
29 Note that the Chinese government had indicated that the telecommunications market could be opened before 2010, regardless China joins the WTO or not.
30 Global One has now become a wholly owned subsidiary of France Télécom.
31 *Financial Times*, 19 November 1997.
32 See Wall Street Journal, http://interactive.wsj.com/articles/SB95306145891976369.htm.
33 Currently there are only two public mobile phone networks operated by China Telecom and Liantong respectively.
34 *China Daily*, April 12, 1998.
35 To be sure, the launch of Liantong as the second carrier was not intended to create a competitor to China Telecom in the first place. Rather, the government made it clear that Liantong's role should be complementary to that of China Telecom.
36 See *CommunicationsWeek International*, 20 April 1998, p. 37.
37 CIIED (1996), Section 6.5.
38 In addition to its central role in coordinating, jointly with the MEI, the national Golden Card Project, the People's Bank of China was said to have been vigorously promoting its own information system in more than 50 cities throughout the country for the purpose of banking clearance since late 1996. *China Electronics News*, April 29, 1998.
39 *Times*, 22 September 1997, p. TD14.
40 For example, the returning to power of Deng Xiaoping in the late 1970s has led to a new age of economic reform and open-door policies, which in turn have made China a country entirely different from Mao's age.

41   European Commission (1998), *Status of Voice Communication on Internet under Community Law and, in Particular, under Directive 90/388/EEC*, OJ No. C6, 1 October.
42   *Ibid.*
43   The Chens charged Rmb6 to 9 yuan per minute depending on which country the customer had dialed. China Telecom's charge for calls to the US was Rmb18.4 yuan per minute in late 1998. The average price of international calls per minute in China is at Rmb29 yuan (approx. £2.23) at present. This is prohibitively expensive for the majority of residential users in China. The average monthly salary in Beijing at the moment is Rmb1,000 yuan, just about enough to make 34.5 minutes of international calls.
44   Article 225 of the Chinese Criminal Law stipulates that, it is illegal 'to undertake trading without approval those products defined by the law and administrative regulations as items exclusively managed and sold or traded with restrictions [by the state]'.
45   For background information about Chen Yan's encountering the local police, see http://personal.gz168.net/blackwhite/background.htm and *People's Daily*, 31 January 1999.
46   Quoted in *Nanfan Daily [South Daily]*, 25 January 1999; *People's Daily*, 5 February 1999.
47   MII official statement quoted in *Guangming Daily*, 23 January 1999.
48   *People's Daily* (Overseas Edition), 2 February 1999.
49   Translation (by the author) in part of the Mawei Police Station's application to the Provincial Public Security Authority for approval to investigate the Chen Yan IP telephony case (see original text in Figure 4.1).
50   Commission of the European Communities (1997a), *Fifth Framework Programme for Research and Technological Development*, COM(97) 553 final, Brussels, 5 November.
51   The Information Society Forum (1996), p. 9.
52   Gore, A. (1991), 'Infrastructure for the Global Village', *Scientific American*, September 1991.

PART II
GOVERNANCE OF THE DIGITAL REVOLUTION

5 Chinese Politics Online: Implications of the Internet

Where there is a policy on the top, there is a counter-policy at the bottom.[1]

Introduction

A leading industrialist once claimed that '[t]he Web reminds me of the early days of the PC industry. No one really knows anything. There are no experts. All the experts have been wrong. There's a tremendous open possibility to the whole thing. And it hasn't been confined, or defined, in too many ways. That's wonderful.'[2] Indeed, 'tremendous open possibility' of the Internet includes its potential to reshape the power structure in countries with a totalitarian regime.

In 1998 two prominent western leaders, US President Bill Clinton and the British Prime Minister Tony Blair, visited China. The purposes of the two state visits might differ but there was at least one item of their agenda in common: both leaders highlighted the importance of electronic communication between China and the Western world. More specifically, President Clinton launched a session of 'virtual surgery' – using the Internet to virtually bring Chinese doctors from the Northwest of China and American doctors to jointly conduct a medical operation. Following this event, Tony Blair launched a high-tech electronic link between Tsinghua University, one of the top Chinese universities, and Manchester University in Britain. The initiative is primarily co-funded by the Chinese Education and Research Network (CERNet, one of the most established and largest Internet Service Providers or ISPs in the country) and the Higher Education Funding Council for England (HEFCE), with commercial sponsorship from Cable and Wireless Communications (C&WC) and China Telecom. The main objective of this electronic link was to provide immediate and direct access between all UK universities and more than 450 Chinese universities.

This initiative has effectively joined up the Joint Academic Network (Janet) of Britain and its Chinese counterpart, i.e., the CERNet.

The implication of both the Clinton and Blair initiatives is evident: the Internet has won the recognition by politicians of western industrialised countries as an important means to 'engage' China in the information age.

This vision reflects the trend that the world in which we live today is becoming increasingly integrated or globalised on many fronts and the interest of Western countries may be better served by engaging, rather than isolating or containing, countries such as China. Some argue that,

> The forces behind globalisation – what Mike Moor of the WTO has dubbed the two Ts' of technology and telecommunications – have uprooted the old boundaries of the nation state. It is clear to many that the familiar coincidence of sovereignty and national interest no longer hold good. Individual states, we know, can achieve greater prosperity under a system of global rules.[3]

It is perhaps for achieving greater prosperity in the globalised world, the Chinese government has demonstrated its willingness to let China become an integral part of the international community[4] and the Internet might provide a convenient and cost-effective technology to achieve this objective.

Some predict that the remaining communist regimes will eventually 'breakdown' in the information age. Al Gore, the US Vice President, compares capitalism with communism in a way massively parallel, decentralised computing compares with a powerful central computer. Capitalism and representative democracy rely on the freedom of the individuals and these systems operate in a manner similar to the principle behind massively parallel computers, which process data not in one central unit but rather in tiny, less powerful units distributed throughout the computer. When millions of individuals process information relevant to their lives and to express their conclusions in free speech and in votes simultaneously, the aggregate result is incredibly accurate and efficient decisions. In contrast, communism attempted to bring all the information to a large and powerful central processor, which collapsed when it was overwhelmed by ever more complex information.[5]

Rupert Murdoch, one of the most influential media tycoons in the world, recently described the Internet as a revolutionary liberator of the individual that would sweep away rather than deepen social inequality and meet all our demands. 'Governments will have to get out of the way of change. Change is not only accelerating, its direction and consequences are becoming less predictable. Central planning is a dangerous game.'[6]

Despite the various attempts by the Chinese government to censor the Internet, some western politicians are firmly convinced that the Internet threatens to bring about political changes:

> Now there's no question China has been trying to crack down on the Internet. Good luck! That's sort of like trying to nail jello [jelly, author] to the wall. But I would argue to you that their effort to do that just proves how real these changes are and how much they threaten the status quo. It's not an argument for slowing down the effort to bring China into the world, it's an argument for accelerating that effort. In the knowledge economy, economic innovation and political empowerment, whether anyone likes it or not, will inevitably go hand in hand.[7]

As far as the western visionaries are concerned, the Internet has not only ushered in the greatest period of wealth creation in human history, but also brings about a brave new world with 'online democracy'.[8] It is widely expected that western liberal democracy will evolve into a digital democracy and the remaining totalitarian regimes will be replaced with democratically created rule of law.

This vision may well be true in that most former communist regimes have already collapsed and capitalist mode of production (or market economy) is prevailing in China. However, the virtue of representative democracy has not landed onto the Chinese soil. With the arrival of the information age, the Chinese Communist Party (CCP) and its government is becoming well equipped with new information and communications technologies, which in turn would become a new means of control. Some academics have made their reservations explicit about the perceived link between technological progress and political democratisation:

> New technologies replace the open plains and encourage a discount of the present for perfect futures. ... Together these dreams bind over the wounds of a corrosive reality neither rational nor egalitarian. Each in its time, the developments of steam energy, electricity, telephones, radio, television, and, even more so, recent developments in computers and telecommunications have sparked new hopes for rapid attainment of these dreams. In the United States the messiah is technology (Laudon, 1977, p. 1).

To be sure, with the ease of use of abundant new information and communications technologies, 'it is possible to evolve societies in which people live in greater freedom, exert great influence on their circumstances, and experience greater dignity, self-esteem, purpose, and well-being' (Sclove, 1995, p. 244). But, in the meantime, realistic hopes should not be inflated into technological hypes because 'common knowledge has it that technologies perform one or perhaps a few intended functions, while also producing a limited range of unintended social and environmental consequences' (*Ibid.*, p. 10).

This chapter examines the recent development of the Internet and its impact on political change in Mainland China. It is argued that the Internet is a double-edged sword: it is indispensable for economic modernisation but the wide spread and mass use of the Internet has also presented unprecedented challenges to the ruling regime. Whilst the government has implemented powerful measures to tame the Internet, this new media appears to be untameable. The Internet has now evolved into uncharted water for political activities – both dissident groups and the government were quick to embrace the power online. With the prospect of joining the WTO, China will find it hard to stay away from the global communications revolution, which would have long-term impact on the political process in the country.

It seems that the networked structure of the Internet – there is neither ownership nor centre on the network – is incompatible with the highly centralised and hierarchical political system operating in China. However, this 'incompatibility' is insufficient to suggest any immediate political change or social revolution towards democratisation in the country. Rather, the social and political impact of the Internet, no matter how profound it may be, should be understood from a long-term perspective and any romanticised 'vision' on the digital age should not be divorced from the harsh reality of Chinese politics. The empirical evidences and discussions presented in this chapter suggest that, whilst the Internet as a new communications tool can be used to liberate human beings from the constraints of time and space, the same technology may also be used to enhance and extend governments' effort to exert efficient control. By examining the development of the Internet, this chapter will also demonstrate who, the state or the individual, controls this new digital media and how it is manipulated in the country.

Growth of the Internet in China

The Internet is a global network of computer networks. Originally developed as a computer network for scientific research during the Cold War era (more precisely 1969), in the United States, the Internet has now been turned into one of the major communications tools used by 201 million people worldwide. The Internet first reached the Chinese academic community in 1988, when the Chinese Institute of High Energy Physics was linked with the European Centre for Nuclear Research *via* a 4.8 Kbps

(Kilobytes per second) line. The capacity of Internet link between China and the rest of the world increased to 241 Mbps (Megabytse per second) in June 1999.[9]

The rapid development of the Internet in China is also in part demonstrated by the fast increase of users. During the period 1994 to 1999, the total number of Internet users increased, as shown in Table 5.1, from 10,000 to 8.9 million. In the last three years of the 1990s the total number of Internet users either more than doubled (1997 and 1998) or more than tripled (1999) the previous year figure. The CNN estimated that, by the year 2005, there would be 141 million people online in China.[10] That would be, if achieved, equivalent to about 10% of the total Chinese population.[11]

Table 5.1   Internet development in China: 1994-1999

Year	1994	1995	1996	1997	1998	1999
Number of Users (,000)	10	80	200	670	2100	8900
Annual Increase (%)	-	700	150	235	213	324

Sources: Based on Ministry of Science and Technology, *Development Report on China's New & High-Tech Industry*, Beijing, The Science Press, 1999; Survey by the China Internet Network Information Centre (CNNIC), December 1999.

Table 5.2   Major Internet Service Providers (ISPs) in China

Network	Sponsor/Owner	Date of Launch	User Community
CSTNet	The Chinese Academy of Science	April 1994	Science and technology institutes
ChinaNet	MPT	May 1995	Commercial users
CERNet	State Commission of Education	November 1995	educational establishments
ChinaGBN	MEI	September 1996	Commercial users

Source: Adapted from Yang (1998).

Internet Service Providers (ISPs) in China were initially confined to four major nationwide networks and these are CSTNet, ChinaNet, CERNet and ChinaGBN. These four ISPs are exclusively state-owned organisations.

Table 5.2 gives the details about the sponsors/owners, date of launch and the user communities of these four networks.

Despite the government's wary attitude towards information published on the World Wide Web (WWW), and the new way of digital communication facilitated by the Internet (e.g. e-mails, mailing lists, online chat rooms and web-based discussion forums), the number of ISPs is increasing rapidly. Up until now, there are about 400 ISPs licensed by the MPT (now a part of the MII – Ministry of Information Industry) (Kynge, J. (1998).

The exponential growth of the Internet in China confirms some analysts' observation that, in many developing countries, the increases are even greater than found in the United States or Nordic countries at a similar point in 'Internet development'.[12] The development of the Internet reflects in part the fast expansion of the overall information and communications technology sector and the national economy in China since the early 1980s. Including the Internet, the average annual growth rates for the main areas of the Chinese ICT sector (e.g., telephone, computers and TV sets) have substantially superseded the country's GDP (Gross Domestic Product) growth, which is averaged at 9.7% during the period 1980 to 1998. In comparison, the average growth rate for telephone users was 24.5% and 61.5% for computers during the same period.

Table 5.3   Growth of the ICT sector and GDP in China: 1980-1998

	1980	1998	Average Growth, %
GDP (Rmb billion)	451.8	7955.3	9.7
Telephone users, (million)	2.1	110.9	24.5
Computers (,000)	0.532	2980	61.5
TV Sets (,000)	2480	42759	17.1

Source: Adapted from Ministry of Science and Technology (1999).

Despite fast growth rate and the potential of the Internet as a new driver for economic development and modernisation, there are factors constraining the spread of the network in China. Among others, high costs for getting connected and surfing the Internet are in part responsible for the relatively lower level of Internet penetration in the country. Commercialisation of the Internet started in 1995 when ChinaNet was launched. ChinaNet is owned by China Telecom but access to the international Internet *via* ChinaNet is provided by Sprint, one of the major long distance telecommunications operators in the US. In part due to the high prices imposed by international carriers,[13] Internet service charges remain prohibitively high in China. For instance, in the mid-1990s, ChinaNet charged Rmb1,500 yuan ($176) of access connection fee plus Rmb100 yuan ($12) of usage fee for 6 hours per month or Rmb300 yuan ($35) per month for 75 hours.[14] Compared to Internet service charges in western industrialised countries (e.g. America Online charges $19,95 as a flat fee for unlimited access hours per month), cost of access to Internet services in China is excessively high. Even if the cost of Internet services is reduced by up to 50%, as the Ministry of Information Industry considers at the moment, it is still well beyond the reach by most ordinary Chinese consumers with a modest annual income.

Another reason affecting Internet access is the very low level of home computer ownership in China. It is estimated that, in 1998, only 3% of Chinese households had a computer (Kynge, 1998). This has resulted in the fact that, among the 8.9 million Internet users in China, half of them access the Internet from locations outside their home.

The government also recognises the fact that the number of Internet Contents Providers (ICPs) and the amount of information provided on the Internet in China is very limited.[15]

Table 5.4   China online: Internet users

Registered Subscribers	8.9 million
Gender	79% male
Marital Status	64% single
Largest User Group	Students (21% of the total)
Educational Level	84% have a college degree
Age Range	86% between 18-35
Beijing and Shanghai Users	32%
Access Location	50% home; Internet café 11%; 37% work/school; 2% other

Source: Based on survey by the China Internet Network Information Centre (CNNIC), December 1999.

According to a recent survey undertaken by the China Internet Network Information Centre, the current Internet user community in China is largely dominated by young (86% between 18-35 years old) and unmarried (64%) male (79%) individuals with a college degree (84%).

Compared to the total numbers of people with access to the Internet all over the world, which is at 201 million at the moment, China's share is still very low indeed. To be sure, the spread of Internet access at the global level is uneven: More than half of the Internet users are from the US, which makes up only 4.7% of the total world population. In the US, over one-third of the population now have Internet access. According to the United Nations (UN), with only 15% of the world's population, western industrialised countries are home to 88% of all Internet users. This suggests that the 'Internet boom' is largely confined to the major industrialised countries and, despite the trend that the Internet is transforming the global economy into a digital economy, the North-South divide remains unchanged. With 739 million people living in Africa, there are only 14 million phone lines (fewer than Manhattan or Tokyo) and 1 million Internet users (compared with 10.5 million in the UK at the moment). Overall, up until now, more than 80% of people in the world have never heard a dial tone, let alone surfing the Web; and this digital divide between the information-haves and have-nots is still widening.[16]

Despite the gap between China, as a developing country, and its western industrialised counterparts on the information superhighway, it is widely believed that the high growth rate of the Internet holds great potential for economic development and political democratisation in countries such as China. As far as the future spread of the Internet in China is concerned, it should be viewed as an integral part of the country's economic development in the new millennium. So long as the Chinese economy remains dynamic, there will be ground for an optimistic view about the future development of the Internet in the country.

It used to be a luxurious fashion for many Chinese couples in the 1980s to buy a piano for their sole child, the 'little emperor'. In the 1990s, the centre pierce of household items in China has become a personal computer (PC), mainly for the purpose of supporting the child's education. Increasingly, more and more PCs are linked to the Internet and getting online has become a new fashion for the growing army of the new social elite (e.g. party/government officials, intellectuals and those who have become rich). For thousands of years the most popular social greeting between friends and other acquaints has been simply 'Have you eaten?' – when 'food is people's heaven'. Nowadays, however, the new and fashionable social greeting is 'Are you online?'. The Internet has not replaced food to become people's heaven but it is already quietly changing the Chinese society.

In June 1997, under the auspices of the State Council Information Office (SCIO), the China Internet Network Information Centre (CNNIC) was founded. As a not-for-profit organisation for administration and service, the mission of the CNNIC is to 'serve for Chinese Internet users and promote Chinese Internet developing more healthily and orderly.'[17] What seems important, though, is the fact that any information and communication on the Internet not in line with the Party and government policy would be deemed 'unhealthy'. The term 'orderly' means the development of the Internet should not be detrimental to social stability.

Hierarchical Control and Networked Communication

'Jumping into the sea to make a dry spot.' This is a Chinese proverb describing any unreasonable demand or unrealistic expectation. By accepting the Internet, China has jumped into the sea of online digital communications revolution, which is intrinsically not governable by any individual nation state. However, the Chinese government appears determined to put the global computer network under its control.[18]

To be sure, attempts by states and governments (in both the world's democracies and totalitarian regimes) to unilaterally put the Internet under their own national control are not rare. In February 1996 the American President Bill Clinton signed the Communications Decency Act (CDA), which stipulates that transmission of 'indecent' materials (such as child pornography) over the Internet would be a crime and could be subject to fines (maximum $25,000) and imprisonment (up to two years). This has caused widespread protest by the freedom of information activists and, in less than a year's time, the CDA collapsed when a Supreme Court judge ruled that the CDA was unconstitutional.

Many governments in western industrialised countries have taken severe actions to censor the Internet. In November 1999, the FBI of the United States demanded a website with a 6-minute video clip showing a plan to ignite race riots be removed and the ISP in question complied. The FBI did not ask for a court order to shut down this site and took its own initiative to censor it.[19] In Britain, in November 1999, the Lord Chancellor ordered Kingston Internet, an ISP based in Hull to remove a website on its sever where an open letter by a local resident was published criticising the Crown Court judges' decision on a particular case. Kingston Net followed the Lord Chancellor's order and removed the open letter from its sever. The local resident believes this action has breached his right to freedom of speech and decided to take his case to the European Court of Justice. The German Government ordered CompuServe, now part of America Online (AOL), to shut down 200 news groups hosted by the ISP two years ago. There are many incidents of this type showing some governments' willingness to exercise their power to censor the Internet.

The situation in Asia is even bleaker. The Singaporean government has adopted a range of technical measures to restrict access to certain types of information on the Internet, such as pornography. In Singapore, sending any message, which is offensive on moral, religious, communal or political grounds *via* the Internet, is illegal. 'The Singapore government knows that it cannot do much to censor the Internet. But it refuses to give up without a fight' (cited in Finnie, 1995). In Burma, government regulation requires Internet users to register with the police. Web sites without government authorisation and the transmission of material deemed harmful to the state are illegal.[20] Whilst dial up for Internet services is taken for granted in many countries, the ownership of an unauthorised modem could bring a Burmese citizen a lengthy jail term.[21] In Vietnam, Web sites offering politically sensitive and morally harmful materials are blocked and Internet users must seek government approval for going online. The communist regime in North Korea is more adamant than any other government in dealing with the challenge of the Internet – private use of the Internet is simply not allowed in the country.

While the Chinese government is strongly promoting the construction of a nationwide information superhighway, it is not so much prepared to give equal priority to contents[22] provision on the communications network. On the contrary, political consideration always supersedes the exploitation of economic benefits. The rapid and wide spread of cable and satellite services, which are now available to more than 10% of TV households, will potentially enable more and more residents to have access to global TV news broadcasting such as channels provided by the CNN and the BBC. This is believed not in the favour of the government. In response, the State Council, the Chinese cabinet, issued Proclamation 129, which imposed a ban on receiving direct foreign broadcasting and severe restrictions on private satellite dish ownership. This has led to that CNN news broadcast can only be viewed in hotels and compounds that house foreigners (e.g. foreign diplomats and journalists), which needs special government permit to provide it anyway.[23]

Rupert Murdoch, the owner of News Corp., once commented in public that the spread of satellite TV broadcasting would eventually become a major threat to any totalitarian regime in the world. But before his prophecy becomes true, News Corp. bent to the pressure from Beijing and reluctantly abandoned its planned transmission of BBC news from Star TV, its Hong Kong subsidiary. News Corp. subsequently succeeded in securing a joint venture, called Xinren Information Technology, with *People's Daily*, the Chinese Communist Party's top propaganda newspaper, with a combined investment of $5.4 million specialising in electronic publishing and on-line data services (Dai, 1997, p. 84).

Generally speaking, government control over the Internet in China is achieved mainly by means of: contents and access regulation; technical measures and end user control; and government online.

Contents and Access Regulation

Whilst the Internet is increasingly proving to be a thorny issue for many public authorities throughout the world, the Chinese government had no hesitation to regulate the Internet. The overall approach adopted by the Chinese government is rather simple – it announced in February 1996 that the Chinese laws against pornography, social disturbances and breaches of state security apply on the Internet.[24] In addition, the central government has adopted a few pierces of regulation in order to harness the growth and use of the Internet:

- The computer information system security protection rules (State Council Order No. 147, 1994)
- Gateway administration of computer information network's international connection (MPT, No. 492, 1996)
- Administrative rules for international connection *via* ChinaNet (MPT, No. 493, 1996)
- Administrative rules for product tests and sales licensing related to computer information system (Ministry of Public Security, No. 32, 1997)
- Administrative rules for multimedia communications (MPT, 1997)
- Security protection administration of computer information network's international connection (Ministry of Public Security, 1997)
- Temporary rules concerning the administration of the Chinese Internet domain name registration (State Council).

Since the mid-1990s, the Chinese government has ordered that, firstly, all Internet Service Providers in China go through the Ministry of Posts and Telecommunications. Secondly, all types of foreign-owned economic news services must be distributed through the country's sole news agency, Xinhua (New China) News Agency, which has been strictly controlled by the CCP. Government control over the Internet in China goes even further: all Internet users are ordered to register with the police. Registration of end-users constitutes the core of the Chinese system of control and represents a typical approach to the problem of security within China (Muellor and Tan, 1997, p. 95). Beijing Telecom, the Beijing municipality branch of the former MPT, are given the task to operate the servers that allow computer users to gain access to the Internet. More specifically, the Chinese government's regulation of the Internet, among others, stipulates a number of points as follows:

- Organisations and individuals are not allowed to use the computer systems to undertake activities against the interest of the state or the security of computer information systems;
- Organisations and individuals are not allowed to use the Internet to search, copy, produce and disseminate information detrimental to state security or information of a pornographic nature;
- Computer systems with international connection must be registered with the provincial government or higher level;
- Transporting, carrying or posting computer information media should be reported to the customs offices;
- International connection to the Internet must use the international gateways provided by the MPT's telecommunications network; organisations and individuals are not allowed to set up or use any other gateways (including satellite gateways).

With regard to the nature of Internet mediated contents, the Chinese government regulation specifically outlaws the flowing information:

- Information provoking protest and sabotage of the application of the constitution, law and administrative rules;
- Information provoking the toppling of the government and overthrowing of the socialist system;
- Information detrimental to the unity of the country;
- Information provoking national hatred, national discrimination and detrimental to national solidarity;
- Fabricating or distorting facts, spreading rumours and disturbing social order;

- Promoting criminal activities such as superstitions, pornography, gambling, violence, murdering, etc.;
- Information insulting or slandering to others;
- Information damaging the reputation of government agencies;
- Any other information breaching the constitution, law and administrative rules.

The specific government regulations over the Internet in China appears to be comparable with those in Burma.[25] One would consider the Chinese government's regulation is more than sufficient to censor the Internet and deprive any degree of freedom of expression. Ironically, the same regulation stipulates that 'the users' freedom and privacy of correspondence are protected by the law. No organisations and individuals are allowed to use the Internet to invade the freedom and privacy of correspondence, which is against the law.'[26]

The 'Great Firewall': Technical Measures

The Chinese sense of security and defence is traditionally linked with walls. The irony is, as a Chinese proverb says, the walls have ears!

The Beijing Telecom servers are known among the Chinese Internet users as the 'Great Firewall',[27] a nick name obviously derived from China's Great Wall, which was used by Chinese armies since the Qin Dynasty (221-206 BC)[28] to defend the country's borders stretching from the Northwest to the Northeast. The function of the 'firewall' (*fanghuo qiang* in Chinese), literally 'Netwall' (*wangguan* in Chinese), is to block unauthorised access to Chinese government or corporate websites but also to block access by Chinese citizens to undesirable foreign websites. This centralised approach has apparently made it possible to a certain extent for the government to broadly censor the Internet. It was reported that, in 1996, more than 100 websites in China were blocked by the government and, among others, these include:

- US news media such as the *Los Angeles Times*, *Wall Street Journal*, *Washington Post*, Voice of America, CNN;
- Politically sensitive sites, including the Taiwan Government Information Office;
- Home pages of groups that monitor human rights issues in China;

- The U.S.-based China News Digest (CND), a site provides information about China and has become extremely popular among overseas Chinese intellectuals;
- Pornographic sources such as the *Playboy*.[29]

In May1999 agents from the Ministry of State Security (MSS) paid unannounced visits to Internet Service Providers and connected them to two new monitoring devices, which are used to track individual e-mail accounts and aid the government's attempts to block undesirable materials on the Internet.[30] In a similar move, the Ministry of Public Security (MPS) has recently ordered a 24-hour watch on popular online chat rooms. It also stipulated that 'as soon as counter-revolutionary discussions are discovered, the police should contact the managers and cut the service as well as investigate the real name of those who put up the message'.[31] There is no doubt that the Chinese government would take the advantage of any new technology available to enhance its efforts in online surveillance.

Some argue that electronic media, including the Internet, makes no exception in so far as government control or censorship is concerned:

> Electronic media, as they are coming to be, are dispersed in use and abundant in supply. They allow for more knowledge, easier access, and freer speech than were ever enjoyed before. They fit the free practices of print. The characteristics of media shape what is done with them, so one might anticipate that these technologies of freedom will overwhelm all attempts to control them. Technology, however, shapes the structure of the battle, but not every outcome. While the printing press was without doubt the foundation of modern democracy, the response to the flood of publishing that it brought forth has been censorship as often as press freedom. In some times and places the more capacious new media will open wider the floodgates for discourse, but in other times and places, in fear of that flood, attempts will be made to shut the gates (Pool, 1983, p. 251).

Largely because of the implementation of state control measures, the number of victims of the Chinese government's crack down of 'illegal' use of the Internet is increasing. Lin Hai, a computer engineer in Shanghai was sentenced in early 1999 to two years of imprisonment for supplying a list of Chinese e-mail addresses a pro-democracy organisation based in the US. Qi Yanchen, a Chinese dissident, was jailed in September 1999 for reproducing information on human rights downloaded from the Internet. The leader of the new China Democracy Party (CDP), Wang Youcai, was recently sentenced to over 10 years of imprisonment for 'crimes' including sending pro-democracy literature abroad via e-mail and accepting $800 from foreigners to buy a computer.[32]

The Chinese government's unilateral effort to regulate and control the Internet runs into conflict with the fact that the part of the Internet on the Chinese soil is actually an integral part of the global network of computers. For the time being, there is a lack of internationally accepted agreement, which could be readily applied to the Internet or the 'cyberspace':

> There is yet no law of cyberspace. But it is clear that a genuine revolution is brewing in which the revolutionaries are unwilling to recognize and unlikely to observe laws imposed upon them by outside jurisdictions. They are coming to realize that cyberspace is a place or a universe of many places where users are making their own jurisdictional boundaries and developing their own standards of fair play and acceptable-use policies. It is not necessarily a lawless place, but lawless places do exit in cyberspace as well as in the real world. The real clash will come between the geopolitical boundaries (which the technologies of information ignore) and the electronic boundaries (which have no geopolitical counterpart). Whose rules and regulation will apply? And what sanctions are appropriate (Branscomb, 1994, pp. 6-7)?

Undoubtedly, there is a long way to go before any cyber law is agreed upon by the international community. Until then, individual countries, such as China, will likely work out their own way to deal with the Internet.

Government Online

If you can't beat them, join them! In late 1998 the Chinese government launched a nationwide Programme called 'Government Online'[33] and the year 1999 was officially chosen as the 'Year of Government Online'. The main objectives of this Programme include:

- 80% of government organisations at all levels throughout the country have their official websites;
- to provide online civil information services which would lead to the creation of an electronic government;
- to provide the basis for the development of a networked society.

The 'Government Online' Programme is a new dimension of the Informatisation of the National Economy Programme.[34] In the meantime, the increased presence of government information and official propaganda would rival, if not exclude, the growing liberal and anti-government content on the Internet – this might be the untold reason behind the 'Government Online' Programme.

The Internet and Democratisation

It is claimed that '[n]ot a decade goes by in free countries, and not a day in the world, without grim oppressions that bring protesters once more to picket lines and demonstrations. Vigilance that must be so eternal becomes routine, and citizens grow callous' (Pool, 1983, p. 10). The birth and popular usage of the Internet has not solved this problem; rather, it is adding a new dimension to the tension between the state and its citizens in each country and increasingly broadening the horizon of the conflict to the global level.

Many believe that Technologically speaking, with the arrival of the Internet age, the state is rapidly loosing its conventional advantage of political control:

> Within this territory, different developments in communication technology are tending to reduce all transmitted information, whether pictures, speech, software or text, to a common digital form. This convergence in the form of transmitted information has limited the technical capacity of the state to regulate flows of information across [and within] national boundaries reducing, as they do, the traffic across the state's boundaries to a featureless stream of binary bits. The trend presents a difficult challenge to the sovereignty of the state, reducing its capacity to control what is increasingly valuable and voluminous flow of electronic commodities (Camilleri and Falk, 1992, p. 121).

The Internet and Transnational Political Mobilisation

Dissident groups and anti-government forces throughout the world are quick to recognise the convenience and importance of the Internet.

At the global level, the Internet has been used to organise and coordinate large-scale protests. One of the widely reported events was the anti-capitalism protest coordinated by the 'J18' group during the summer 1999 in central London. 'J18' is not any type of conventional dissident organisation; rather, it is merely a website[35] on the Internet, to which anybody anywhere in the world could access *via* the Internet for information regarding the protesting activities. 'J18' claimed that the day 18 June 1999 was an 'international day of action, protest and carnival aimed at the heart of the global economy'.[36] The objective of the 'J18' actions was that 'across Europe, in Canada, Nigeria, Venezuela, Argentina, Mexico, South Korea, Indonesia, Brazil, Australia and many more nations, activists will occupy and transform their local financial districts (stock exchanges, banks, corporate HQs)'.[37]

Thanks to the publicity on the Internet the 'J18' campaign has led to a large-scale demonstration, which was joined by thousands of people in the financial City of London and caused damages to many corporate office buildings. In the wake of the event, the British authorities found it hard to place charges on any individual(s) for organising the activities – the main 'organiser' was the Internet!

The experience of the 'J18' in using the Internet to organise global activities against liberal capitalism was repeated by the 'n30' at a much more sophisticated level. The 'n30', announced the day 30 November 1999, when 150 governments joined the 3rd conference of the World Trade Organisation (WTO) in Seattle, a 'Global Day of Action, Resistance, and Carnival Against the Global Capitalist System'.[38] Activists from diverse groups and movement all over the world used 'n30' as a forum to exchange information, network with each other and organise activities in Seattle. In many ways the Internet played a pivotal role in making 'n30' an effective channel of communication. For instance, 'n30' set up electronic mailing lists for discussions among participants *via* the Internet.[39] Meanwhile, 'n30' used its designated website (http://go.to/n30/) to disseminate information and news about the preparations around the world for actions on the 30 November. The 1999 WTO conference in Seattle turned out to be a *debâcle*, for which the 'no30' was in part responsible.

The 'J18' and 'n30' cases suggest that the Internet is already being used by various organisations and movements to coordinate their political campaigns at a global level. It could be argued that there might not be such movements as 'J18' and 'n30', if the Internet were not available. It is anticipated that more global political activities will be organised *via* the Internet in the future.

Chinese Dissidents Online

The political implications of the Internet in China are also becoming increasingly evident. Almost as soon as Internet connections to China were opened, there were reports of incidents regarding the dissemination of anti-government information from overseas sources – Chinese Internet users received e-mail messages discussing taboo subjects such as the Tiananmen Square crackdown and the independence of Taiwan and Tibet. Officials at the ISPs were so 'nervous' that they 'voluntarily' reported the incidents to the authorities (Mueller and Tan, 1997).

A group of Chinese dissidents manage to distribute an on-line magazine, entitled *Suidao* (Chinese for 'Tunnel'), dedicated to defying government censorship. During the occasion of the eighth Tiananmen Square crackdown on 4 June 1997, *Suidao* was launched as the first electronic underground journal in China.

From a technical point of view, any attempt to assume absolute control by any government over the Internet may eventually prove a difficult, if not impossible, task. Wei Jingsheng, arguably the most prominent dissident who had spent 14 and half years in prison before his exile to the US, has started using the Internet in his political campaign. In September 1999, it was reported that Wei had sent e-mail messages from a cyber café in Paris to the Chinese government bodies in Beijing.[40] Wei's e-mail messages contained the text of Article 19 of the Universal Declaration of Human Rights.[41]

In order to advocate social change in China, a former Tiananmen Square activist helps publish a newsletter called 'VIP Reference', an electronic newsletter, that he sends from the United States to over 250,000 Chinese e-mail accounts on a daily base.[42]

Human rights campaigners have recently launched the Digital Freedom Network, which is a website devoted to collecting and posting banned literature and news reports from around the world, including China. Bao Ge, a Chinese dissident who sent a letter to Jiang Zemin in September 1997 calling for multi-party democracy and freedom of press, used the Digital Freedom Network website to make his letter accessible by the public. In Bao Ge's view, 'no voice of opposition will be allowed to be heard. Therefore, attempts by the Digital Freedom Network to break through such censorship are extraordinarily significant.'[43] Some argue that,

> China's dissident movement, battered by crackdowns since 1989, has found a refuge in cyberspace. Party leaders are battling back by erecting a system of computer blocks and filters dubbed the 'great firewall of China', but it still has many holes. Cybercritics include supporters of everything the communists hold taboo, from democracy to independence for Tibet and Taiwan, and the recently banned spiritual group, *Fulun Gong*.[44]

Dissidents and human rights activists based outside China may be able to reach only a small percentage of the Chinese population, but they maintain that in a Chinese society, where Internet access is available only to the rich, the intellectuals and the students, it is not about how many people they reach, but which ones.[45]

The Falun Gong Movement

Perhaps the most widely cited case recently is the *Falun Gong* movement, which has been effectively using the Internet and other communications technologies (e.g. pagers and mobile phones) to coordinate its nationwide and international operations.

Falun Gong (otherwise known as *Falun Dafa*) was introduced by Li Hongzhi in 1992 as a new way of meditation based on a mixture of ancient Chinese philosophies, *qigong* and Buddhism. It advocates the spirit of *zhen* (truthfulness), *shan* (benevolence) and *ren* (forbearance). By the end of 1999, the number of followers worldwide was estimated at over 100 million. This is significantly more than the total number of the Chinese Communist Party members, which is about 60 million. In July 1999 the government decided to ban *Falun Gong*, which caused worldwide protest by its followers and sympathisers.

On 25 April 1999, over 10,000 *Falun Gong* practitioners took to the street and gathered outside the Chinese government headquarters, the Zhongnanhai compound in Beijing, petitioning the government for official recognition of the *Falun Gong* movement. Although the demonstration was quiet and peaceful, the sheer scale and the sudden appearance of the crowd frightened the Communist Party and Government leaders. *Falun Gong* leader Li Hongzhi confirmed that the peaceful protest was 'spontaneous' and it 'was organized through the Internet'.[46] The Chinese authorities believe a few *Falun Gong* movement leaders with access to the Internet used e-mail to plot strategy and then relayed instructions *via* telephone and word of mouth to their members.[47]

Since the official ban, the Chinese government has ordered to block access to all *Falun Gong* websites and individuals who used the Internet to publicise the movement have been punished. Zhang Haitao, a computer engineer in the northeast city Changchun, was accused of setting up a website promoting *Falun Gong* and charged with inciting subversion against state power.[48] Local government authorities in Changchun shut down Zhang's website on 24 July 1999 and detained him a few days later. In October 1999, Zhang Ji, a student at Qiqihar University in Heilongjiang Province, was arrested for sending information *via* the Internet to the United States and Canada on what was happening to *Falun Gong* in his home Province.[49]

Whilst the government authorities in China are endeavouring to shut down and block access to websites promoting *Falun Gong* inside China, *Falun Gong* websites have been flourishing in the cyberspace hosted by millions of followers and supporters in other countries.[50] These websites contains detailed information about every aspect of the exercise and the development of the movement both inside and outside China.

The Holes in the 'Great Firewall'

Given the heavy-handed regulation of the Internet in China, how could 'illegal' information posted by organisations such as the *Falun Gong* become accessible to people inside the country? This chapter is not intended to explore the technical details but the following points, among others, might throw some light on the issue.

First, heavy regulation of the Internet in China is coupled with a lack of clearly defined implementation mechanisms. The involvement of a large number of government ministries and administrations in controlling the Internet has resulted in the overlapping of responsibilities and inefficiency. The Interim Regulations for Connections to International Networks, issued in January 1996, initially granted the former MPT the exclusive power to operate and manage international links to the Internet. When the Ministry of Information Industry (MII, which subsumed the MPT) was established in 1998 the new Ministry also announced that it would assume full control of the websites operating in China. Meanwhile, other ministries are also determined to make themselves heard.[51] One of the competing state departments is the Ministry of Public Security (MPS), which requires that Internet users must register with its agencies. This kind of internal turf struggle has resulted in that what China threatens and what it actually does can differ:

> ... so many government agencies are vying for control over the Internet – and its economic benefits – that a ruling by one agency can be changed another.[52]

Whilst government ministries are scrambling for power and control, loopholes are likely to be created – in interpreting government policy on the Internet, for instance, a wide variety of voices could be heard about what should and should not be permitted.

Second, certain aspects of state regulation, such as the MPS's user registration requirement, do not apply to employees of foreign companies. Foreign companies are allowed to provide Internet access on their own corporate networks (routed through the state-authorised interconnecting networks), so long as they do not offer commercial services in China. Potentially there are opportunities for employees at foreign-owned companies to obtain information from the Internet and then pass it on to people outside.[53]

Third, the 'great firewall of China' has many holes in it.[54] Although the government has attempted to control access to foreign websites by routing international Internet access through government-controlled gateway computers and subjecting Chinese ISPs to monitoring and administration by the Chinese authorities, users can get around this by dialing an Internet service provider outside the country *via* a simple modem.[55]

Fourth, compared to gaining access to websites, e-mail is more difficult to monitor and control. E-mail messages can be sent anonymously and in a coded format (with the help of encryption technologies), which can be next to impossible to crack.[56] By the end of 1999, there were 35.6 million e-mail accounts, of which 26.7 million were free mail accounts.[57] It is not hard to see that the government cannot keep up with all messages or necessarily trace them to particular individuals – many users gain access to the Internet through computers of Internet cafes, universities or government offices, which are used by many individuals.[58]

Fifth, certain websites may have been closed but new ones are also being created. With the ease of use of Web page authoring tools, it takes little effort to set up new websites or add new pages on to the Web. In October 1994, the Chinese government discovered its official website defending China's human rights record had been replaced with a new page denouncing it as propaganda and linking visitors to the Amnesty International website.[59]

Finally, with 8.9 million Internet users, it is an extremely daunting, if not inconceivable, task for the Chinese authorities to monitor every user's online discussion across every 'chat room' and every bulletin board. While most domestic websites concentrate on safe topics such as sports and entertainment, recent online discussions in Internet 'chat rooms' have included sensitive topics (e.g., major corruption scandals, atrocities during the Cultural Revolution) that are not raised in the state media.[60] In a chat room run by the *People's Daily* newspaper (the mouthpiece of the CCP) Chinese Internet users dared to express their opinions which are politically sensitive:

> Three users banter about Taiwan's upcoming election and express grudging respect for a candidate the Chinese government loathes. Another makes an impassioned cry for freedom of speech in a nation where voicing unauthorized opinions can mean a prison term. Still another posts a poem that pokes fun at the 'cleaning ladies' – censors who come online to scrub away comments that go too far in criticizing the government.[61]

Despite its zeal to control the Internet, as it has done to other conventional media such as the newspapers, book publishing, radio and TV broadcasting, the Chinese authorities are faced with a number of dilemmas:

First of all, there is apparently a difficult compromise which the Chinese government would have to make between its economic policy and political interest. Heavy regulation and centralised state control over the Internet would potentially slow down the growth in the number of Internet users and Internet-based commercial activities. The Internet, in particular the World Wide Web, is widely dabbed the largest free economic zone in the world. Failure in promoting electronic commerce would put China in a potentially very disadvantaged position on the Internet in comparison with other countries, who are mobilising their business communities to make the most of the Internet. For the time being, the US has seized a substantial lead in exploiting commercial opportunities offered by the Internet and the European Union is fast becoming increasingly competitive – it predicts a sharp boost from the introduction of a single European currency by the turn of the Century (Nelson, 1997).

The fact that China is lagging behind in on-line electronic commerce will be in odd with the Chinese government's own technology policies on informatisation of the national economy. The Chinese government has made it clear that it would be in favour of promoting the commercial use of the Internet. However, government actions such as blocking the Web sites offering access to up-to-date economic and financial information (e.g. the *Wall Street Journal* and CNN business news) suggest the opposite – it throws away the baby with the bath water. Among major ICT technologies, the Internet is perhaps the cheapest, easiest to use and holds arguably the most lucrative business potential. To reject the Internet, even in part, means to substantially devalue the significance of the government's informatisation programme to the national economic growth in the long run. Chinese policymakers and cybercops need to mind the growing gap in electronic commerce between China and its industrialised counterparts.

Secondly, the 'global design' of the Internet network does not seem to accommodate national control. Because of the very nature of the design of the Internet, which is a global network of computer networks, it does not belong to anybody and makes almost impossible for any national government authority to unilaterally insert absolute control over the Internet. The Chinese government might still be able to ensure control of the Internet at the moment through a centralised approach, but the growing number of Internet users will certainly make state policing a difficult task.

The technical complexity and network structure of the Internet makes it harder, if not impossible, for any government to win the online censorship battle. Equipped with first rate ICT technologies and a world class intelligence network, the American law enforcement agencies, such as the FBI, have been engaged in a hard-fought battle against online financial fraud activities ever since the Internet has become a global communications network. But the truth is, according to the FBI's own estimate, computer-using thieves make off with as much as $10 billion a year in the US alone.[62]

Thirdly, globalisation and international communication in the digital age is rendering totalitarian regimes increasingly vulnerable in terms of political control. China's further progress in economic reform (e.g. opening up) at the domestic level and joining the WTO at the international level will undoubtedly further integrate the Chinese economy into the global economy. The Chinese government has no objection to (actually it is endeavouring to promote) the economic use of the Internet at the moment, despite its attempt to curb the political side of the network. It is foreseeable that an Internet boom will arrive in China in the not too distant future in parallel with the rapid rise of telephone connection and PC purchase. A consequence of this will be internal and cross-border voluminous flow of digitised information, in the simplest form of '1s' and '0s'. When these binary codes reach a networked computer located anywhere in the world, the information displayed on the screen could be of an economic nature, or a political nature. This digitised, globalised and networked process of flow of information and communication is certainly empowering, in particular to the non-state and anti-state forces. A new war has just started in the cyberspace: the bullets are made of 1s and 0s; the state and individuals are equally powerful commanders. As a matter of fact, the Internet could be used as an effective tool for organising large-scale anti-government movements, as demonstrated by the case of *Falun Gong* and many other international events. It is argued that:

New ways of thinking, of communicating, of organizing people and information – the Net takes aim squarely at things that since Mao's earliest days have been the state's exclusive domain. ... [T]he technology that China needs to build the most powerful country on earth in the 21st century could also undermine the monolith state itself. Where the quest by Deng's successors to control the Net and its consequences will lead, no one knows. But no one doubts that the Net, that amorphous and unpredictable messenger, holds out tantalizing possibilities for a country so long turned in upon itself (Barme and Ye, 1997).

In the age of the Internet, 'the state's monopoly over the use of coercive technology is progressively undermined by the emergence of non-state actors who have access to the same technology' (Camilleri and Falk, 1992, p. 114). The Internet, as a technology, can be used as a coercive technology by the state for purposes such as surveillance. 'Big brothers' are certainly watching their citizens. But, in the meantime, where access to the Internet is available, individual users and state organisations can be equal actors in the cyberspace. As an extreme case, a sophisticate hacker may have the ability to disable strategic computer networks, upon which important state organs carry out their routine function.

The Internet as a New Media: The WTO Effect

As the number of daily newspapers continues to dwindle and media companies of all stripe race to consolidate, the Internet is often seen as the last venue in which alternative and independent journalists can have a voice.[63] The potential of non-traditional news sources to offer a diversity of timely, hard-hitting information perhaps reached a peak when the World Trade Organisation met in Seattle:

> With new, relatively inexpensive technologies – including video cameras, Web cams, audio recorders, lap top computers and cell phones – journalists produced and distributed thousands of stories and images not available from mainstream media.[64]

Largely due to the tight government control and censorship, traditional news sources, such as newspapers, magazines and broadcasting, have never been adequate for Chinese citizens to keep themselves informed of current affairs. The Internet is important as an alternative source of information for not only facilitating public debate on the WTO issues in China but also enabling the Chinese people to reach the sea of digital information which is otherwise unthinkable. As far as China is concerned, the new challenges brought by the Internet and the new opportunities offered by the future WTO membership are becoming increasingly interwoven. Apparently, together, the Internet and China's WTO membership provide a new angle for critically assessing the prospect of political change in the country.

In November 1999, China and the United States reached an important trade agreement, which successfully opened the way for China to join the WTO ending its 13 years of hard-fought struggle in international diplomacy. Under the new China-US bilateral agreement, foreign direct investment of up to 49%, to rise to 50% after two years, in Chinese telecommunications and Internet companies would be allowed. Prior to this agreement, foreign investment in both telecommunications and Internet infrastructures and services was officially banned.[65]

The China-US deal on the WTO has spurred a fever of interest, from both domestic and foreign organisations, to seek new opportunities of investing in the Internet sector. For instance, the IT Office of the Shanghai municipality government, set up a Rmb1bn (equivalent to $121m) venture capital fund to assist the creation of Internet and other IT companies in November 1999, following the WTO news. A Shanghai government official suggests that the Internet will be a major investment target – both Internet content providers and e-commerce.[66]

In relation to the development of the Internet, China's WTO membership will have a number of important implications:

First of all, the entry into the Chinese telecommunications and Internet markets by foreign investors would potentially increase competition for the provision of services in both sectors and, therefore, drive down cost for users. High cost for telecommunications and Internet service is one of the major reasons prohibiting many ordinary Chinese citizens from getting online. Currently, despite the rapid grow in the last few years, the residential telephony penetration rate is only at about 10%, which is very low compared with that of the industrialised countries where Internet penetrate rate is significantly higher. Western politicians attach great importance to the long-term impact on the Chinese society of cheaper communications technology after China joins the WTO:

> When China joins the W.T.O., by 2005 it will eliminate tariffs on information technology products, making the tools of communication even cheaper, better, and more widely available. We know how much the Internet has changed America, and we are already an open society. Imagine how much it could change China.[67]

Second, if the WTO membership opens China's customs gate for the new middle class, the Internet, facilitated by potentially much cheaper telecommunications services, will become an important and fast route for these cash-rich consumers to reach cheaper cars and other expensive consumer items. This might be one of the reasons why many Chinese care about the tense process of WTO negotiations. In late November 1999, sina.com, a popular Chinese portal, recorded 1.5 million hits in 24 hours.[68] The result of this development would be an increased penetration of western (capitalist) cultures and life style into the Chinese society. Although the 'import' of western consumer culture and life style might not necessarily lead to the acceptance of western way of thinking, the change in the 'base', in Karl Marx's term, will eventually produce the momentum for the change in the 'superstructure'.

Third, foreign Internet service providers such as Yahoo!, which is already operating in China, would potentially open a new floodgate, arguably uncontrollable, for foreign media and foreign information to flow into the Chinese territory.[69] Meanwhile, the arrival of electronic commerce and, more broadly, the digital economy suggests that digital media and digital information would be more widely treated as 'digital goods'.[70] Consequently, cross-border flow of digital information *via* the Internet would gradually become an economic and trade activity and, therefore, digital goods would be subject to the scrutiny of WTO rules. Joining the

WTO club in the information age implies that China would be engaged in a process of trading an increasingly large amount of 'digital goods' with other countries. Under the new circumstances, Beijing would find existing government bans on foreign media and foreign information could run into conflict with the WTO rules. As China is determined to become a member of the WTO, 'digital goods', including digital media, would undoubtedly come into China in the form of information age commodities.

With the increased availability of digital media on the Internet and ever lowering telecommunications cost, Chinese citizens would have the opportunity to read foreign newspapers and magazines, listening to foreign radio programmes and watching TV broadcasting online. Unfortunately, due to the government's political concerns, most of these foreign media are currently kept outside the Chinese borders.[71]

As a new media, the potential importance of the Internet should not be underestimated. The April 5th political movement in 1976, which started as a mass memorial of the late Chinese Premier Zhou Enlai but secretly cracked down by the government in the Tiananmen Square, was hardly known to the outside world. Likewise, the pro-democracy movement of December 1986, which had led to the removal of the then Communist Party head Hu Yaobang from the country's leadership, received very little media coverage. The reason was simple: the Chinese government was able to ensure absolute control over the media and information flow between China and other countries. In contrast, the June 4th movement in 1989 was much better covered by foreign media – people abroad were quite well informed of the on-going situation in Beijing and the rest of China until the moment when the Chinese Government shut down the satellite transmission of foreign TV broadcasting. The crackdown of the *Falun Gong* movement since the summer 1999 has received wide publicity *via* the Internet which, arguably, the Chinese government was unable to shut down.

Although censorship of the Internet is already in place, the Chinese government could not claim overall and final success due to the nature of the Internet. Increasingly, the growing number of Internet users and the blossoming of digital information available on the network is overwhelming the government censor machine, which has been effective in controlling conventional, analogue and domestic media. The Chinese Communist Party's Central Propaganda Department has a firm grip on domestic information providers and network infrastructure, but this control, as argued by Mueller and Tan (1997), is threatened by the ease with which computers can retrieve information from anywhere:

If Internet access were to continue its path of uncontrolled growth, China's government would find it difficult to control either the economic supply of information or the content of messages and publications (Mueller and Tan, 1997, p. 90).

This, however, does not suggest that the Chinese would make any substantial political compromise in order to secure the WTO deal. On the contrary, removing the ban on foreign investment would not alter the fact that the Internet is still regarded with suspicion by many Chinese government officials, who are currently discussing how to license Internet companies and review contents on Chinese websites, areas that existing laws do not address.[72] This suggests that, in assessing the role of the Internet in political change, any optimistic view should not be divorced from a cautious approach.

The 'big character posters' (BCPs) can be said a unique Chinese media, which has played an important role in contemporary Chinese political history. The BCPs were always home made and, once they were put up on the walls in the street, they would normally convey important political messages with immediate effect. Mao Zedong put up one BCP, entitled 'My Big Character Poster: Bombarding the [Bourgeois] Headquarters', in the beginning of the Cultural Revolution in the 1960s and this has eventually led to the demise and jail of the then Chinese President, Liu Shaoqi. BCPs were not transmissible – their life was confined to the space of walls. However, the effectiveness of Mao's BCP could hardly be matched by any electronic media, which has the capacity of transmitting messages from one place to another at any distance almost instantly. Wei Jingsheng, Deng Xiaoping's most hated political dissident, wrote big character posters in 1979 urging his fellow countrymen be aware of the 'new dictatorship' (by Deng Xiaoping) and the 'Four Modernisations'[73] should be extended to five – with the fifth being political democratisation. Despite long-term imprisonment, his BCPs have planted the seeds for future dissident movements in China. If we compare Wei's 1979 BCPs with his recent e-mail messages sent from Paris to Beijing, the effectiveness of the former might exceed that of the latter.

Nevertheless, it has become a truism that the mobility of capital, labour, goods and services undermines the ability of individual states to set their own rules. The development of the Internet certainly fits with this argument. 'The Internet is further eroding that autonomy. So to preserve national freedom of action, governments increasingly will have to set [and accept] multilateral rules. Only this way will they be able to reclaim the control over their own affairs that has been lost to globalisation' (Stephens, 1999). Joining the WTO will undoubtedly push China into this kind of position, where the Chinese government would be obliged to observe the international club's rules. The prevailing of rule of law for economic affairs might help pave the way towards the rule of law for domestic political affairs.

Conclusion

Started with a brief review of the rapid growth the Internet in China, this chapter has discussed the Chinese government's various attempts to bring the Internet under its control. This effort includes the introduction of harsh regulations on contents and access; the wide use of technical measures (e.g. 'firewall') to filter the flow of information and monitor users' online activities; and a nationwide programme to provide official information online (in part to rival undesirable information). Whilst strict government control of the Internet has indeed led to a large number of individuals being punished for their political use of the Internet, this chapter also demonstrated the extent to which the Internet can be used as a powerful communications tool by political activists and human rights campaigners within and outside China. This is largely because China's 'great firewall' has many 'holes' in it. Further, the development of the Internet in China is coupled with the country's progress towards becoming a member of the WTO. It was argued in this chapter that joining the WTO would potentially make the Chinese government's restrictions on foreign digital media unattainable and the Internet could become an important and alternative media. Chiefly among others, the Internet would play an indispensable role in terms of fostering online public debate, which is crucial for any democratic change in the long run.

The discussions presented in this chapter have raised a number of important issues. First of all, Chinese politics is being significantly affected, if yet changed, by the power of ubiquitous digital information. In summarising his experience in establishing and ruling the People's Republic of China (PRC) *via* violent revolution, Mao made it explicit that political power rests with the gun; and the Communist Party, rather than the government, must assume absolute command of the People's Liberation Army (PLA). Whilst this still hold its truth, the dawning of the information age has brought with it the emergence of another equally important power, i.e., the power of information.

It has already become the top government officials' knowledge in many countries with a totalitarian regime that maintaining absolute rule would depend, to a great extent, upon their control of information. Countering to these rulers' willingness, new ICTs are opening new ways of disseminating information and ever growing communication among individual citizens and social groups. In this respect, new ICTs are a double-edged sword: they are indispensable to national economic development but they can also be used in a way detrimental to the power of the state. This is exactly the dilemma faced by the Chinese government. On the one hand, the Internet is officially recognised as an important element to the Informatisation of the National Economy Programme. Accordingly, the Chinese government recognised the commercial potential of the Internet and encouraged the economic use of the network. On the other hand, the Internet is poised to become a new challenging power to the government and the political system. Whilst the Chinese government is determined to harness the development of the Internet and explore this global network's economic potential, dissident information is also being disseminated *via* the same network. This is the 'unwanted' side of the Internet.

Second, the Internet is poised to act as a virtual public sphere accommodating free express of ideas. Internet 'chat rooms', online discussion forums and e-mail lists, which exist all over the Internet, are already being used by many Chinese to communicate with each other and with participants from other countries. Websites hosted by both Chinese and foreign ISPs can be used for publishing news, discussion papers and other information, which otherwise might not get published under current government censorship rules. The Internet has the potential to serve the Chinese citizens as a public sphere, in which freedom of express may be achieved (although to a limited degree at the moment).

Third, China's national control of the Internet is becoming increasingly at odd with globalisation. The Internet may be compared with the global environment. The quality of the air depends on the way it is protected collectively by all nations and all human beings on the earth. Whilst everybody has access to the air, nobody owns it and nobody can exert control. This is more or less the situation faced by the global community regarding the Internet. The Chinese government can issue regulations and intervene the development of the Internet but this does not suggest it has absolute control over the network. The truth is, the Chinese part of the Internet is an integral part of the global Internet and, within the cyberspace, there are no borders dividing China from the rest of the world. The Internet is poised to become the most dynamic force driving and deepening globalisation in the new millennium. If any nation, including China, wish to have a say in governing the Internet, the only way forward is to be engaged in global cooperation of rule making for the Internet.

Finally, the Internet is becoming increasingly important to facilitating the flow of information by-passing government control but it is not a panacea to solve all of the problems associated with the democratic deficit in China. The Benton Foundation claims that the establishment of adequate communications and education systems is the most important condition to the success of democracy:

> Nothing is more important to the success of democracy than robust systems of communications and education. Communications bind society together. Education expands its cconscience. Without an effective system of communication, we cannot engage in collective action or acquire the information we need to make sound decisions. Without a strong system of education, we cannot cultivate citizens with the knowledge and skills they need to govern themselves.[74]

In the meantime, the relationship between new communications technologies and democratic change is recognised but with caution:

> The interaction over the past two centuries between the changing technologies of communication and the practice of free speech, ... fits a pattern that is sometimes described as 'soft technological determinism'. Freedom is fostered when the means of communication are dispersed, decentralized, and easily available, as are printing presses or microcomputers. Central control is more likely when the means of communication are concentrated, monopolized, and scarce, as are great networks. But the relationship between technology and institutions is not simple or unidirectional, nor are the effects immediate (Pool, 1983, p. 5).

In short, the social and political impact of the Internet should be understood from a long-term perspective and any optimistic 'vision' on the digital age needs to take into account the harsh reality of Chinese politics. Whilst the Internet holds a great potential for economic development and democratisation in China, the same technology might also be used by the government to add a new dimension of control, i.e., digital and networked control, to a plethora of conventional means of control.

The next chapter will further examine the politics of technology governance with a focus on the global competition for new TV technologies, i.e., High Definition TV and Digital TV.

Notes

[1] Contemporary Chinese proverb.
[2] Steve Jobs, http://www.connected.org/pandora/publi.html.

3   Stephens, P. (1999), 'Broken Borders of the Nation State', *Financial Times*, 3 December.
4   This can be demonstrated in part by the long-lasting effort of the Chinese government to joint the World Trade Organization (WTO).
5   Gore, A. (1991), 'Infrastructure for the Global Village', *Scientific American*, September 1991.
6   Lecture by Rupert Murdoch at Oxford University, 1 December 1999, cited in *Yahoo! News*, http://dailynews.yahoo.com/h/nm/19991201/wr/tech_murdoch_1.html.
7   Bill Clinton (2000), Full Text of Clinton's Speech on China Trade Bill, *The New York Times*, March 9, http://www.nytimes.com/library/world/asia/030900clinton-china-text.html.
8   BBC News Online, 14 October 1999. http://news.bbc.co.uk/.
9   Cited in Qiu, J. L. (1999/2000) 'Virtual Censorship in China: Keeping the Gate Between the Cyberspaces', *International Journal of Communications Law and Policy*, Issue 4, Winter, pp. 1-25, available at http://www.ijclp.org.
10 http://cnn.com/TECH/computing/9909/22/china.web.idg/index.html.
11 The total population of Mainland China is about 1.3 billion at the moment, excluding Hong Kong.
12 Tony Rutkowski, executive director of the Centre for Next Generation Internet, cited in *CommunicationsWeek International*, 1 March 1999, p. 10.
13 It is believed that Chinese operators have to pay $95,100 per month to international carriers for a 2Mb/second link to the Internet in the United States. See *CommunicationsWeek International*, 2 February 1998.
14 Information on prices is from Xu and Armstrong (1995) and *CommunicationsWeek International* (1998). Exchange rate used in calculation is $1 = Rmb8.5 yuan.
15 Ministry of Science and technology (1999), p. 78.
16 North America (US and Canada) accounts for 56% of the 201 million world total Internet access; Europe 23.5%; Asia-Pacific 16.5%; Latin America 2.7%; Africa 0.9%; Middle East 0.4%. Figures cited in this paragraph are from the BBC New Online, October-November 1999, http://news.bbc.uk/.
17 The CNNIC's official website is: http://www.cnnic.cn/english/CNNIC-4.htm. The CNNIC is the organisation in charge of China's top-level domain name registration, IP address allocation, and sets the Internet service standards.
18 In *The Control Revolution* James Beniger (1986) defines 'control' as 'purposive influence toward a predetermined goal' (p. 39).
19 Information was supplied to the 'Politech' e-mail list (politech@vorlon.mit.edu) on 24 November 1999.
20 Myanmar Post and Telecommunications (MPT, currently the sole Internet Service Provider), on behalf of the Burmese government, has recently issued regulations for users of its Internet service. They are:

- Any writings detrimental to the interests of the Union of Myanmar (Burma) are not to be posted;
- Any writings directly or indirectly detrimental to the current policies and secret security affairs of the Government of the Union of Myanmar are not to be posted;
- Writings related to politics are not to be posted;
- Only the person who is granted an internet account is to use the internet; no other person is allowed to use the internet;

- The person who is granted an internet account is held responsible for all internet use on that account;
- A person with an internet account is prohibited from hacking the web and entering and destroying the security system of MPT;
- Hacking the web and entering and destroying the security system of other internet users is prohibited;
- Persons who hold an internet account are forbidden to misuse the account of other internet users;
- Internet users are to inform MPT of any threat on the internet;
- Internet users are to obtain prior permission from the organisation designated by the state to create web pages;
- Applicants for an internet account are held accountable for the veracity of facts contained in the application form;
- MPT has the right to amend and change regulations on the use of the internet without prior notice;
- Application can be filed for compensation for any damage or loss;
- Internet use will be terminated and legal action will be taken for violation of any of these regulations.

The above points are originally reported in *Communications Law in Transition Newsletter*, Vol. 1, No. 4, 12 February 2000, http://pcmlp.socleg.ox.ac.uk/transition/issue04/updates.htm.

[21] BBC News, 29 January 2000, http://news2.thls.bbc.co.uk/.
[22] Mainly those politically sensitive contents.
[23] See Schoof, R (1996). 'China Tightens Control of the Internet', *Amarillo Globe-News*, http://amarillonet.com/news/china9996.html.
[24] Schoof (1996).
[25] See Note 20 above in this chapter.
[26] Ministry of Public Security (1997), *Security protection administration of computer information network's international connection*, 30 December, Chapter 1, Article 7.
[27] Kurtenbach, E. (1997), 'Chinese Government Spreads Propaganda through Internet: Leaders Learning to Live with the Web', *Myrtle Beach Access*, http://www.myrtlebeachaccess.com/news/97-7-24/chinanet2.htm.
[28] Shi Huangdi, the first Qin emperor who unified China, ordered the burning of Confucian books and the purge of Confucius' followers in order to consolidate his power.
[29] Schoof (1996), http://amarillonet.com/news/china9996.html.
[30] *Managing Information*, Vol. 6, No.7, September 1999, p. 21.
[31] Yahoo! News, 31 January 1999, http://dailynews.yahoo.com/headlines/w...y.html?s=v/nm/19990131/wr/china_3.html. Note that most participants in online chat rooms and authors of Internet bulletin boards use pseudonyms in fear of persecution for their radical views.
[32] Liu, M. (1999), 'The Great Firewall of China', *Newsweek International*, 11 October, http://www.newsweek.com/nw-srv/printed/int/wb/ov1315_htm.
[33] The official website is: http://www.gov.cn/.

³⁴ See *Guangming Daily*, 27 January 1999. The 'Government Online' Programme has already developed a testing site at: http://www.gov.cn/.
³⁵ The 'J18' website is http://www.j18.org. 'J18' was derived from the date of the protest, i.e., June the 18th 1999. This was the date when the G8 industrialised nations met in Kohn, Germany.
³⁶ See http://www.greennet.org.uk/june18/.
³⁷ *Ibid*.
³⁸ Quoted from http://www.seattlewto.org/n30/call/eng.html.
³⁹ The 'November 30' Discussion List, which could be subscribed *via* the website http://n30.listbot.com/, allows for participants around the world to discuss and coordinate their actions in Seattle. Similarly, the 'No2WTO' Discussion List (subscription *via* http://no2wto.listbot.com/) was set up to facilitate networking among people interested in radical mobilisation in Seattle against the WTO.
⁴⁰ *San Jose Mercury News*, 30 September 1999. The Government bodies to which Wei's emails were sent to include the Chinese Foreign Ministry, CCTV (Chinese Central TV), *People's Daily*, *China Daily* and the Chinese Internet Information Centre [China Internet Network Information Centre].
⁴¹ Article 19 of the Universal Declaration of Human Rights, adopted in 1948, stipulates that "Everyone has the right to freedom of opinion and expression; this right includes freedom to hold opinions without interference and to seek, receive, and impart information and ideas through any media and regardless of frontiers.' Ironically, China is a signatory of the Declaration.
⁴² Liu, M. (1999), 'The Great Firewall of China', *Newsweek*, 11 October, http://www.newsweek.com/nw-srv/printed/int/wb/ov1315_htm. Written in Chinese, 'VIP Reference' offers a daily critique of Beijing's communist leaders.
⁴³ *The New York Times*, 8 May 1998.
⁴⁴ Liu (1999), 'The Great Firewall of China', *op cit*.
⁴⁵ CNN, 'The Great Fire Wall of China', 22 September 1999, http://cnn.com/TECH/computing/9909/22/china.web.idg/index.html.
⁴⁶ Liu (1999), 'The Great Firewall of China', *op cit*.
⁴⁷ *Ibid*.
⁴⁸ 'China-sect *Falun Gong* Web site creator charged with subversion in northern China', http://falunwisdom.net/main/index.html.
⁴⁹ Reuters: 'China Charges Student on Falun Gong E-Mail-Report', posted at http://fulunwisdom.net/main/index.html.
⁵⁰ Just a few examples of *Falun Gong* websites: www.falundafa.org; www.falundafa.ca; www.falundafa.au; www.falundafa.de; www.falundafa-china.org; www.stanford.edu/group/falun/; etc.
⁵¹ *Far East Economic Review*, 10 February 2000.
⁵² *USA Today*, 15 March 2000, http://www.usatoday.com/usatonline/20000315/2031918s.htm.
⁵³ According to a survey by the China Internet Network Information Centre (CNNIC, http://www.cnnic.net.cn/), 8.7% of Internet users were employees at foreign and joint venture firms by the end of 1999.
⁵⁴ *Newsweek*, 11 October 1999.
⁵⁵ BBC News, 4 December 1998, http://news2.thls.bbc.co.uk/.
⁵⁶ *Ibid*.
⁵⁷ CNNIC Survey, December 1999.
⁵⁸ *The New York Times*, 27 January 2000, http://www.nytimes.com/.
⁵⁹ BBC News, 4 December 1998, *op cit*.

60 *Far East Economic Review*, 10 February 2000.
61 Report in *USA Today*, 15 March 2000, http://www.usatoday.com/usatonline/20000315/2031918s.htm.
62 Cited in Nelson (1997).
63 Mailing list: BENTON-COMPOLICY@CDINET.COM, 13 January 2000.
64 *Ibid.*
65 Note that a large number of foreign companies had invested in the telecommunications and Internet companies *via* their local partners in the form of so-called CCF (China-China-Foreign) contracts. Officials from the Ministry of Information Industry claimed the CCFs were illegal shortly before the China-US WTO agreement. This agreement would certainly provide new arguments for legitimizing the existing foreign stakes in the Chinese telecommunications and Internet companies.
66 *Financial Times*, 24 November 1999.
67 Bill Clinton (2000), 'Full Text of Clinton's Speech on China Trade Bill', *The New York Times*, March 9, http://www.nytimes.com/library/world/asia/030900clinton-china-text.html.
68 *Newsweek International*, 29 November 1999.
69 It was reported that in 1997 China was still serious about cutting its Internet off from the rest of the world with a China-only Intranet in fear of the flowing in of undesirable foreign media and information. See *USA Today*, 15 March 2000, http://www.usatoday.com/usatonline/20000315/2031918s.htm.
70 The term 'Digital goods' refers to a wide range of 'commodities' packaged in a digital form. Among others, computer software and games, digital music, digital video, online publications, online broadcasting, online advertising and other types of commercial online information provision, etc., are important categories of 'digital goods'.
71 Note that, to a certain extent, the Internet has already arrived as a 'rescuer' – with the availability of new software free of charge, Chinese users can watch TV channels, listing to radio broadcasting and enjoying digital music on the Internet – if they are not blocked by the government!
72 *Wall Street Journal*, http://interactive.wsj.com/articles/SB942867426523651360.htm.
73 The 'Four Modernisations', as discussed in Chapter 4, were launched by Zhou Enlai. Deng Xiaoping further developed this by suggesting that, to achieving the 'Four Modernisations', science and technology is the key. The central point of Wei Jingsheng's Big Character Poster was that economic development can not be achieved without political democratisation and the latter should be regarded as the 'fifth modernisation'.
74 The Benton Foundation (2000), *The E-rate in America: The Tales of Four Cities*, February.

6 Shaping the Screen: The Politics of Digital TV[1]

We can't hamper technology by legislation and even if you can you fail.[2]

Introduction

Television broadcasting has been traditionally viewed as an indisputable territory of state regulation. This is because there is a perception that television broadcasting is one of the typical industrial sectors where market failure exists. As far as colour TV broadcasting systems are concerned, the world has been subject to three major variants of standards, i.e., the NTSC (National Television Systems Committee) system invented in the US, the PAL (Phase Alteration by Line) system invented in Germany and the French SECAM (*Systèm Electronique Couleur avec Mémoire*) standard.[3] These broadcasting standards had not been challenged until the mid-1980s, when the quest for new TV broadcasting technologies reached high definition television (HDTV), which has led to the breakthrough in digital TV technologies.

An important outcome of the global competition for a new generation of TV technology was, perhaps, the rapid development of fully digital TV,[4] a revolutionary technology first discovered by scientists and engineers at the laboratory of General Instrument (GI) in the US in 1990. Subsequently, the course of mainstream HDTV development has changed from analogue technologies to fully digital systems. The application of digital compression techniques has made possible that a large number of TV channels can be transmitted using narrow bandwidth. The 1990s witnessed a plethora of commercial launches of multi-channel digital broadcasting across different platforms (e.g., digital terrestrial, digital satellite and digital cable services) in some parts of the world. Meanwhile, a large number of national governments are deciding or have decided on a definitive date for 'digital switch over' – to phase out all analogue TV broadcasting and change to digital TV broadcasting.

Conventional TV programmes are transmitted, either terrestrially or *via* satellite or through cable networks, in an analogue format and viewers have no control over the viewing process. In contrast, digital TV offers higher picture quality and digital sound as well as interactivity – viewers would have control over the picture on the screen by cropping a scene, zooming in on a particular detail or, in the case of sports, for example, choosing which camera angle they want to watch.[5] Another aspect, perhaps the most important one, is that fully digitised TV transmission technologies will make the convergence of the computer industry and the TV industry a reality. This would have important implications for the conventional TV broadcasters, electronics manufacturers and consumers. In order not to miss the bandwagon of digital broadcasting, all the major terrestrial broadcasters in the UK have committed themselves to the government's 1996 Broadcasting Act by reserving digital channel space on the condition that they would digitise all of their analogue transmission for digital broadcasting in due course.

The arrival of the digital age means that the traditional paradigm of the global TV broadcasting industry will be changed and the conventional regulatory structure will become increasingly incompatible with the new reality of technical change centred on digital convergence.

This chapter analyses the involvement of the European public authorities in the process of technological standardisation for HDTV and digital broadcasting in a global context. Among others, the effectiveness of the major European policy initiatives and regulatory regimes will be discussed. In particular, questions will be asked about the outcomes of the European audiovisual and technology policy since the mid-19980s and the role played by market forces in determining what technologies should reach the viewer's living room.

Global Competition for HDTV: The Genesis of Digital TV

Following the launch of black and white TV and colour TV (CTV) services, i.e. NTSC in the US in the 1950s and PAL/SECAM in Europe in the 1960s, the development of TV technology reached its third major stage in the 1980s – that is the emergence of HDTV. From a technical point of view, there are four major aspects associated with HDTV:

- Studio equipment used for storing and editing source materials;
- Transmission standard for sending out programme signals;
- Production standard for programme making;
- Receiving equipment, i.e. HDTV set and associated peripheral products.

Generally speaking, HDTV is a new generation of TV system designed to provide the viewer with high resolution pictures (using about 1,000 horizontal scanning lines) displayed on a widescreen TV set (with an aspect ratio or dimension of 16/9 as that of modern cinema screen)[6] – eventually a hung-on-the-wall flat panel display – plus digital stereo sound effect. In other words, HDTV is to offer the consumer the so-called 'home cinema' experience. In comparison, a conventional CTV picture is transmitted with 525 horizontal scanning lines on the NTSC system and 625 lines in the case of the PAL/SECAM format. The doubling (or close to doubling) the number of horizontal scanning lines is the major element to achieve the high resolution picture of any HDTV system. The level of picture resolution achieved with an HDTV system is about four to five times that on a conventional CTV screen. Whilst the major HDTV systems were initially designed to transmit TV pictures of an analogue format, digital stereo sound was promised as a universal characteristic of any HDTV system. Although stereo sound effect is nowadays also offered by the NICAM sets, neither the NTSC system nor the PAL/SECAM system was built to provide this technical feature.

What seems interesting is the fact that HDTV has added a new dimension to the global hi-tech competition since the mid-1980s. The technological contest for HDTV has involved not only the leading world economies, including Japan, Western Europe and North America, but also the newly industrialised countries (NIC) and some developing countries. On the one hand, the HDTV format battle was characterised by the shift from analogue technologies to fully digital systems. On the other hand, the process of global competition for HDTV witnessed a high level of government intervention.

During the second half of the 1980s the major challenge, as far as the European industry and European public authorities are concerned, was the Japanese HDTV technology. Accordingly, the global competition was between the Japanese system (which was already technically established) and the European system (merely a proposal) at this stage. Both the Japanese and European systems were mainly analogue technologies. The breakthrough in digital compression technology achieved in the US in 1990 radically changed the course of HDTV development. In other words, the global competition for HDTV (between Japan and Europe) has given way to a new contest between digital TV technology and analogue systems since the beginning of the 1990s. Consequently, both the Japanese and European official standards have become technologically disadvantaged.[7]

The outcome of the HDTV competition, as the following discussion will show, seems to suggest that inflexible state regulation and ill-defined government subsidy to one side of the competing technologies may not lead to the choice of the best technologies. To a certain extent the winning digital technology over analogue systems might not have become reality without the dynamism of market forces.

The Hi-Vision System

As a state-owned public broadcaster, NHK (Nippon Hoso Kyokai, or Japan Broadcasting Corp.) launched a study project on the next generation TV, i.e., HDTV, at its Science and Technical Research Laboratories in 1964,[8] to follow the current TV transmission standard (NTSC, a technology developed in the US). The Laboratories' aim was to create a system that would give a sense of 'being there' – the viewer would feel as if he or she were really at the stadium watching a sporting event, for example. The results of these studies showed that HDTV required a vertical viewing angle of 20 degrees, a horizontal viewing angle of 30 degrees, a viewing distance of 3 times the height of the screen, and around 1,000 scanning lines. The studies further showed that a field frequency of 60 Hz enabled images to be reproduced smoothly without flickering.[9] The NHK engineers also realised that the NTSC screen with an aspect ratio of 4/3 did not fit in the natural vision range of human beings, which is believed to be a 16/9 frame. In order to improve the colour TV technology, NHK started its long journey towards higher picture resolution with wider screen format.

In line with the conclusions of its study, NHK started HDTV development in 1970. The NHK initiative was warmly responded by the Japanese consumer electronics manufacturers, among whom Sony was the most enthusiastic company. By 1984, Sony and NHK had already fully defined the world's first HDTV system, called Hi-Vision. The transmission system to be adopted for Hi-Vision was MUSE (Multiple Sub-nyquist Sampling Encoding). The major technical parameters of the MUSE transmission standard are as follows:

- 1125 horizontal scanning lines;

- 16/9 screen aspect ratio;
- using DBS (Direct Broadcast by Satellite);
- interlaced scanning;
- incompatible with conventional CTV receivers;
- 60 field frequency;
- digital stereo sound.

In 1981, NHK brought its HDTV technology to the US for demonstrations in order to raise public awareness, and the company announced its MUSE satellite transmission system for Hi-Vision three years later. In 1986, the Japanese industry, led by NHK and Sony, proposed a world studio standard for HDTV but the CCIR (Consultative Committee for International Radio) Plenary in Dubrovnik rejected this initiative mainly due to objections from the European governments. However, this did not stop the Japanese industry's HDTV campaign. The frequently enhanced 'experimental' broadcasting demonstrates the Japanese industry's determination to promote MUSE and Hi-Vision, regardless the unfavourable response from the European countries and, later, the US and the constantly changing technological environment:

- March 1985: Experimental broadcasting with MUSE at Tsukuba Science Expo;
- December 4, 1986: Experimental satellite broadcasting with MUSE using BS-2 (Broadcasting Satellite);
- September 1988: MUSE relay transmission of Seoul Olympic Games;
- June 3, 1989: NHK regular test broadcasting for 1 hour daily on channel BS-11;
- November 25, 1991: Hi-Vision Promotion Association begins test broadcasting 8 hours daily;
- November 25, 1994: Test broadcasting 10 hours daily begins through split license among NHK and other 8 commercial broadcasters;
- April 10, 1995: Test broadcasting extended to 11 hours a day;
- April 8, 1996: Test broadcasting extended to 13 hours a day (14 hours on Saturdays and Sundays);
- July 1996: Live coverage of Atlanta Olympic Games;
- April 7, 1997: Test broadcasting extended to 14 hours daily;

- October 6, 1997: Test broadcasting extended to 17 hours daily;
- February 1998: 272 hours of broadcasting of Nagano Winter Olympic Games;
- June-July 1998: Live coverage of World Cup Soccer France'98.[10]

Following the lead of NHK, major Japanese consumer electronics companies, such as Sony, Matsushita, Hitachi, Toshiba, NEC and Mitsubishi, etc., built HDTV sets based on the conventional CRT (Cathode Ray Tube) technology for the home market by 1991 (although prices remained high). As a matter of fact, Japan is the only country where real HDTV broadcasting is available on a regular base, despite that the global race for HDTV has been going on for over a decade.[11]

The Japanese vision of HDTV goes even farther than Hi-Vision. In July 1990, a group of Japanese organisations[12] proposed a new system, i.e., the so-called second generation HDTV, at a conference held in Japan. The screen resolution of the proposed second generation HDTV was promised twice as high as that of NHK's Hi-Vision system and the ultra high resolution would make it a reality that HDTV sets can be used as a video conferencing display and computer monitor in the home. The planned launch timetable for the second generation HDTV is around 2015. This plan has not achieved much publicity nationally and internationally.

The HD-MAC System

The Japanese proposal for a global HDTV standard encountered fierce objection from the allied European governments at the CCIR Plenary held in Dubrovnik of the former Yugoslavia during 12-23 May 1986. In the meantime, the CCIR asked the European countries to work out an alternative HDTV system in competition with the Japanese system by 1990.

In the wake of the 1986 CCIR conference, a group of European companies, including Philips, Thomson, Bosch and Thorn EMI, submitted an HDTV proposal to the Eureka Secretariat. This proposal was proposal was accepted and established as the Eureka 95 HDTV Project (or EU95). Funding for EU95 was made available *via* the Eureka framework, i.e. home country governments of the participating firms would provide financial support for their R&D activities towards HDTV.

The European version of HDTV was named HD-MAC (High Definition

Multiplexed Analogue Component). HD-MAC was an extended version of the European MAC (Multiplexed Analogue Component) standard family, which has several other versions such as C-MAC, D-MAC and D2-MAC. D2-MAC had already been adopted in some European countries such as France and Scandinavia for DBS. MAC uses the same number of horizontal scanning lines with that for PAL, i.e. 625. Therefore, MAC is compatible with PAL, although a set-top satellite converter is still needed for PAL sets to receive MAC DBS transmission.

The major technical configuration for HD-MAC, as initially proposed, includes the following aspects:

- 1250 horizontal scanning lines;
- 16/9 aspect ratio for the screen;
- backward compatibility with MAC receivers;
- satellite transmission only;
- Digital stereo sound effect.

The EU95 consortium initially proposed HD-MAC as a world standard to replace the Japan's MUSE system, on the ground that the Japanese system was technically revolutionary, i.e., not compatible with either NTSC or PAL/SECAM. In contrast, HD-MAC was promised to be backward compatible with conventional CTV sets, therefore, evolutionary and would not make already exiting TV sets obsolete. As a matter of fact, because HD-MAC adopted 1250 lines (doubling the 625 scanning lines) it would be technically easy to achieve backward compatibility with MAC receivers.

The EU95 consortium's 'evolutionary' approach was to make MAC as the intermediate step towards HD-MAC. In other words, the expected commercial success of HD-MAC would be contingent upon the popularity of MAC transmissions within European countries. MAC transmission was not available at all until May 1990, when BSB (British Satellite Broadcasting) was launched.

HD-MAC was favoured by various European public authorities, in particular the European Commission, the French Government and the Dutch government. The British government repeatedly used its veto power against EU Council decisions on providing EU funding towards HD-MAC and MAC. Despite this, it is estimated that €1bn was provided by the EU and European governments to support the development of HD-MAC. This amount was met by another sum of €1bn of R&D investment from leading

European manufacturers such as Philips and Thomson involved within the EU95 consortium. To further boost EU95 and HD-MAC, the European Commission proposed an 'Action Plan' to provide €850m of EU subsidy to the European consortium. This plan was supported by most Continental EU Member States but the British government strongly objected to the package. The DTI (Department of Trade and Industry) of Britain claimed that MAC and HD-MAC were both technologically out of date thanks to new developments in digital technologies. As a compromise, a substantially reduced sum of €228m was approved by the Council of Ministers in 1993 on the condition that EU funding would be available to new programme making of any widescreen format.

In early 1993, Philips announced that it would halt its plan to manufacture HD-MAC sets due to insufficient public support to high definition programme making. Following this announcement, the European Commission also made public of its intention to drop HD-MAC as the official European HDTV standard, in favour of new digital technologies.

To be sure, the EU95 consortium achieved tremendous technological progress in bring out a fully defined HDTV system within a short period of time (1986-93). The problem, among many others, associated with the death of HD-MAC was that European public authorities used their technology policy making power to pick winner at the early stage of innovation and, when mainstream technology shifted from analogue HDTV to digital TV, public policy failed to reflect this change at an opportune time.[13]

HDTV Development in the US

The American response to the issue of HDTV had been subject to the influence of Sony and NHK prior to the CCIR Dubrovnik Plenary in 1986. Although the SMPTE (Society of Motion Picture and Television Engineers) had set up a study group on HDTV in as early as 1977, and the American broadcasters' Advanced Television Systems Committee (ATSC) was formed in 1983 to investigate the need for advanced television standards, the pre-Dubrovnik HDTV discussions in the US were mainly focused on the Japanese system. In 1985, for instance, the ATSC recommended a studio production standard for HDTV to be adopted in the US with parameters of 1125 horizontal scanning lines and a field rate of 60 Hz or 30 frames per second. This was essentially a Japanese standard. At the CCIR Dubrovnik Plenary, representatives of the American federal government decided to fully support the Japanese HDTV proposal as a world production standard. After the Japanese proposal was blocked by allied representatives of European governments, the American government assigned the FCC (Federal Communications Commission) the task to coordinate HDTV development in the US.

The FCC responded by setting up an Advisory Committee for Advanced Television to develop policy recommendations regarding the introduction of HDTV services in the US. The main points of FCC policies for HDTV in the 1980s were as follows:

First, and most importantly, the FCC ruled in 1989 that HDTV must be transmitted terrestrially. This was in part due to the fact the FCC's ruling power covers terrestrial TV transmission only; cable and DBS transmissions are not the responsibilities of the FCC. In the meantime, this policy was intended to protect the interests of the existing powerful terrestrial TV broadcasting networks. This differs from the European and Japanese approaches, which used DBS for HDTV transmission.

Second, due to the very limited channel space for terrestrial TV broadcasting, the FCC ruled in 1989 that future HDTV transmission must not exceed the bandwidth of 6MHz. In comparison, the Japanese MUSE and the European HD-MAC systems would initially require 30MHz and 27MHz respectively. The FCC ruling was based on a report by its Office of Engineering and Technology that most existing TV stations would be allocated with an additional 6MHz channel without causing unacceptable technical problems in terrestrial transmission. Accordingly, new HDTV systems requiring more 6MHz of bandwidth would not be authorised for terrestrial broadcasting in the US.

Third, instead of claiming 'revolutionary' or 'evolutionary', the FCC stipulated that future HDTV services must be directly compatible with the existing NTSC sets or 'simulcast' (simultaneous broadcasting). This meant that all HDTV programmes must be simultaneously transmitted on the NTSC standard, so that owners of conventional CTV sets would not be excluded from watching new programmes transmitted on the HDTV standard. The transitional period of 'simulcast' would be 15 years from the date HDTV services begin.

Fourth, in 1990, the FCC indicated that it was looking for a genuine HDTV system rather than initially an EDTV (Extended Definition TV) first. This led to the withdraw of about 20 EDTV proposals from the FCC bidding process.

Finally, unlike Japan and Europe, foreign companies were invited to join the bidding process for the future HDTV standard in the US. Above all, federal government financial subsidy was not promised for HDTV R&D activities.

These FCC rulings actually made it extremely challenging for firms who were involved in the bidding process. Technically speaking, to press the huge amount of information required for transmitting HDTV pictures into the bandwidth of 6MHz was a difficult objective for any scientific laboratory to achieve in the 1980s.

In June 1990, engineers at General Instrument (GI) took the lead in digital compression – they managed to compress HDTV signals into the desired 6MHz bandwidth and met the FCC requirement. GI's breakthrough in digital compression had a great impact on the course of HDTV development all over the world. Most noticeably, the FCC responded immediately by announcing that the American standard for HDTV would be a fully digital system. This new ruling effectively excluded any possibility for the non-digital systems, such as the NHK's Narrow MUSE and the Philips/Thomson analogue proposal based on the HD-MAC system, to win the bidding. These non-digital or analogue HDTV proposals were subsequently withdrawn from the bidding process.

HDTV in Other Countries

HDTV development is mainly carried out in the Triad economies: Japan, Europe and the US. However, evidence shows that some newly industrialise countries and developing countries have also made their efforts to catch up with the big three in terms of HDTV development. Most noticeably, South Korea and Taiwan have been actively making investment to follow up HDTV activities. China also intends to become a player on the global HDTV arena. HDTV research and development activities in these countries are not directed towards establishing an independent systems; rather, getting ready and making an optimal choice amongst competing technologies weighs more in terms of government policymaking.

In the beginning of the 1990s, an HDTV R&D and promotion consortium was set up under the coordination of the Korean government. This consortium draws expertise from the Korean electronics manufacturing industry, research institutes and academic organisations. The Korean government contributed 40% towards this consortium's running cost, which was set at Korean Won 100bn by the end of 1992. In 1990, Samsung and Lucky Goldstar signed a contract with NHK to import signalling technologies needed for HDTV from Japan. The Korean consortium also proposed to export HDTV sets from the mid-1990s.

The Taiwanese government has also been involved in promoting HDTV research activities since the beginning of the 1990s. HDTV activities have been coordinated between the Industrial Bureau, which is a branch of the government's Ministry of Economy, and the Research Institute of Industrial Technologies (RIIT). The RIIT proposed to invest NT$6.5bn (approx. $260m) to employ 2,200 technical and engineering staff to develop HDTV during a period 1992-95. It is known that NT$6bn (or 92.3%) of the RIIT investment for HDTV came from government budget. The Taiwanese HDTV system would be developed based on the major technical parameters of the US system. As far as the infrastructure is concerned, the Ministry of Transportation, which administers the Telephone and Telecommunications Bureau, decided to launch its quasi-DBS satellite in the mid-1990s, on which HDTV signals would be transmitted. In addition, the RIIT also invests NT$300m (approx. $16m) on an annual base in its own HDTV laboratories located in the US.

The Mainland Chinese government has also been following the process of HDTV development *via* the former Ministry of Broadcasting, Film and Television (MBFT) and the former Ministry of Posts and Telecommunications (MPT).[14] In the early 1990s, the Chinese government signed a contract with the Eureka 95 consortium to licence the latter's MAC transmission technology to be used for satellite broadcasting in the vast northwest area, Xinjiang Autonomous Region. The Research Institute of Broadcasting Technologies sent delegations to major international HDTV events, such as the 1990 International Broadcasting Convention in Brighton, to follow up HDTV development. The MPT and the University of Posts and Telecommunications in Beijing have research projects undergoing designated to HDTV system evaluation. Under the Chinese government's 8th Five-Year Planning (1992-96), HDTV, and other advanced communications technologies, was targeted as a priority area of development. China has planned to assemble and export HDTV sets by the turn of the century. Bilateral meetings and negotiations between Mainland China and Taiwan have also been held with the intention to jointly explore HDTV.

European Public Policy for New TV Technologies

The spectrum of the HDTV competition was so wide that hardly any aspect of the information and communications technology (ICT) sector has not been touched upon. The global competition for HDTV did not confine itself to technologies and commercial organisations. On the contrary, regulators and policymakers have become important players during the race for HDTV standardisation. From an international perspective, HDTV was widely perceived as a strategic technology. The strategic aspect of

HDTV, on the one hand, was that HDTV was promised to unveil a new chapter for the world consumer electronics industry. On the other hand, HDTV was believed a generic technology in a sense that it would trigger off a range of important technical innovations in areas such as digital compression techniques, large size flat panel displays (FPDs) and advanced semiconductor components. Governments and firms in many parts of the world had an untold fear of a possible domino phenomenon: missing out in the HDTV competition would make a country or a firm become technologically dependent upon its competitors in a number of high tech component areas in the 21st Century.

As far as Europe is concerned, HDTV came at a time when technology policymaking began to shift gradually from the national government level to the European level within the EU. This change in the process of European policymaking was manifested in, firstly, the large number of European research and technological programmes (in particular relevant to the information and communications technology sector). Secondly, leading European manufacturers (e.g. Philips, Thomson and Nokia) in the audiovisual technology sector wanted to become European industrial champions, rather than just national champions. Thirdly, the European Commission has been actively promoting the formation of a 'European audiovisual space', in which previously fragmented national markets would be integrated into a single European market for audiovisual technologies and services.

In sum, the European Union 'recognised the strategic importance of high definition television (HDTV) for the European consumer electronics industry and for the European television and film industries and established the strategy framework for the introduction of European HDTV'.[15] Meanwhile, 'the objectives of the strategy for the introduction of HDTV in Europe are an integral part of the Community audiovisual policy' and 'they must take into account other objectives of this policy within the perspective of the development of Europe's audiovisual capacity...'.[16] This section aims to provide a brief review of the European policy context for TV broadcasting and TV technologies.

Legal Foundations

The usage of the term 'audiovisual' within the European Unions' official documents refers to the film and television sector. Accordingly, broadcasting and/or audiovisual policy is policy for the film and television sector.[17] It is widely accepted that under the Treaty of Rome the Community did not enjoy any real powers in the matter of audiovisual policy and, thus, the situation did not change until the late 1980s.[18] This view interprets the European audiovisual policy mainly in terms of its relevance to European cultural policy, which was not a Community policy area under the Treaty of Rome.

This chapter sees the audiovisual sector as consisting of mainly two different domains, i.e., audiovisual technologies ('hardware') and audiovisual contents ('software'). This is in line with the European Commission's definition of audiovisual:

> The audiovisual sector which covers programme production and distribution ('software'), to which equipment manufacturing ('hardware') can be added, has an economic importance that is often underestimated as compared to its unquestionable cultural significance.[19]

In the absence of a clearly defined legal basis under the Treaty of Rome for policy intervention in the audiovisual sector at the European level, Community actions aimed at promoting the competitiveness of European producers (in particular 'hardware' manufacturers) were carried out as a part of the European industrial policy and common market policy prior to the Maastricht Treaty.

Since the late 1970s, and in particular the mid-1980s, the European audiovisual sector has been facing increased competitive pressure from two main forces in a global context. On the one hand, the European consumer electronic manufacturers have been challenged by the Japanese suppliers. On the other hand, the European film and television programme makers have been severely squeezed by the Hollywood studios. With the whole world becoming Japanised in consumer electronics manufacturing and Americanised in film and TV programme making, the survival of the European audiovisual sector seems increasingly dependent upon non-market forces.

On the consumer electronics market, Philips' V2000 home video system, was wiped out by the Japanese Betamax (of Sony) and VHS (of JVC) systems with the latter having been accepted as the *de facto* world standard in the early 1980s. In a comparable way, the Philips DCC (Digital Compact Cassette) technology failed to become a commercial success largely due to the competition from a rival Japanese system, i.e., Sony's MiniDisc digital audio system in the early 1990s.[20] It appears that the European consumer electronics manufacturers were unable to turn their own technologies into commercial success. Meanwhile, the very existence of European manufacturers also became questionable by the 1980s. For instance, by the mid-1980s all of the British-owned colour TV manufacturers had disappeared and the top ten TV makers in the UK were exclusively non-British a decade later.

As far as the film and TV programme industry is concerned, the European Commission has identified four major weaknesses as follows:

- Fragmentation into national markets and producers are too small to compete on European and world markets;
- A low rate of cross-border programme distribution and circulation;
- A spiralling and chronic deficit;
- Inability to attract the financial resources for recovery.[21]

Incorporating three generation of constitutional development,[22] the Treaties on the European Union (TEU),[23] the Community is now well equipped with a legal framework and eligible to take actions in order to help improve the competitiveness situation of both the consumer electronics manufacturers and the audiovisual programming industry. More specifically, under the TEU, Article 2 stipulates that the Community 'shall have as its task, by establishing a common market and an economic and monetary union and by implementing common policies or activities ... to promote throughout the Community ... a high degree of competitiveness and convergence of economic performance...'. Articles 3(m), 3(n), 157 (m) and 163-173 grant the Community the authority to strengthen the competitiveness of Community industry and promote research and technological development. A large number of Community industrial policy measures, including policies for new TV broadcasting systems, have been implemented in line with the TEU.

The TEU, in particular Article 151, now stipulates that the Community 'shall contribute to the flowering of the cultures of the Member States, while respecting their national and regional diversity and at the same time bringing the common cultural heritage to the fore.' More specifically, the European Community, when necessary, may take action aimed at encouraging 'dissemination of the culture and history of the European peoples' and 'artistic and literary creation, including in the audiovisual sector'. In other words, the 'cultural' industry and the 'audiovisual' sector have been added to the list of policy domains of the Community under the TEU. Before the Maastricht Treaty, Community actions targeting the audiovisual and broadcasting market were proposed on the ground of creating a 'common market' in terms of freedom of services across the Member States as stipulated by Articles 2, 3(c), 40 and 50.

With the constitutional framework laid down by the TEU, the development of the EU's audiovisual policy currently has three main objectives, i.e.,

- Establishing and ensuring the functioning of a true European space for audiovisual services;
- Contributing to developing a strong, forward-looking programme industry that can compete on world markets and help European culture to flourish and create jobs for Europe;
- Closely monitoring the emergence and development of new audiovisual and information services, with emphasis on their impact on creation, communication and fundamental rights.[24]

European Activism: Defining the Rules of the Game

The principles of establishing an internal market and promoting the competitiveness of European producers, as embraced by the Treaty of Rome, which have been extended by the later versions of the EU Treaties, have led to the emergence of a policy framework governing the European audiovisual sector. This policy framework consists of two different, but closely related, dimensions: supporting European efforts in establishing European standards for audiovisual systems and fostering the formation of a single European audiovisual market.

The first major piece of Community legislation on the technological aspect of the audiovisual sector was the Council Directive of 1986 on the adoption of the MAC/packet family of standards[25] as the 'common specifications' for direct broadcasting by satellite (DBS), i.e., the widely known 'MAC Directive'.[26] The MAC Directive stipulates that, among others,

- Member States shall ensure the use of *only* [emphasis by the author] the MAC/packet systems for DBS;
- The MAC cable system should be preferred for redistribution by cable of DBS programmes;
- Member States shall ensure the use of any systems, which evolve from, and operationally compatible with those MAC/packet systems.

The primary aim of the MAC Directive was, firstly, to ensure, by EU legislation, the exclusive use of the European MAC/packet systems for all satellite television broadcasting throughout the Member States. Secondly, in view of the emergent Japanese technology for a new generation of TV broadcasting *via* satellite, the MAC Directive would shield the MAC family of standards from foreign competition. Thirdly, the wording 'systems evolve from those MAC/packet systems' and 'operationally compatible with them [i.e., MAC/packet systems] specifically created a protective legal environment to ensure the success of HD-MAC, which was proposed by a European consortium competing with the Japanese proposal regarding a world standard of high definition TV. Finally, the MAC Directive was intended to help create a high level of penetration by MAC TV receivers in Europe so that the future high definition TV standard 'evolved' from the MAC family would have a strong backward compatible market base.

The MAC Directive suffered from a few drawbacks. First of all, the Directive defines direct broadcasting by satellite as 'a broadcasting satellite service as defined in the Radio Regulations of the International Telecommunications Union (ITU), i.e. using channels assigned to Member States in the 11.7 to 12.5 GHz band at the World Broadcasting Satellite Administrative Radio Conference (Geneva 1977) [WARC BS-77] and intended for display on 625 lines domestic TV receivers.'[27] In other words, the MAC Directive confines DBS services to the channels defined by WARC BS-77 in the 11.7 to 12.5 GHz, which are essentially high-powered satellite transmission channels. The EU authorities would soon learn that DBS services could also be achieved by using cost effective low-powered satellite channels transmitting to old standards (e.g. PAL) rather than any of the MAC family of systems. This point is widely regarded as a legal loophole within the MAC Directive.[28]

The second drawback, with hindsight, is that the MAC Directive did not foresee the potential challenge of digital broadcasting technologies, which was pioneered by GI of the United States. The British government subsequently criticised the EU's MAC strategy for its backing an 'obsolete' technology – all members of the MAC/packet family were essentially analogue transmission systems. In view of technical change and pressures from many quarters of the Community, the MAC Directive had to take into account fully digital TV systems in 1992, when the Directive was renewed.[29] On the one hand, the renewed MAC Directive set a regulatory framework of standards for advanced television broadcasting services based on the HD-MAC standard and D2-MAC standard.[30] On the other hand, the renewed MAC Directive left room for the development of fully digital systems. Under the renewed MAC Directive, both the HD-

MAC and D2-MAC standards would be required only for 'non-fully digital' satellite and cable transmission in Europe.

A new Community Directive[31] published by the European Parliament and the Council of Ministers in November 1995 on the use of standards for the transmission of TV signals further differentiates between 'non-fully digital' standards and 'fully digital' systems. The 1995 Directive continues to require that television services transmitted in the Community shall use the HD-MAC transmission system, only 'if they are in high definition, and are not fully digital'. The irony is that, by late 1995, it seemed highly unlikely that any broadcaster, including those from the EU, would adopt the HD-MAC system to transmit high definition TV programmes in Europe, given the rapid development of fully digital (both high definition and standard definition) TV technologies in the US and Europe. As for fully digital TV services, using 'a transmission system which has been standardised by a recognised European standardisation body' is allowed by the new Directive.[32] In other words, there is no specific standard stipulated by the new Directive as the only official choice for fully digital TV transmission, so long as the service is in a wide-screen format (16/9).

The third drawback lies in the fact that the original MAC Directive was focused on TV broadcasting *via* satellite plus cable re-distribution. That is to say, the interest of terrestrial broadcasters was not taken into account. This would potentially trigger wide spread of unhappiness within the terrestrial broadcasting sector in Europe. In the mid-1980s, the provision of DBS services was still very limited. In the UK, for instance, there were no DBS services until 1989 and 1990, when Sky Television and British Satellite Broadcasting (BSB) were launched respectively.

Another critical drawback associated with the 1986 MAC Directive was the excessive desire of the EU authorities to intervene in the process of innovation and the premature choice of the MAC/packet family. This protectionist policy approach has effectively eliminated the dynamics of market forces, which might have benefited the innovation process. The EU authorities eventually realised and corrected this mistake when reconsidering the TV standards issue, although at a much later time:

> Whereas it is essential to establish common standards for the digital transmission of television signals whether by cable or by satellite or by terrestrial means as an enabling element for effective free-market competition and *this is best achieved by mandating a recognized European Standardization body taking account, as appropriate, of the outcome of the consensus processes under way among market parties* [emphasis by author].[33]

Finally, the 1986 MAC Directive was focused single-mindedly on the strategic importance of common technical specifications, which would 'be of great economic benefit for the European consumer electronics industry as regards its competitiveness' and make 'a significant contribution to European unification and to the development of a true European identity'.[34] It failed to recognise that any success of the 'common technical specifications' for TV broadcasting would have to be accepted by the market. The adoption of the MAC standard was also potentially detrimental to the interests of the viewers, who had already invested in equipment manufactured to the PAL/SECAM standard in Europe, considering the very insignificant improvement of viewing experience the MAC standard would have achieved.

In parallel with the rule making for protecting and promoting European originated audiovisual technologies, such as the MAC/packet family of advanced TV broadcasting standards, the EU authorities have also committed great efforts to creating a common European space for producing and distributing audiovisual services. As mentioned earlier, the legal foundation on which the EU authorities exercise intervention in the broadcasting sector is the provisions laid down within the Treaty of Rome concerning the establishment of common market and the freedom of movement for services. The 1989 Council Directive,[35] the so-called 'TV without Frontiers' Directive, represents the most significant legislation by the EU in this respect.

The principal objectives of the 'TV without Frontiers' Directive included, among others, the abolition of restrictions on freedom to provide broadcasting services across national borders within the Community:

> Each Member State shall ensure freedom of reception and shall not restrict retransmission on their territory of television broadcasts from other Member States for reasons which fall within the fields coordinated by this Directive.[36]

Another important provision within the 1989 Council Directive was its requirement that,

> Member Sates shall ensure where practicable and by appropriate means, that broadcasters reserve for European works, within the meaning of Article 6, a majority proportion of their transmission time, ...[37]

It is clear that the fundamental purpose of the 'TV without Frontiers' Directive was not different from that of the 'MAC Directive', which was to create an internal market without frontiers among the Member States for

European producers. Because of the legal requirement, as stipulated by these legislation, foreign (or non-EU) technologies and television programmes would be either barred from or at a reduced level in entering the EU market. Therefore, if the 'TV without Frontiers' legislation were ever enforceable, it would be enforced in part by the establishment of a common European frontier in a global context, which is sometimes referred to as the 'Fortress Europe'. Given that the 'TV without Frontiers' Directive was renewed with minor amendments in June 1997, the European audiovisual sector is likely to be governed by the above rules for a long time to come.

The EU authorities have learned the lesson, a costly one, from its own experience in technology policy making for HD-MAC. The European Commission recently admitted that 'the earlier European model', i.e., the MAC and HD-MAC model, was 'driven by technology and extensive regulation'.[38]

Supporting Measures

In addition to its proactive legislation and financial supports, the European public authorities have devised other supporting measures in order to secure the success of new European technologies for TV broadcasting and production. Among others, Vision 1250 is worth mentioning.

Vision 1250 was initiated by the European Commission and set up in July 1990 as a special European Economic Interest Grouping (EEIG) based in Brussels. Members of Vision 1250 included consumer electronic manufacturers, independent producers, broadcasters, professional equipment manufacturers, telecommunications operators, etc.

The objective of Vision 1250 was 'to organise and to provide the basis for the development of the 16/9 market, for which digital video technologies provide high quality production for both the new 16/9 widescreen broadcast services and for forthcoming multimedia applications'.[39] In essence, Vision 1250 promotes the adoption of new broadcasting and production technologies and equipment:

> Within this framework, it undertakes a full range of actions to facilitate the setting up of high quality professional 16/9 infrastructure (notably Digital High Definition Video) and it actively promotes to the European independent producers the use of digital 16/9 production and post-production technologies.[40]

Bearing in mind that Vision 1250 was launched at a time (1990) when the global competition (among Japan, Europe and the US), it is beyond any doubt that the primary mission of the organisation was to promote the adoption of broadcasting and post-production equipment manufactured to the European HDTV standard, i.e., HD-MAC. The organisational name 'Vision 1250' is self-evident: 1250 is exactly the number of horizontal scanning lines of the proposed HD-MAC transmission standard.

Table 6.1 EU audiovisual policy on TV technologies and programme making

Audio-visual Policy	Hardware/Technologies	Software/Programmes
Overall objective	Improving the competitiveness of European producers	Improving the competitiveness of European producers
EU Treaty (legal foundations)	Common market: Article 2; Competitiveness of industry: Articles 3(m) and 157; Research and technological development: Articles 3(n) and 163-173.	Common market: Article 2; Competitiveness of industry: Articles 3(m) & 157; Freedom of services: Articles 3c, 49 & 50; Culture/audiovisual: Article 151.
Rules of the game (legislation)	86/529/EEC:Council Directive, OJ L311; 89/337/EEC: Council Decision, OJ L142; 89/630/EEC: Council Decision, OJ L363; 92/38/EEC: Council Directive, OJ L137; 93/424/EC: Council Decision, OJ L196; Council Resolution, 1993: OJ C209; Council Resolution, 1994: OJ C181: 95/47/EC: Council Directive, OJ C281.	89/552/EEC (Council Directive, OJ L298); 97/36/EC (Council Directive, OJ L202); 90/685/EEC (Council Decision, OJ L380).
Promotional measures	The Action Plan (1993) Vision 1250 (1990)	The MEDIA (I & II) Programme
Pan-European synergy	Eureka (technological): EU 95-HDTV (1986); EU 15-CERISE (1987) EU 256-DIGITRANS (1988); EU 283-SYNTHETIC TV (1988) EU 625-VADIS EU 637-PAL+ (1991); EU 775-TVMIX (1991); EU 851-HDTV Projector (1993); EU 1187-ADTT (1994) EU 127-JESSI EU 1041-LIMELIGHT	Audiovisual Eureka

In an attempt to ensure the success of the European HDTV standard, the EU and the European governments have also launched other initiatives. For instance, the EU's MEDIA Programme, including MEDIA I and MEDIA II, has made specific provision to encourage and support programme making to the 16/9 and high definition format. The European Commission hoped that, through the support under the MEDIA Programme, a stock of high definition programmes could have been built up before the proposed introduction of HDTV services in Europe by 1995.[41]

European Public Policy vis-à-vis Market Forces

In the past few years, digital satellite broadcasting has also added a new dimension to the development of digital TV. News Corp., among others, has been making great effort to build up a global empire of digital TV broadcasting *via* satellite.

News Corp.'s interest in satellite broadcasting can be traced back to the late 1980s, when the company successfully launched Sky Television in Britain.

To the surprise of the EU public authorities, particularly the European Commission, Sky Television was launched in 1989 and its programmes were transmitted to the conventional PAL standard through Astra, a low-powered telecommunication satellite. Sky's DBS transmission using the old PAL format apparently did not violate the MAC Directive adopted in 1986, because the latter was limited in scope to high-powered DBS services as defined in the WARC-77 document. The fact that Rupert Murdoch managed to launch his DBS services and was not constrained by the 1986 MAC Directive was widely believed to be a regulatory 'loophole'.[42]

In contrast to Sky Television, BSB (British Satellite Broadcasting), launched in May 1990 and transmitted *via* the Marco Polo satellite, was the only DBS service using the D-MAC format, a variant of the MAC/packet, in Britain. It was anticipated that the launch of BSB would increase the popularity of the MAC standards and, therefore, would enhance the European HDTV strategy. Unfortunately, BSB quickly ran into financial crisis. In order to secure its shareholders' interests, BSB merged with Rupert Murdoch's Sky Television. The new company incorporating Sky Television and BSB was given a new name BSkyB (British Sky Broadcasting), in which News Corp. owns 40% of the stake.

As a result of the merger, the previous 5-channel services from BSB were incorporated into the 4-channel services from Sky to form a new 6-channel DBS service, which were all transmitted in the PAL format from

Astra. As part of the deal, the previous small squarial dishes used by BSB were replaced with the bigger and round-shaped Astra dishes. As far as the transmission format was concerned, the BSB-Sky deal was effectively a takeover of BSB by Sky, rather than a merger of the two. From a technological point of view, the first, and most interesting, implication of the BSB-Sky affair was that Astra and PAL, the existing CTV broadcasting standard, have won the victory over the more technologically sophisticated (and officially promoted) D-MAC system. The deal marked the virtual end of D-MAC as a European satellite standard.[43]

The victory of Astra and PAL and the collapse of D-MAC, to some extent, resembled the VCR format battle, where the VHS system won the victory over the so-called technologically more sophisticated Betamax and V2000 systems. In both cases market forces and the choice of the consumers played a significant role.

In terms of financial losses, it was the manufacturers of squarial dishes and D-MAC receivers used for BSB reception who suffered from the merger. Because the BSB equipment was not able to receive signals transmitted from Astra, producers had to stop production and their previous stock could no longer be sold. Philips, who had produced 150,000 receivers for BSB, and Thomson claimed £50m and £20m of compensation respectively from BSB on the grounds of breaching contract by the latter after the merger.[44]

The failure of BSB has led to criticisms from some industrialists on EU policy makers for leaving a 'loophole' in the MAC Directive and, as Philips commented, 'did not prevent the improper use of telecommunication satellites for transmission of TV signals in the old PAL standard', and 'it was the cause of a regrettable loss of time and much unproductive debate'.[45] It seems that this corporate view of Philips over DBS regulations was very different from that of some commentators:

> Regulate only for safety and anti-trust reasons; let markets decide who gets which rights of way and what technology is used. ... there is no reason for regulators to stop broadcasters from choosing among a growing family of technologies instead of insisting on one.[46]

Given the wide criticisms and the controversies caused by the coercive MAC Directive, the EU authorities decided to continue to support MAC but left room for alternative technologies (e.g. digital TV) to develop in the renewed version of the MAC Directive. Among others, the renewed MAC Directive stipulates that D2-MAC is only compulsory for 'not completely digital' DBS with a 16/9 aspect ratio of widescreen TV format. This implies that old systems, such as PAL and SECAM, with an aspect ratio of 4/3 might still be used for DBS services. The new Directive also requires that any 'not completely digital' TV transmission of 625 lines must be accompanied by D2-MAC transmission of the same programmes after 1 January 1995, but the extra costs of simulcast services would likely be compensated by EU subsidy.

The BSkyB deal was, indeed, politically controversial, but the new venture has already brought financial benefits to its shareholders. By the time when BSB and Sky Television were merging, both companies were heavily losing money and their independent operations were believed to be at risk.[47] BSkyB has now become the largest DBS broadcaster in Europe. In March 1996 BSkyB reached 5.35 million subscribers in the UK and reported an operating profit of £315m for the financial year ending June 1996.[48]

As a survivor (and winner) in the gap of Europe's regulatory regime, BSkyB now functions as the springboard, from which News Corp. (the parent company of BSkyB) is poised to transmit digital TV signals that can be received from every corner of the earth under his 'Sky' in the age of digital broadcasting.

Rupert Murdoch announced his plan of launching 200 digital TV channels in the UK *via* satellite by the end of 1997.[49] In the meantime, BSkyB has also teamed up with the Granada Group and Carlton Communications in a consortium bidding for terrestrial digital channels in the UK. The consortium, called British Digital Broadcasting (BDB) confirmed that, if it won the bidding, it would be subsidising the manufacturers of the 'set-top boxes' which would enable the conventional TV sets to receive the new digital channels.[50] In order to facilitate the launch of 200 digital channels, BSkyB put an order to the electronics manufacturers[51] for 1 million 'set-top boxes' (STBs) at a total cost of £250m. It is believed that the genuine cost per unit of the set-top decoders is about £400; but BSkyB negotiated subsidy deals with BT, Midland Band and Matsushita by offering access to the boxes for interactive services.

BSkyB's announcement coincided with the UK government's plan to start digital terrestrial broadcasting as a type of pay-TV in 1998. What seemed interesting was the joining forces between the BBC, which is a state-owned and non-commercial broadcaster, and BDB. The two organisations have recently reached an agreement to jointly broadcast up to eight subscription channels. This agreement has led to fears that current TV set owners would eventually have to pay for existing 'free-to-air' services. It is rather ironic that, not long ago, the BBC and BSkyB were still engaged in a fierce dispute over the control of the set-top boxes. The

BBC, and other terrestrial broadcasters, was concerned that BSkyB might abuse the power over digital satellite system *via* its 'set-top box' standard.[52]

At a later stage of the bidding process for the digital broadcasting multiplexes, the British government insisted that BSkyB should withdraw from the BDB consortium. The British government was concerned that BSkyB, with a substantial ownership in digital satellite broadcasting and a stake in digital terrestrial broadcasting, might become a monopoly in digital broadcasting. Reluctantly, BSkyB withdrew from the BDB consortium but got compensation from the British government for this change.

Rupert Murdoch's digital satellite TV broadcasting was by no means confined to Britain. On the contrary, Murdoch's ambition was to build up a global empire of digital broadcasting. In April 1996, News Corp. formed a joint venture, named ASkyB (American Sky Broadcasting), with MCI to begin digital broadcasting (direct to home) in autumn 1997 covering all of the 50 states in the US. The ownership of ASkyB was split between News Corp. and MCI – 80% and 20% respectively. In the meantime, News Corp. and MCI also set up SkyMCI, ASkyB's sister company, to offer a range of multimedia information and data services for business customers.[53] In other words, ASkyB would target the residential customers whilst SkyMCI would concentrate on serving business users.

At the moment there are five other DBS companies offering services to a total of 10m subscribers in the US; they are DirecTV (owned by Hughes Electronics), USSB (subsidiary of General Motors), PrimeStar, EchoStar and AlphaStar. Compared with the 66m customers of the cable industry, the satellite broadcasting sector is only at its early stage of development in the US. With a common fear of the cable industry's dominant position, the American DBS industry is undergoing a consolidation process. This process has already made its first significant step: News Corp. recently reached an agreement with EchoStar on a merger between the latter and ASkyB to form a single company named Sky. The new partnership, with a promised sum of investment at $500m from News Corp., would potentially offer 500 digital channels of TV broadcasting, Internet, media, educational and business services in the US.[54] These channels, as estimated, would be able to reach 75% of American homes by 1999 with sharp digital pictures and CD-quality sound, near video-on-demand (VoD) and interactive services (such as home shopping and home banking).[55] Undoubtedly, News Corp. is on the way to becoming one of the major players to promote DBS services and challenge the cable industry in the US.

The Japanese television broadcasting industry used to be most immune from the invasion of digital satellite channels, of which News Corp. would take a lion's share. PerfecTV, the American satellite broadcaster, launched 70-channel services in October 1996. This was followed by News Corp's announcement to launch 12 digital channels by April 1997 *via* its newly formed subsidiary JSkyB (Japan Sky Broadcasting).[56] JSkyB promised to increase the number of its digital channels to 100 by April 1998. Due to the fact that JSkyB shares the same satellite (JCSat-3) with PerfecTV, Japanese viewers are able to receive services from both companies.

News Corp. has also brought its DBS services to some other parts of Asia. The formation of ISkyB (Indian Sky Broadcasting) was intended to serve as an effective conduit for News Corp.'s satellite television programmes to reach every corner of India, a country with the second largest population (after China) in the world.[57] StarTV, another subsidiary of News Corp. based in Hong Kong, appears to be strategically important to its parent company, given its geographical position. StarTV's satellite broadcasting channels has the potential to recruit a substantial number of subscribers outside Hong Kong. In particular, Hong Kong's return to the Chinese sovereignty in July 1997 has made the territory an important springboard for News Corp. to expand its StarTV services into the vast area of Mainland China, where political control over foreign TV broadcasting is still tight.

China's joining the WTO (World Trade Organisation) in the near future, which is widely expected in the wake of the bilateral trade agreement between China and the US signed in November 1999, would seem to add more pressure for Beijing to re-consider its long-standing hard-line attitude towards foreign information and foreign media. Under the recent China-US trade agreement, China would increase its import of Hollywood films, which is currently confined to no more than a dozen per year, and eventually will relax control. It is entirely reasonable to speculate that the WTO deal would have great import on the media sector as a whole and digital satellite broadcasting would be one of the most effective ways to sell digital media to the Chinese population. StarTV is well positioned to benefit from such a positive scenario.[58]

In a strategic move, as mentioned in Chapter 4, News Corp. has already established a joint venture with *People's Daily,* the Chinese Communist Party's top official newspaper. The joint venture, called Beijing Xinren Information Technology, is intended to develop electronic publishing and online data services. The potential synergy between Beijing Xinren and StarTV, and close contacts to be built up by the latter with the Chinese government, would help News Corp. to insert a strong foothold in China's future digital satellite TV and electronic data services market.[59]

Figure 6.1   News Corp.'s digital broadcasting empire

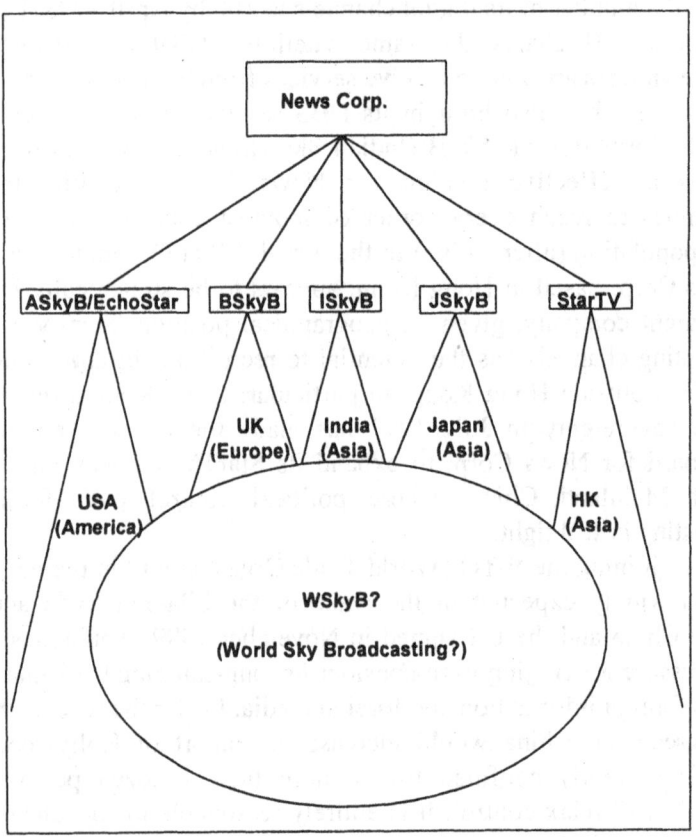

Apparently, the global digital satellite plans now represent the most important part of News Corp's corporate strategy;[60] and Rupert Murdoch is poised to create a digital DBS empire under the roof of his 'Sky'. There will be, undoubtedly, technical, commercial and regulatory challenges to the 'Sky Empire', but 'digital transmission and News Corp's encryption technology open up huge opportunities depending on how much software is installed in people's set-top boxes'.[61] It looks highly likely that, once

News Corp. has made use of the 26 alphabetical letters to name its Sky ventures in different countries, the eventual formation of a *de facto* 'WSkyB' ('World Sky Broadcasting') as a global business empire for digital broadcasting would simply be a matter of time. Some commentators are just beginning to realise the emergence of a global digital satellite empire under the banner News Corp.:

> CBS and Viacom have their cable networks; Time Warner has America Online; even Disney is latching on to the internet. Now Rupert Murdoch wants one, too. A digital distribution platform that is, that can pipe News Corporation's content into homes around the globe. In fact, Mr Murdoch believes News Corp already has one in its worldwide collection of satellite operators. The market just has not recognised it properly.[62]

It was recently reported that Rupert Murdoch, chairman of News Corporation, was moving to consolidate his global satellite TV interests into a new $35bn company in preparation for what is likely to be one of the biggest public offerings of a media business.[63] The News Corp. management confirmed in a statement that they have under serious consideration plans to consolidate their worldwide satellite platforms and certain related assets under one umbrella entity.[64]

Global Competition for Digital TV and the Success of DVB

'The imminent arrival of a digital television future much earlier than anticipated has therefore contributed towards a suspension of any international decision on HD broadcasting standards and, as a result, has led to a relative standstill in the changeover to this new dimension among broadcasters.'[65]

The digital compression breakthrough achieved by GI in 1990 enabling the transmission of HDTV signals through the conventional terrestrial TV broadcasting bandwidth of 6MHz heralded the beginning of a new era for TV technology development.

The birth of digital TV technology contributed significantly to the collapse of the European HD-MAC system, and also threatens the survival of the more established Japanese MUSE system. Thanks to the technical achievement of GI, the US, as a latecomer, stole the lead in diverting the course of HDTV development from largely an analogue approach (as represented by HD-MAC and MUSE) to a new and fully digital approach in the beginning of the 1990s.

The major contenders for digital TV (including digital HDTV) are at the moment the Grand Alliance in the US with the ATSC terrestrial transmission system, the Digital Video Broadcasting (DVB) group with a range of transmission systems in Europe and the Japanese DiBEG group's ISDB terrestrial standard. In addition, there are other initiatives, such as the HD-Divine and some Eureka digital TV projects. For the time being, the DVB group seems to be the most promising winner of the global digital TV format contest.

The Grand Alliance

In the early 1990s, there were three major consortia with four fully digital HDTV proposals submitted to the FCC for tests; these were:

- American Consortium (Zenith and AT&T) with one proposed system called Digital Spectrum Compatible;
- American Alliance (GI and MIT[66]) with two proposed systems and they are the Digicipher system and CC-Digicipher system;
- Advanced Television Research Consortium (ATRC) (Philips, Thomson, Sarnoff Research Centre, Compression Labs and NBC) with one proposed system called Advanced Digital Television (ADTV).

Although joined at a much late stage, Toshiba became the third partner after GI and MIT within the American Alliance.

On 24 May 1993, the three remaining contenders for HDTV, i.e. the American Consortium, the American Alliance and the ATRC group, reached an agreement to end head-to-head competition and announced that they were pooling their technical expertise to form a 'Grand Alliance'.[67] The Grand Alliance, under the auspices of the FCC, would jointly set a fully digital HDTV standard for the US. From the FCC's point of view, the joining forces of the three competing consortia would benefit the future HDTV system if the contenders could bring the best elements of their own systems into a common system.

On the financial side of the Grand Alliance, further R&D and engineering costs were to be met by the seven participants originally from three competing consortia. In principle, the financial responsibility is split even among the three. It was hoped that the R&D costs occurred through the Grand Alliance would be recouped sufficiently from the royalties and licence fee after the common digital TV system is commercially established. Meanwhile, the formation of the Grand Alliance was intended by the participating groups to avoid large-scale financial losses, as any contender was likely to be a loser if they continued to compete against each other. The FCC stays clearly away from the financial aspect of the Grand Alliance, as it did during the bidding and testing period before the combining of the competing systems.

On the technical side, the Grand Alliance supports the ISO's MPEG-2 standard for digital video compression. MPEG-2 is a worldwide standard and is being adopted in the main areas of the ICT sector, such as computer, multimedia, telecommunications and consumer electronics industry. As far as digital TV is concerned, video compression is the key system element.

The establishment of a fully digital HDTV standard through the Grand Alliance would, as perceived, firstly provide the US electronics industry with a competitive advantage on the emergent HDTV market. This would be particularly so when the huge sums of perceived royalties and licence fees are paid to the holders of key digital TV patents when consumer electronics firms start to manufacture HDTV products to the American standard.

Another important point is that the initial triumph of the Grand Alliance was also shared by non-American firms. Within the Grand Alliance, Philips of the Netherlands, the owner of the Magnavox, Philco and Sylvania brand names, and Thomson of France, the owner of RCA, are two important technical and financial contributors to establishing the common standard. Philips and Thomson are also two of the world's four largest consumer electronics manufacturers (the other two are Matsushita and Sony). These two companies will not only share the royalty income with their American collaborators but also bring their expertise gained through participating in the Grand Alliance back to Europe, where digital TV development is gaining momentum.

Digital Video Broadcasting (DVB)

The officially supported European HDTV standard, HD-MAC, was demised in part by the FCC's decision to adopt a fully digital HDTV system for the US. The formation of the Grand Alliance to develop a single standard further enhanced the competitive advantage of the US in fighting the global competition for HDTV standardisation. However, the overwhelming leading position of the US in digital TV development is being increasingly challenged by initiatives from other regions, particularly Europe. The rapid progress in digital TV technology achieved by the European Digital Video Broadcasting (DVB) Group has attracted attention from European policy makers and the industry, including manufacturers and broadcasters.

DVB was initiated by the European Launching Group (ELG) for digital video broadcasting in late 1991. The ELG, led by Peter Kahl from the German Ministry of Telecommunications, was initially an informal grouping intending to establish a fully digital TV system for Europe. The ELG was joined by a range of broadcasters, equipment manufacturers, signal carriers and radio regulators from several European countries. The ELG later renamed itself the 'General Assembly', whose memorandum of understanding was signed by every participating organisation. In September 1995, the 'General Assembly' formally adopted the name Digital Video Broadcasting (DVB).

Figure 6.2   DVB organisational structure

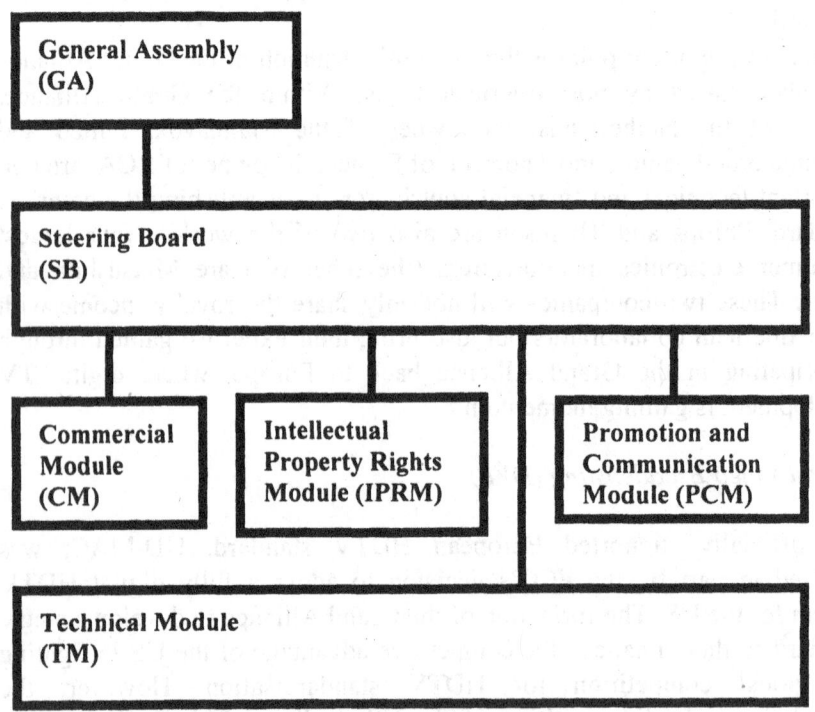

Source: Adapted from DVB Project Office, http://www.dvb.org/.

The main aspects of organisational structure of DVB are as follows:
- the General Assembly: joined by all members of the group;

- the Steering Board: consisting of up to 34 elected members;
- the Technical Module;
- the Commercial Module;
- the Intellectual Property Rights Module;
- the Promotion and Communication Module
- a range of specialised Modules.

Within the DVB group, the Steering Board plays the most significant role and is responsible for issues including budget, regulations, publicity, signal security, intellectual property, etc. The Technical Module (previously called the Working Group on Digital Video Broadcasting) deals with developments associated with the ISO's MPEG and, on behalf of the DVB Group, liases with the EBU and the ETSI (European Telecommunications Standard Institute), etc. The DVB group also contributes to the definition process of MPEG-2 generic video standard.

The specialised Modules operating under the DVB groups include:

- **DVB-S:** the satellite transmission system developed by DVB's Satellite Module. This standard has already been finalised for use in the 11/12GHz band configuration.
- **DVB-C:** the cable transmission system developed by DVB's Cable Module to re-distribute digital video broadcasting programmes.
- **DVB-T:** the digital terrestrial transmission system developed by DVB's Terrestrial Commercial Module for 7-8MHz channels. DVB-T has incorporated some technical elements achieved by other European projects such as HD-Divine, dTTb, VADIS, SPECTRE, etc. The agreement reached by members of the Steering Board of DVB on a common European digital terrestrial television standard on 18 December 1995 was perhaps the most significant achievement of the DVB group since its inception. This has firmly put Europe into a very strong position in terms of digital TV broadcasting.
- **DVB-M(M)DT:** the DVB's Multichannel Microwave Distribution System. DVB-MIDST is aimed to deliver digital video signals using microwave technologies.
- **DVB-CS:** Digital satellite master antenna television (SMATV) distribution systems.
- **DVB-I:** DVB's interactive television module.

- **DVB-DATA:** DVB's Data Broadcasting module, which specifies the transmission of data in DVB bitstreams.
- **DVB-CA:** DVB's Conditional Access module.
- **DVB Subtitling:** This module provides digital broadcasting systems for TV, sound and data services.
- **DVB Interfaces:** This module ensures that DVB interface to PDH and SDH networks.

Figure 6.3 Map of DVB worldwide adoption

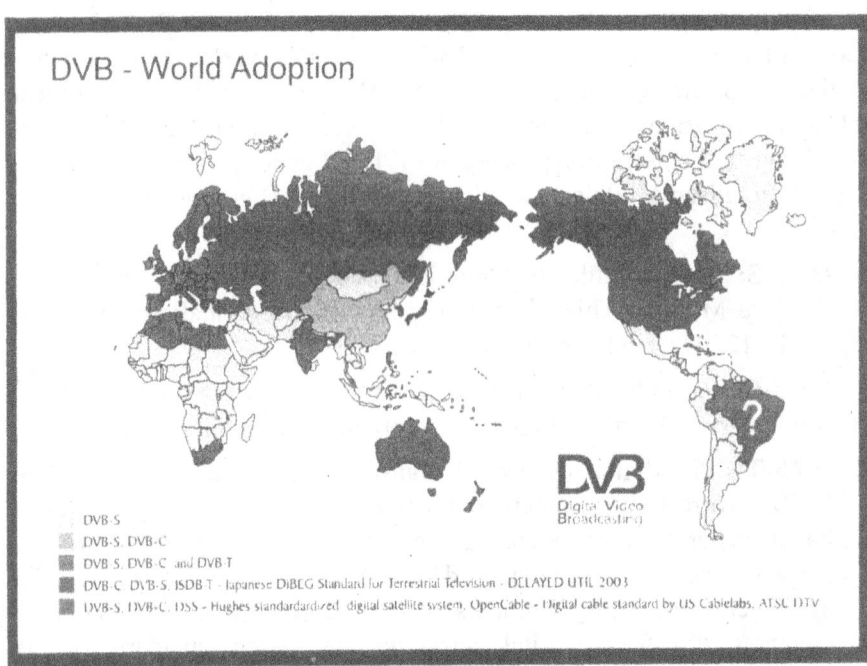

Source: DVB Project Office, Geneva, Switzerland, May 2000.

The steadily rising influence of DVB is in part indicated by the number of participating organisations. In 1993, the DVB group had 85 members. The membership increased to 140 in 1995, 180 in 1996. By 16 February 2000 membership of the DVB group reached 263 involving organisations from over 30 countries.

Apparently DVB is on the way to success. Within Europe, the main elements of the DVB standards family (e.g. DVB-T, DVB-S and DVB-C) have already been adopted by broadcasters. DVB-S for digital satellite broadcasting has reached by far the largest number of countries, including those where competing standards are in place. In the US, for instance, despite that Hughes has developed its proprietary digital satellite system (DSS) and US CableLabs has developed the digital cable standard OpenCable, DVB-S has won the favour of some broadcasters.

The DVB group's digital terrestrial TV standard (DVB-T) has, by the time of writing, won the official blessing and been adopted in 28 countries including Belgium, Croatia, Czech Republic, Denmark, Finland, France, Germany, Greece, Hungary, Ireland, Italy, Lithuania, The Netherlands, Norway, Poland, Portugal, Slovakia, Slovenia, Spain, Sweden, Switzerland, Turkey, Ukraine, United Kingdom, Australia, New Zealand, India and Singapore. In addition, DVB-T trials are presently under way or completed in Hong Kong, Brazil, Cuba, Chile, China, Israel and Taiwan.

In view of the failure of its notorious MAC strategy and the increased popularity of the DVB, the European Commission now extends its support to the latter. The European Commission admitted that it 'recently wrote to the Argentine government to advise a review of its decision to adopt ATSC [i.e., the American digital TV standard] without objective comparative testing of DVB-T and ATSC'.[68]

The most radical development in favour of the DVB standards family is perhaps the recent 'rebellion' of some broadcasters in the US against the mandatory ATSC system. In October 1999, the Sinclair Broadcast Group filed a petition, co-signed by another 250 broadcasting stations, with the FCC, arguing that the nation's digital television standard was seriously flawed because receivers could not easily pick up a viewable television signal in non-ideal circumstances. More specifically, Sinclair asked in its petition that the FCC should revise the digital broadcasting standard, which was approved by the FCC in 1996, by adding a second transmission standard that is now used in Europe, i.e., the DVB-T standard. This would allow television broadcasting stations to choose whichever system they prefer. Sinclair had its own test during the summer 1999, which showed that DVB-T worked better than the ATSC system. By early November 1999, 750 of the nation's 1600 television stations had joined the Sinclair campaign.[69] Sinclair itself owns or operates a total of 59 television stations, more than any other company in the sector.

The Sinclair tests result and its subsequent petition was certainly a powerful challenge to the FCC and its DTV policy. Bruce Franca, deputy chief of the FCC's engineering and technology office, said, 'It certainly

Table 6.2   DVB digital broadcasting standards

Standard	Title	Reference
DVB-S *Satellite*	Digital satellite transmission systems	ETS 3000 421
DVB-C *Cable*	Digital cable delivery system	ETS 300 429
DVB-T *Terrestrial*	Digital terrestrial broadcasting system	ETS 3000 744
DVB (M)MDS *Multipoint (microwave) distribution system*	Digital multipoint distribution systems at and above 10 GHz Digital multipoint distribution systems at or below 10 GHz	ETS 300 748 ETS 300 749
DVB-CS *(Satellite) Master Antenna TV (SMATV)*	Digital satellite master antenna television (SMATV) distribution systems	ETS 300 470
DVB-I *Interactive Television*	Return channels in CATV systems (DVB-RCC) Network-Independent interactive protocols (DVB-NIP) Interaction channel for SMATV Return channels in PSTN/ISDN systems (DVB-RCT) Interfacing to PDH networks Interfacing to SDH networks	ETS 300 800 ETS 300 801 Draft ETS 300 803 ETS 300 802 ETS 300 813 ETS 300814
DVB-DATA *Data Broadcasting*	Specification for the transmission of data in DVB bitstreams	TS/EN 301 192
DVB-CA *Conditional Access*	Common Interface for conditional access and other applications Technical specification of SimulCrypt in DVB systems	EN50221 TS101 197
DVB Subtitling	Digital broadcasting systems for TV, sound and data services, Subtitling systems	prETS 300 743
DVB Interfaces	DVB interfaces to PDH DVB interfaces to SDH networks Interfaces for CATV/SMATV headends and similar professional Equipment	prETS 300 813 prETS300 814 EN 50083-9

Source: Adapted from DVB Project Office, http://www.dvb.org/.

makes you step back and think. But I'm not sure it's enough to convince us that we made a mistake.'[70] The Consumer Electronics Manufacturers

Association (CEA) strongly opposed the Sinclair petition and filed a motion to dismiss it. The CEA argued in its motion,

> Reopening the proceeding on a DTV standard years after its adoption by the commission will benefit no one but the handful of broadcasters desiring to delay the transition to digital broadcasting.[71]

Believing that the current ATSC transmission standard was adequate, the FCC decided to deny the Sinclair petition by a 5-0 vote in the early February 2000.[72]

Despite the FCC verdict and the CEA's motion, the Sinclair campaign would certainly become a very positive signal at the global level advantageous to DVB. Any country now would have to be cautious when they make a decision on the choice of DTV broadcasting standard. The popular response by a large number of countries to the DVB-T standard for digital terrestrial broadcasting already suggests that the standard is on the way to become an international standard, despite that DVB was originally intended to be standards platform for Europe.

There were three major factors contributing to the rapid expansion of DVB. First, the breakthrough of digital compression techniques at General Instrument in the US had led to the belief embraced by the industry that digital TV holds the future for TV broadcasting. Meanwhile, There was an uncertainty associated with the MAC and HD-MAC approach adopted in Europe. This uncertainty was in part created by the collapse of BSB in Britain, which was using D-MAC in the beginning of the 1990s.

Second, the EU's MAC and HD-MAC strategies were formulated mainly to protect the interest of equipment manufacturers in the European consumer electronics industry, and the interest of TV broadcasters was not sufficiently accommodated. In comparison, within the DVB group the interest of broadcasters is well represented. By April 1994, 120 European broadcasters had already joined the DVB group. As a matter of fact, the DVB group is headquartered within the European Broadcasting Union (EBU), which delegates the collective interest of public and commercial broadcasters from Europe.

Third, the direct influence of the Germany Ministry of Telecommunications was an important force behind DVB.[73]

Apart from the strong backing from the German government, the European Commission also supports DVB. Although the Commission is not a signatory of DVB's Memorandum of Understanding, it has been represented at the DVB group's meetings since the early days. In addition, the European Commission, *via* its 'Euro-Image Project', provides financial support to the DVB group's operation. But the main financing of DVB comes from its members.

It is worth noting that, although the Grand Alliance of the US and DVB of Europe both supports the generic MPEG-2 standard, MPEG-2 in the US is not necessarily the same in Europe as far as digital transmission is concerned. As a generic standard, MPEG-2 does not preclude many technical variations contained within specific digital video systems. For instance, digital video broadcasting is closely linked with 'conditional access', which is realised *via* the 'set-top box' (STB). The European Union public authorities, in particular the European Commission, have been pushing hard to achieve a common European standard for STBs. But there is still a long way towards a globally accepted common standard for this.

According to the DVB Project Office, both DVB and the ATSC systems use MPEG-2 for compressing the video information, although the US system proposes a table of 18 different formats for digital television images, one of which (1080P) is not supported by MPEG-2. The US ATSC system makes use of the proprietary Dolby AC-3 audio encoding system, where DVB uses MPEG layer II audio, a system sometimes known as 'MUSICAM', developed by the international partners of the MPEG group. This is a significant difference as it means that DVB is 100% MPEG-2 compliant, whereas the ATSC DTV system is not. Meanwhile, the most important difference between the two standards is the RF modulation or transmission technology used. The ATSC DTV system uses the single-carrier modulation technique known as 8-Vestigial Sideband (8-VSB), where DVB-T makes use of the state of the art multiple carrier technology Coded Orthogonal Frequency Division Multiplexing (COFDM).[74]

Apart from DVB, there are a few other digital TV initiates in Europe, which were important in the early days of digital TV development. First of all, HD-Divine (High Definition Digital Video Narrowband Emission), is a fully digital HDTV system proposed by a Scandinavian consortium in the early 1990s. The HD-Divine consortium was initiated by the Swedish Broadcasting Corporation, Telia Research, Teracom, Telecom Denmark and Telecom Norway.

The HD-Divine consortium demonstrated a fully working system for the first time in Amsterdam in July 1992 during the International Broadcasting Convention. The HD-Divine group managed to digitally compress HDTV signals for terrestrial transmission using an 8MHz channel.

Secondly, proposed for funding under the European RACE (Research on Advanced Communications for Europe) programme, the dTTb (digital Terrestrial Television broadcasting) has been existing for years since the beginning of the 1990s but had never been favoured by the European Commission prior to the collapse of HD-MAC in 1993. The EU's attention had almost exclusively directed to the development of the HD-MAC system.

Thirdly, in parallel with the EU95 project, two other Eureka projects, EU256 and EU625, are dedicated to defining a fully digital HDTV system including a transmission standard and a production standard. In particular, the EU625 consortium has been joined by 32 European organisations including TV broadcasters, electronics manufacturers, software houses, telecommunications companies and some academic institutions. EU625 is financed with a total budget of $24m to develop VADIS, short for Video-Audio Digital Interactive System. VADIS was intended to become a European digital HDTV system. In a similar way, EU256, led by RAI, the Italian broadcasting organisation, was launched to develop a fully digital HDTV transmission system for Europe.

Digital TV in Japan

Digital TV, including digital HDTV, has not gained as much momentum in Japan until recently as it has in the US and Europe. The major reason, among others, is the fact that the NHK's Hi-Vision broadcasting using the MUSE transmission standard has been launched and many consumer electronics manufacturers have already built commercial HDTV sets using the conventional CRT (Cathode Ray Tube) technology.

The MPT (Ministry of Posts and Telecommunications) did have attempted to introduce a fully digital system to replace the Hi-Vision system but has met with fierce resistance and criticism from the consumer electronics industry. The MPT recently suggests that digital terrestrial TV broadcasting will be possible in Japan sometime during the period year 2000 to 2005. But, in the meantime, the MPT stipulated that digital HDTV broadcasting by satellite should commence after year 2007 so that a window of opportunity will be maintained for the struggling analogue Hi-Vision system. Further more, the MPT policy may not be seen as the final and definitive ruling of the Japanese government. As in some other countries, the MPT is not the only government body involved in regulating the TV broadcasting sector in Japan. On the contrary, other government agencies, such as the MITI (Ministry of International Trade and Industry), are also involved.

The Japanese government's plan is that national digital switchover will be made once 85% of the public are equipped with digital TV reception equipment. Japan also planned to start test broadcasting of digital TV in 2000 with a commercial launch in 2003. National coverage would be achieved by 2006 under this plan. The challenge comes from the terrestrial broadcasters, who have so far shown little interest in digital terrestrial TV.[75]

Nevertheless, the DiBEG group in Japan has developed their own terrestrial transmission system, i.e., ISDB-T (Integrated Services Digital Broadcasting-Terrestrial). The DiBEG standards group has adopted COFDM as the transmission technology for its ISDB-T system. Because of this, the Japanese digital terrestrial standard is said to be very similar to the DVB-T standard. There were industry discussions about combining ISDB-T with DVB-T but the timing of the European launch of digital terrestrial TV services did not permit this to happen.[76] Consequently, so far as digital terrestrial TV standards are concerned, Europe, the US and Japan have all gone their own way. This has effectively opened a new era of global competition for digital TV standardisation with the rest of the world outside the 'Triad' left to make their own choice among the competing standards.

DVB as a de facto Standards Family for the EU

The success of DVB is in part manifested in the launch of digital pay-TV services in the European Union. During the second half of the 1990s, 11 out of the 15 EU Member States launched digital satellite broadcasting to the DVB-S standards. Meanwhile, six EU Member States launched digital cable services using the DVB-C standard. Although only three EU Member States (UK, Spain and Sweden) introduced digital terrestrial TV broadcasting (DVB-T) in the late 1990s, nine other Member States have a plan to implement DVB-T in the beginning of the 21st Century. It appears that the three major DVB platforms, i.e., DVB-S, DVB-C and DVB-T, have already become the *de facto* standards family for digital TV broadcasting throughout the European Union. In other words, there doe not seem to be any chance for the American digital TV standards (for both SDTV – Standard Definition TV and HDTV) to be adopted in the European Union. In view of the recent controversy over the technical validity of the ATSC system in the US represented by the Sinclair petition against the FCC policy, the DVB standards family are gaining advantage in winning the global standardisation war for digital TV.

Compared to the development of digital satellite and digital cable broadcasting in the EU, the pace of digital terrestrial TV adoption has been much slower. The introduction of digital terrestrial TV broadcasting in Britain in November 1998 was pioneering in Europe.

Despite its previous objection to the EU's further subsidies towards HD-MAC, Britain has become the first country in the world to launch digital terrestrial TV services, which complements digital DBS and digital cable TV. The coexistence of different forms of digital TV broadcasting has led to the emergence of a competitive market for new services, which would likely benefit the consumer.

Research and development towards DTV was in part manifested in the British industry, led by NTL (National Transcommunications Limited), the demerged engineering arm of the former Independent Broadcasting Authorities (now re-named the Independent Television Commission). NTL had been pushing its digital terrestrial television technologies for a few years prior to the commercial launch of services in Britain.[77]

Table 6.3 Introduction of digital TV in the European Union

Country	Digital Satellite TV Introduction Date	Digital Cable TV Introduction Date	Digital Terrestrial TV Introduction Date (Estimated)	Digital Switch-over Date (Expected)
Austria	1996	1997	2002	NA
Belgium	XX	1998	2001	NA
Denmark	1998	1998	2000	2008-2013
Finland	1998	XX	2000	2006
France	1996	1996	2000	2010
Germany	1997	1997	2001	NA
Greece	XX	XX	NA	NA
Ireland	XX	XX	2000	2010
Italy	1996	1996	NA	2006
Luxembourg	XX	XX	NA	NA
Netherlands	1998	XX	2000	NA
Portugal	1998	X	2000	NA
Spain	1998	X	1999	2010
Sweden	1998	1998	1999	NA
UK	1998	X	1998	2010

Keys: X: Service unavailable in 1997; XX: Service unavailable in 1998; NA: Information not available.
Source: Adapted from European Commission (1999c), *The Development of the Market for Digital Television in the European Union*, COM(1999) 540, Brussels, 9 November.

The BBC was another important player in the field of digital TV transmission technologies. In the summer 1995, the BBC succeeded in digitally transmitting high quality widescreen pictures from its London Television Centre to the Crystal Palace transmitter. The digital signals were received by a TV set with a digital-analogue decoder and a portable set-top aerial.

With the intention to boost digital terrestrial TV broadcasting and reap the benefit associated with 'early mover advantage', the British government set out proposals in autumn 1995 to launch at least 18 digital terrestrial channels within two years. The new digital terrestrial TV channels were expected to cover up to 60-90% of the British population. The British government's digital terrestrial TV proposal stipulated the following aspects:

- Six frequency channels, i.e. 'multiplexes', would be made available and each would be used to transmit at least three digital terrestrial channels. The first licence, if granted, would be free of charge for 12 years.
- The four existing terrestrial broadcasters, and the forthcoming channel 5, were guaranteed to have access to the new digital frequencies on the condition that at least 80% of their analogue broadcasting programmes were broadcast on the new digital services. The percentage of simulcast was revised in the beginning of 1996 by the British government to 100%, i.e. all analogue TV programmes offered by the current terrestrial channels must be transmitted digitally.
- Companies bidding for the digital channels would be assessed according to how fast and how widely they provide digital services. Bidders were expected to subsidise the consumer's purchase of the new 'set-top' decoders.
- A single company may not control more than 25% of the available digital terrestrial capacity and 15% of total TV audience with the exception of the BBC. In the meantime, up to 10% of the digital terrestrial transmission capacity would be allowed for non-broadcast facilities, such as digital telecommunications and interactive services.
- The ITC (Independent Television Commission) and the Radio Authority have been tasked to allocate channel capacity.[78]

The initial problem with the British proposal to launch digital terrestrial services, however, might not be who should be responsible for allocating the channels; rather, it was the question of what kind of content to be available in order to sufficiently fill in the bandwidth reserved for these new channels. If the solution was simply to make the existing analogue broadcasting programmes available on the new digital channels, then another question arises: would there be enough programmes? What would be the incentive and benefit for the customer to invest in the new digital channels? In other words, would the customer be prepared to pay for the new channels or new equipment for the kind of programme that they were getting from conventional analogue broadcasting, be it terrestrial or satellite, anyway? There were no convincing answers to these questions at the outset.

Some companies might consider this issue otherwise. For instance, the legally much confined BT (British Telecom) immediately responded to the British government's digital broadcasting proposal by showing interest in becoming a multiplex owner. It is understandable that BT has been banned from entering the television broadcasting service business; owning a digital broadcasting multiplex could potentially offer BT a window of opportunity to explore the overlap in technology between digital TV services and its nascent video-on-demand (VoD) trials in Ipswich and Colchester. However, BT's VoD trials, as those undertaken in the US, are yet showing any immediate market prospect.

In the wake of launching its digital terrestrial broadcasting programme, the British government has also made public its plan requiring the BBC to sell off its terrestrial transmitter network and raise money to invest in digital production technology, which is key to the development of digital terrestrial television in Britain.

Up until now, there is no state subsidy earmarked by the British government towards the development of digital TV services.[79] On the contrary, the government was hoping to increase its revenue by charging the digital terrestrial TV broadcasters licence fees in 12 years after the licence was granted. The British policy agenda for digital terrestrial broadcasting is reminiscent of the FCC'S earlier approach in dealing with the HDTV competition in the US.

Following the commercial launch of SkyDigital by BSkyB in October 1998, the British Digital Broadcasting (BDB) Group, consisting of Granada and Calton Communications, launched ONdigital a month later. ONdigital is the first fully digital terrestrial TV service in Europe and, for the first time, put the DVB-T broadcasting standard into real commercial test. By the end of 1999, ONdigital reported a total of 552,000 subscribers to the new service.

Government policy on digital TV that future terrestrial digital channel licence holders were expected to subsidise the consumer's purchase of the new 'set-top boxes' (the digital decoders or 'digibox' in BSkyB's term) has been translated into reality. In part due to the head-on competition between the two different digital broadcasting platforms, i.e., SkyDigital and ONdigital, customers were initially promised a 'set-top box' at a retailing price of just under £200 for either service. BSkyB did have levied a charge of this price on its first group of customers who had subscribed to its SkyDigital services. In order to promote digital broadcasting, BDB and BSkyB later decided to give their STBs away – future customers of SkyDigital and ONdigital can pick up an STB for either service free of charge with a subscription agreement.

The rapid development of both digital satellite and digital terrestrial TV broadcasting in Britain appears to herald the beginning of the end to the legacy of free-to-air TV broadcasting and viewing. By the year 2010, a time when analogue TV broadcasting will be switched over entirely to digital broadcasting, as the British government has proposed, access to any TV channels, satellite, terrestrial or cable, would be controlled by an STB, which links the viewer's living room with the broadcaster. It is likely that the 'digital switch over' in 2010 will also be a 'pay TV switch over' (or the end of public service) in Britain.

Nevertheless, the successful launch of ONdigital in the UK proves that the DVB-T standard is both technically and commercially viable. This will be a significant booster to the DVB standards family. The challenge ahead, as far as digital terrestrial broadcasting in Britain is concerned, is whether ONdigital could sustain its current success and survive the fierce competition from SkyDigital, which has a much larger customer base.

Conclusion

It is clear that the new age of digital broadcasting is strongly characterised by a mixture of state regulation and market forces. Although the broadcasting sector has been traditionally perceived as a typical area of market failure, the role of the state is difficult to define. As far as technology and the process of innovation are concerned, 'picking winners' in dynamic markets even with the best intentions is very risky.[80] In particular, picking winners *via* financial subsidy and regulatory measures is certainly not always the most optimal choice by government. As a matter of fact, the initial victory of the American digital HDTV standard, i.e.,

ATSC, over Europe's HD-MAC and Japan's MUSE and the rapid progress achieved by the European Digital Video Broadcasting consortium were both built upon the dynamics of market competition rather than generous state subsidy or heavy regulation. In addition, the rise of Rupert Murdoch's digital satellite broadcasting empire further demonstrated that market forces sometimes could be more effective than state intervention in pushing forward new technologies and inserting influence on the outcomes of the innovation process.

HDTV was viewed by not only the consumer electronics industry but also governments since the mid-1980s as a strategic technology, which would affect the way of strategic trade for a nation (Tyson, 1992; Dai, Cawson and Holmes, 1996). HDTV was believed vital to revitalising the already saturated world consumer electronics market and boosting the growth of many other industries such as high-tech components (e.g. flat panel displays, advanced semiconductors and high quality digital coding/decoding equipment) and new programme-making corresponding to the new broadcasting standards. These are some of the powerful arguments used by public authorities (e.g. the European Commission) to justify their close involvement in the process of HDTV development and heavy subsidies to indigenous technologies.

Shortly after the formation of the Eureka 95 HDTV Project, the European Union enacted the notorious MAC Directive in 1986 with a view to fostering the success of MAC and, eventually, HD-MAC in Europe. When Rupert Murdoch was launching his Sky Television and subsequently took over BSB, the European Commission appeared to be helpless to the leading manufacturers within the EU95 consortium, who were responsible for technically establishing HD-MAC and would depend upon the success of the new technology for recouping their investment. The MAC Directive stipulated that all DBS services transmitted *via* 'high-powered' satellites must adopt the European MAC standard. But the European Commission failed to foresee that Astra, a 'low-powered' communications satellite, could be used by Sky Television to transmit programmes to the old PAL standard. The leading companies within the EU95 HD-MAC consortium accused the EU authorities of having left a loophole in the MAC Directive, which was detrimental to the success of MAC and HD-MAC. The other side of the coin is that this incident demonstrated the extent to which the new TV technologies (i.e., the MAC family) of Europe and the companies behind them were relying upon the power of legislation for their commercial success.

In the beginning of the 1990s digital technology started to point to a new direction for HDTV development. The FCC in the US was quick to embrace the opportunity by making it clear that the future American HDTV standard would be a fully digital one; whilst the European Commission continued to promote its HD-MAC strategy. The European Commission was not prepared to accept the argument that analogue HDTV would be dead soon and digital technology would be the future.[81] Rather, the European Commission proposed an 'Action Plan' which would make €850m available for promoting HD-MAC for a further period of five years (1992-97). Thanks to the British government's strong objection, the 'Action Plan' was watered down to a final sum of €228m in June 1993 on the condition that future EU funding would be available to any widescreen (16/9) programme making to any transmission standard. HD-MAC effectively died in early 1993 when Philips announced that it would halt its planned manufacturing of HD-MAC sets and the European Commission indicated its policy change in favour of digital TV being developed in the United States.

In contrast to the disastrous ending of HD-MAC, DVB, the largest European digital TV consortium, is poised to become the *de facto* European standards family with the possibility of becoming adopted worldwide. DVB offers the flexibility of multichannel broadcasting using different platforms (including digital terrestrial, digital DBS, digital cable networks, etc.). Differing from the EU95 HD-MAC consortium, which excluded participation by non-European companies, such as those from Japan, the DVB consortium was open to any organisation with an interest in digital TV broadcasting. To a certain extent, the rapid development of digital HDTV in the US initially benefited from the FCC policy that foreign firms, European or Japanese, were invited to participate in the research and development process. Foreign firms brought in with them capitals and expertise badly needed for HDTV development in the US. In return, foreign companies, such as Philips and Thomson, were also among the leading members and patents holders in the latest ATSC digital HDTV system, which was officially approved by the FCC as the single HDTV standard for the US in December 1996.

Having learned lessons from the collapse of HD-MAC, the EU at the moment is declined to pick any digital system as the official standard in Europe. Rather, it leaves the standardisation process largely open to market competition. In the meantime, EU policies are now mainly concerned with that digital TV including digital HDTV transmission should become an integral part of the emergent European information and communications technology infrastructure. In other words, new EU policies are moving towards incorporating the traditionally separated information, communication and audiovisual industries into a single sector. Among others, interoperability, common access (e.g. compatible 'set-top boxes') based on new digital techniques are strongly pushed by the European Commission through its information society programme.

Compared to the US and Japan, however, the regulatory process in Europe is much more complicated. On the one hand, the broadcasting industry is still largely governed by the Member States with different regulatory regimes. On the other hand, the adoption of HDTV and other new TV technology standards is increasingly subject to stipulation by EU laws. Therefore, there are pressures on the European authorities from time to time to harmonise European technology policy and regulatory regimes established by individual Member States, whose national interests are often different or even in conflict.[82] It is also known that the same EU regulation is not always implemented to the same extent in different Member States.

At the international level, the shift of HDTV development from analogue systems to digital approaches since the beginning of the 1990s does seem to suggest an opportunity for the international standard bodies, such as the CCIR or the ITU, to play a more active role. However, the digitisation of HDTV production and transmission standards does not necessarily mean that a single global HDTV or digital TV standard would be adopted without further fight. The reason is rather simple: there does not exist an international regulatory body or legal framework to deal with new TV technologies. The establishment of an appropriate regulatory authority at an international level could possibly avoid this from happening without sacrificing the benefit of market competition. However, the complexity of international politics would render this a desirable but at most wishful thinking for the time being. The politics related to the idea of creating a single European Regulatory Authority would discourage any comparable move at the global level.

We are living in an age characterised in part by the digital revolution, which serves as an important dynamic force driving forward the process of globalisation. The emergent global information infrastructure will be increasingly used to facilitate the international flow of capital, information and communications services. This is widely believed to have a significant impact on the way we understand about and interpret the concepts such as national borders and state authorities. In other words, the arrival of the digital age and the process of globalisation dictate that there needs to be an entirely new approach towards the process of innovation. One of the implications of the global competition for HDTV and digital TV standards is that multinational companies might not consider the process of innovation in the same way policy makers think – whilst the European Commission was endeavouring to promote HD-MAC, European multinational companies wasted no time to join the American effort for developing digital HDTV. In a similar way, when the EU authorities were still obsessed with European ownership of new broadcasting technologies, the DVB group has evolved into a truly international club of business organisations and has developed a set of digital TV standards, which had hardly anything in common with the officially supported HD-MAC system in Europe.

This chapter has shown the weaknesses and, arguably, some flaws associated with state interventionism, as manifested in the European activism since the mid-1980s, in terms of technology policy making. Meanwhile, to a great extent, the dynamics of market forces constitutes an important factor in promoting and governing technical change. However, it would be misguided to suggest that the governance of digital technologies should be entrusted entirely to the 'invisible hands'. The global innovation process for the next generation of optical disc-based digital media, as presented in the next chapter, might suggest otherwise.

Notes

[1] An earlier version of this chapter presented at the 18th Annual Conference of the International Association of Media and History (IAMHIS) on *Television and History* at the University of Leeds, 14-17 July 1999.

[2] Erkki Liikanen, European Commissioner in charge of the enterprise and the information society, quoted in *Financial Times*, 16 November 1999.

[3] As PAL and SECAM are compatible now, the world of TV broadcasting is divided into two major technical camps, either NTSC or PAL/SECAM, in terms of transmission standards.

[4] Digital TV, throughout, refers to any fully digital television transmission system such as digital terrestrial TV, digital satellite TV, digital cable TV and digital high definition TV, etc.

[5] *Guardian Education*, 29 October 1996.

[6] In contrast, the conventional colour TV set has an aspect ratio of 4/3.

[7] See Dai, Cawson and Holmes (1994), p. 28.

[8] Note that this is more than two decades earlier than either its European or American Counterparts.

[9] Information is from NHK.

[10] *Ibid.*

[11] As from 1986 until now.

[12] These include NTT, Nippon Electric, Hitachi, Fujitsu, Mitsubishi, Toshiba, Sony, ITT, Fuji, and Tokyo University.

13 After the GI breakthrough in digital compression technology, all major contenders (including the consortium led by Philips and Thomson) in the US responded swiftly by abandoning their analogue systems and changing to fully digital system proposals. The FCC also changed its policy in favour of digital technology. In contrast, the European Commission continued to argue that HD-MAC would not become obsolete and, therefore, further regulatory and financial support to this official European standard was needed. Despite the growing challenge of digital TV technologies coming from within and outside Europe, the European Commission managed to keep HD-MAC untainted until 1993, when it officially announced the Death of the European technology. It is interesting to note that leading European manufacturers, such as Philips, maintained the same argument suggesting that the only system capable of showing HDTV pictures by the mid-1980s was HD-MAC and the same might not be achieved by digital technology. It's clear that the corporate strategy at both Philips and Thomson was to maintain HD-MAC (mainly by government subsidy) and, in the meantime, to become the technology leaders in digital systems in the US with exclusive private investment. For more detailed discussion about European technology policy and corporate strategy towards HDTV and digital TV, see Dai, Cawson and Holmes (1996).

14 Both ministries have now been incorporated into the Ministry of Information Industry.

15 Council of the European Communities (1993a), *Decision on an Action Plan for the Introduction of Advanced Television Services in Europe*, 93/424/EEC, OJ L196, 5 August.

16 *Ibid*.

17 Collins, R. (1994), p. 1, note 1.

18 European Commission information, http://europa.eu.int/scadplus/leg/en/lvb/124109.htm.

19 European Commission (1993a), *White Paper on Growth, Competitiveness, and Employment: The Challenges and Ways forward into the 21st Century*, COM(93) 700 final, Brussels, December.

20 For more detailed discussion about the home video format and the competition between DCC and MiniDisc, see Dai (1996a), *Corporate Strategies, Public Policy and New Technologies*.

21 European Commission, 'Audiovisual Policy', http://europa.eu.int/pol/av/info_en.htm.

22 This includes the Treaty of Rome (1957), the Maastricht Treaty (1993) and the Treaty of Amsterdam (1997).

23 The numbering of EU Treaty articles is based on the consolidated text incorporating the Treaty of Amsterdam.

24 European Commission, 'Audiovisual Policy', *op cit*.

25 The members of the MAC/packet family adopted by the MAC-Directive include C-MAC, D2-MAC, both for DBS, and D-MAC (for cable distribution).

26 Council of the European Communities (1986), *Directive on the Adoption of Common Technical Specifications of the MAC/packet Family of Standards for Direct Satellite Television Broadcasting*, 86/529/EEC, OJ L311, 6 November.

27 The MAC Directive (1986), Article 2.

28 Rupert Murdoch actually used this loophole to launch his DBS services in the UK in 1989, three years after the publication of the MAC Directive. This point will be further discussed later.

29 Council of the European Communities (1992), *Directive on the Adoption of Standards for Satellite Broadcasting of Television Signals*, 92/38/EEC, OJ L137, 20 May.
30 Note that, unlike Japan where daily HDTV broadcasting has been transmitted to the MUSE standard and can be viewed in many public places and some private homes, HDTV broadcasting service to the HD-MAC standard (or, indeed any other standard) has never been launched in Europe.
31 Council of the European Communities (1995), *Directive on the Use of Standards for the Transmission of Television Signals*, 95/47/EC, OJ C281, 23 November.
32 *Ibid.*
33 *Ibid.*
34 Council of the European Communities (1986), the MAC Directive, *op cit.*
35 Council of the European Communities (1989), *Directive on the coordination of certain provisions laid down by law, regulation or administrative action in Member States concerning the pursuit of television broadcasting activities*, 89/552/EEC, OJ L 298, 17 October.
36 *Ibid.*, Article 2(2).
37 *Ibid.*, Article 4(1).
38 European Commission (1999c), *The Development of the Market for Digital Television in the European Union*, COM(1999) 540, 9 November.
39 Information is from http://www.microresearch.be/hdtv/vision1250/index.htm.
40 *Ibid.*
41 Dai, X. (1996a), *Corporate Strategy, Public Policy and New Technologies*, p. 219.
42 Rupert Murdoch certainly explored the difference in wording between 'high-powered' satellite (such as the Marco Polo) used for TV broadcasting and the 'low-powered' satellite (such as the Astra), which he chose to use.
43 *Financial Times*, 5 November 1990.
44 *The Guardian*, 20 April 1991.
45 See *Philips News*, Vol. 21, No. 10, 10 August 1992.
46 *The Economist*, 16 March 1991.
47 It is believed that, in the early days of its operation, BSkyB was losing up to £10m per week.
48 *Guardian Education*, 29 October 1996.
49 Note that BSkyB did not launch its digital broadcasting until about a year later.
50 *Financial Times*, 14 February 1997.
51 The manufacturers are Pace, Nokia, Sony and Panasonic.
52 *Financial Times*, 20 November 1997. This argument seems to have become less substantiated since the end of 1996 when a unanimous conclusion was reached by the Technical Committee of the EBU (European Broadcasting Union) and EACEM (European Association of the Consumer Electronics Manufacturers) on digital television related to access. This conclusion suggests that, in order to make it easiest and cheapest for consumers to receive digital TV services Europe has to achieve as soon as possible a common receiver platform open (or free to air) television. More specifically, the decision emphasises that, as far as the receiver is concerned, any proprietary elements in software and hardware would have to be avoided and standardisation efforts have to be pursued.
53 The reason why News Corp. has chosen MCI as a partner could well be the fact that the latter had spent $682m for the right to the final direct broadcast satellite licence issued by the FCC in 1996. A joint venture with MCI would offer News Corp.

54 immediate access to the MCI DBS licence. The justification behind the launch of SkyMCI was that the Internet was still a low bandwidth world – low bandwidth means low speed for data transmission in an inhospitable world for audio and video. In contrast, satellite-based multimedia services (including audio, video, graphics and text data) could offer the time-conscious business customers faster access to information services.
55 *Financial Times*, 27 February 1997.
56 *The Sunday Times*, 2 March 1997. Note that both *The Sunday Times* and *The Times* are also owned by Rupert Murdoch's News Corp.
57 JSkyB is jointly owned by News Corporation and Softbank Corporation, a major Japanese venture capital company.
58 This proved to be a difficult move and News Corp. later aborted its Indian Venture.
59 Note that StarTV has already got 300 million viewers in the Asian region.
60 China, with a population of close to 1.3 billion (excluding Hong Kong), is widely believed to have the potential of becoming the world's largest and most important TV market.
61 *Financial Times*, 26 February 1997.
62 *The Sunday Times*, 2 March 1997.
63 *Financial Times*, 14 February 2000.
64 *Financial Times*, 15 February 2000.
65 Statement by News Corp., http://www.newscorp.com/public/news/news_101.htm.
66 *Eureka News*, January 1995. http://www.eureka.be/home/ek-news/av-dos.htm.
67 Massachusetts Institute of Technology.
68 More specifically, the Grand Alliance are joined by 7 giant organisations: AT&T, Zenith, GI, MIT, Philips, Thomson, and David Sarnoff Laboratories.
69 European Commission (1999c), *The Development of the Market for Digital Television in the European Union*, COM(1999) 540, 9 November.
70 *The New York Times*, 1 November 1999.
71 *The New York Times*, 12 July 1999.
72 *The New York Times*, 1 November 1999.
73 *The New York Times*, 7 February 2000.
74 As a matter of fact, Peter Kahl, a senior official in the German Federal Ministry of Communications, personally initiated the formation of the European Launching Group for Digital Video Broadcasting in 1991. The Steering Group of DVB was also chaired by Peter Kahl. See Cawson (1995), p. 169.
75 Information on the technical difference between DVB and ATSC is from the DVB Project Office, http://www.dvb.org/.
76 European Commission (1999c), *The Development of the Market for Digital Television in the European Union*, op cit.
77 Ibid.
78 Based on its research and development work, NTL is already able to export its digital compression technology products used for transmission of new digital satellite services with the capacity of 200-500 channels.
79 The regulatory structure for the digital age is not clear at all in the UK. Oftel, for example, the UK government's monitoring organisation responsible for the telecommunications industry, has been arguing that the authority for allocating the new digital terrestrial broadcasting channels should be given to the itself rather than the ITC or any other organisation.

[79] The only exception is that the BBC is a state-owned broadcaster and it has been relying heavily on viewers' licence fee to finance its operation.
[80] European Commission (1999c), *The Development of the Market for Digital Television in the European Union, op cit.*
[81] Interviews with European Commission officials, Brussels, November 1991.
[82] For instance, the French government was always in favour of promoting MAC and HD-MAC; whilst the British government strongly objected to using public money to subsidise new broadcasting technologies at the European level.

7 Global Governance of Innovation: The Case of DVD[1]

Introduction

The most significant drivers of strategic change in the world today are globalisation and technological innovation (Bradley, Hausman and Nolan, 1993). The impact of these two drivers is becoming increasingly profound on companies operating in the new information and communications technology (ICT) sector. One of the widely cited strategic changes of ICT companies today is their gradual adaptation to the information economy and the network society.

On the one hand, companies, in particular those large multinational corporations (MNCs), are reshaping their corporate structure to become truly global organisations taking the advantage of new communications technologies (e.g., telecommunications networks and the Internet), so that corporate headquarters can have effective control over their global operations. On the other hand, thanks to rapid technical change such as digitisation and technological convergence within the ICT sector, a single company would find it increasingly difficult, if not impossible, to control the process of technical change and market development at the global level. This has prompted the wide adoption of a unique type of competitive strategy, i.e., seeking strategic alliance arrangements with competitors. Corporate strategic alliance is, perhaps, best described by the term 'hostile brotherhood' (See Cawson *et al*, 1990).

The information and communications technology sector has seen numerous events of strategic alliances, joint ventures, mergers and takeovers in recent years. Among others, Microsoft recently sought partnerships with British Telecom (BT) and Ericsson of Sweden in order to establish a foothold in telecommunications and the standardisation process for the emergent mobile Internet communications sector respectively. AT&T and BT have agreed to team up in a joint venture to provide global telecommunications services for the MNCs. AT&T has also been the leading player in the much troubled GlobalPartnership for telecommunications. BSkyB has led the establishment of the British Interactive Broadcasting (BIB) consortium, in which BT, the Hong Kong and Shanghai Bank Corporation (HSBC) and Matsushita are the core members. The objective of BIB was to promote a proprietary interactive digital TV standard. The list of strategic alliances within the ICT sector can be a very long one. What is emerging at the moment, at the global level, is a digital communications revolution driven by a cluster of inter-firm business networks. To a large extent, these business networks, often created around a particular new technology or new product or new dimension of service, are poised to control the course of technical change and the development of the global market by means of, for instance, manipulating the process of standardisation or standard setting.

One result of technological innovation, as a *Financial Times* columnist recently commented, is that companies have been able to extend their global reach drastically in recent years (Jackson, 1999). As a matter of course, 'democracies have been slower to respond. Building global institutions, as the WTO [World Trade Organisation] found in Seattle, is tougher than building a global business' (*Ibid.*).

The main objective of this chapter is to explore the extent to which globally networked businesses dictate the course of technical change and market development in a collective manner. It is argued that business networking involving a large number of companies, in the name of promoting global standardisation, within a particular technological domain or market segment has already become a formidable force beyond the political control at the national government level. With the lack of an alternative, i.e., international level of, regulation, the existence of large-scale strategic alliances might be detrimental to competition and consumer interest.

However, the declining or receding control over the process of technical change and, more broadly, globalisation does not necessarily suggest the absence of global 'governance'. Rather, there is a growing trend towards global governance, which is a process of technological and market agenda-setting *via* allied or networked businesses in a global context. This chapter starts with a review of the recent debate about strategic alliances in the next section. This is followed by a brief discussion about the national systems of innovation theory *vis-à-vis* the globalisation argument. Further, these theories are put into test through a major case study on the global standardisation process related to Digital Versatile Disc (DVD), a new digital technology which is poised to revolutionise the video distribution and computer storage media in the near future.

Strategic Alliances and the Governance of Technical Change

Strategic Alliances and the ICT Sector

Compared with the situation several decades ago, new technologies become generally available more quickly since the 1980s; time has become even more of a critical element in corporate strategy and nothing stays proprietary for long and no one player can master everything (Ohmae, 1990). Thus, 'operating globally means operating with partners — and that in turn means a further spread of technology' (Ohmae, 1990, pp. 5-6). Life cycle for new products is becoming increasingly shortened; technologies (e.g. components) and techniques (involved in the manufacturing process) required for new products are becoming increasingly complicated. It is certainly becoming more and more difficult for firms in the hi-tech sectors to survive the competition on their own. In response, strategic alliances and industrial collaboration have been widely adopted by companies to promote new technologies and new products and have, hence, become the most important component of corporate strategy in the 1980s (Mytelka, 1991, p. 15).

According to Hagedoorn (1993), strategic (technology) alliances[2] and partnerships are cooperative agreements which are aimed at improving the long-term perspective of the product market combinations of the companies involved (p. 375). In a slightly different way, Dodgson (1993) defines collaboration as any activity where two or more partners contribute differential resources and know-how to agreed complementary aims (p. 13). There are two main categories of strategic alliance between firms: vertical collaboration and horizontal collaboration (Dodgson, 1993). Vertical collaboration occurs throughout the chain of production for particular products; whist horizontal collaboration occurs between partners at the same level in the production process. Unlike mergers and takeovers, strategic alliances always preserve a relatively large degree of formal decision-making independence for the partners (Gerlach, 1992, p. 3). Sharp (1989) suggests that, while the 1960s and 1970s could well be called 'the Age of National Champion', the 1980s may earn the title of 'the Age of Collaboration' (p. 202). To extend the Sharp argument, the 1990s could be called a decade of networking – both as a means of communication (e.g., the Internet) and a means of competition (e.g. various global business networks promoting technology/product standardisation).

To be sure, since the 1980s, the world have witnessed fierce competition over technological standards at a global scale (at least within the Triad consisting of the US, Western Europe and Japan) as new technologies and products themselves become increasingly globalised (Dai, 1996a). Empirical researches (e.g. Cawson *et al*, 1990; Dai, 1996a) suggest that competition in the consumer electronics industry has been dominated by standards battles or competition for *de facto* formats, which have been fought by large-scale allied corporate groups. In the information technology sector as a whole, many of the strategic partnerships are also centred on standardisation (Delapierre and Zimmerman, 1991). The information-processing products (e.g. complex systems, computing, data storage, data capture, data retrieval and data transfer units) are characterised to a large extent by the nature that even the largest integrated industrial groups can no longer be capable to cover the entire range of applications. Therefore, strategic partnerships are believed to be a positive sum game (*Ibid.*). Gomes-Casseres (1993) shows that, in the computer industry, inter-firm strategic alliances have been increasingly used by leading firms to dramatically change the competitive pattern of this sector at a global level since the early 1980s.

Some argue that alliances are worth the effort and properly managed alliances are among the best mechanisms that companies have found to bring strategy to bear in global markets (Ohmae, 1990, p. 136).

Why Strategic Alliance?

There are a number of reasons why firms, particularly those MNCs, have joined forces through strategic alliances and industrial collaboration. Among others, the following aspects are widely discussed in the literature in terms of explaining the reasons behind strategic alliances:

First of all, strategic alliance is a strategic response by firms to the challenges brought by technical change. The process of technical change enabled by digitisation has led to the convergence of products, industrial sectors and markets. In turn, the convergence phenomenon has made previously sector- or product-specific strategies of firms much less effective. This is particularly the case of the European consumer electronics and semiconductor industries, and increasingly so of the European telecommunications industry. As Morgan (1989) suggests, at the forefront of technological change, the convergence of computer and telecommunications has made the previously single-product service — voice telephony — grow into a diversity of services — voice, data, video, facsimile (p. 19). Consequently, 'firms are increasingly looking towards cooperative solutions in the form of mergers, joint ventures, and alliances' (Cawson *et al.*, 1990, p. 377). Strategic alliances allow the systematic combination of distinctly specialised skills to be achieved, and it enables participating firms to remain competitive by creating the flexibility needed to react to a changing environment and by enhancing the capacity to manage the process of change itself (Delapierre and Zimmerman, 1991, p. 108).

It is argued that, compared with conventional competitive strategies, strategic alliances are often an effective and efficient way for firms to obtain access to certain specialised assets needed for technical innovation (e.g. Teece, 1986; Jorde and Teece, 1992a; Dodgson, 1993). Technical change extends not only sectoral boundaries but also the boundaries of the firm and, therefore, without participating in inter-firm cooperative arrangements even the most advanced companies may lose their leadership position (Dodgson, 1989, pp. 6-7).

Secondly, in the age of globalisation, internationally organised corporate alliances are fast becoming one of the driving forces to the development of an 'internationally linked economy' (Ohmae, 1990). As far as companies are concerned, 'the pattern is obvious: a product, non-equity-dependent set of arrangements through which globally active companies can maximise the contribution to their fixed costs. These alliances are an important part of the way companies get back to strategy' (Ohmae, 1990, pp. 127-128).

Thirdly, an 'internationally linked economy' certainly becomes a pressure, as well as an opportunity, for firms to internationalise their operation. It is argued that internationalisation through alliance, rather than equity investment, is more cost effective. In making acquisition, the acquirer must pay both for the critical skills it wants and for skills it may already have hence the costs and problems of integrating cultures and harmonising policy prove much larger in an acquisition than that in an alliance (Hamel and Prahalad, 1993, p. 80). Contrary to this, the growth of global competition in technology-related areas makes the strategy of sole reliance on internally financed and internally conducted R&D insufficient and perhaps suicidal (Link and Tassey, 1987, p. 10).

Fourthly, strategic alliance is a necessary and important way of co-opting potential competitors to fight for the same course. This is particular the case when a new technological standard is being established. 'Enticing a potential competitor into a fight against a common enemy, working collectively to establish a new standard or develop a new technology, building a coalition around a particular legislative issue — in these and other cases, the goal is to co-opt the resources of other companies and thereby extend one's own influence' (Hamel and Prahalad, 1993, p. 82).

Finally, inter-firm collaboration may reduce the cost for research and development (R&D) associated with new technologies. 'The development of new technological systems is extremely costly. ... It is very difficult for one firm independently to cover the risks of such a financial burden. This provides another reason for the increased emphasis on collaboration within industry. Firms increasingly are looking for complementary funds from within industry and from government' (Dodgson, 1989, p. 4).

Although there are a large number of motives for firms to engage in partnership, Hagedoorn (1993) argues that two basic categories, i.e., market and technology-related motives are predominant (p. 381). Alic (1990) suggests that the most important among the factors leading to cooperation in R&D are the risks of independent efforts and the costs of continued participation in some technologies (p. 327).

After all, it is probably the unknown likelihood of success in research that leads some companies to combine their efforts (Hagedoorn, 1993). In other words, strategic alliances and other forms of inter-firm collaborations are critical to technological standardisation, which is a prerequisite for almost all types of complex products or systems to succeed. At the pre-competitive R&D stage, industrial collaboration plays an important role to ensure harmonisation of technical solutions and enable participating firms to develop compatible products (Mytelka, 1991a, p. 197). This point is shared by Dodgson:

> With many new technical standards being created, both domestic and international, firms may feel their cases for the adoption of particular technical standards may be improved by their promotion by a number of firms, rather than singly. ... Collaboration provides an effective mechanism for the joint creation and promotion of standards (1993, p. 30).

Competition, Collaboration and the Role of the State

Reasons or motivations for firms to participate in strategic alliance might be many-fold. But the ultimate objective of strategic alliances is to strengthen partners' competitive position. However, there is no guarantee that strategic alliances are always not anti-competitive. For this reason, there might be argument for the state's involvement in technology-related alliances.

The role of the state in inter-firm collaboration may be understood from the following points:

First, in order to improve the so-called 'national competitiveness', in many cases the state is the 'sponsor' or 'promoter' of inter-firm collaborations. Since the 1980s, it is often the development of technology policies that best exemplify the role the state plays as promoters of strategic partnership (Mytelka, 1991, p. 25). Some of the widely cited and typical examples are the defence-related institutions in the United States, ministries of finance [MOF], industry [MITI] and telecommunications [MPT] in Japan,[3] ministries of industry and of research and development in France and DG XIII in the European Union. These are exclusively powerful technology policy makers. It is believed that the 1980s witnessed a 'veritable explosion' of government-supported research (Levy and Samuels, 1991). National and supra-national governments have used a variety of methods to actively promote technological collaboration, including the formation of research associations and consortia, the relaxation of legislative restrictions, the creation of a variety of technology transfer organisations, and taxation policies (Dodgson, 1993, p. 87).

Second, strategic alliances, in many cases, show a degree of government-business collusion. It is argued that inter-business cooperation in recent years is encouraged by policymakers in each country to enhance economies of scale and by creating linkages between their domestic firms rather than between their own firms and foreign firms (Alic, 1990, p. 320). In other words, there is a perception that domestic firms best represent national economic interest. However, against this kind of parochial government thinking, as some scholars argue, cooperation among competitors itself will not necessarily enable firms to rebuild their competitiveness or, even worse, will undermine competitive advantages (Alic, 1990, p. 330; Porter, 1990, p. 122).

The worst case, perhaps, is that R&D 'cooperation' among private firms has sometimes shaded off into behaviour seemingly aimed at retarding rather than accelerating technological progress (Alic, 1990, p. 322). Whilst strategically managed inter-firm associations can promote the long-term development and competitiveness of a sector; non-strategically managed inter-firm associations will likely have the opposite effect (1990, pp. 18-19).

Government-business collusion is often established in activities associated with standards setting in favour of domestic firms. It is true that parallel standards can exist side-by-side and there is obviously the case of *de facto* standards controlled by single firms. However, there are also examples of collusion on the part of firms and governments to provide exclusionary standards. This exclusion of non-participants (competitors) in the process of standards formation may explain why firms feel the pressure to collaborate to avoid the high costs of them not doing so (Dodgson, 1993, p. 78).

Third, although cooperative R&D programmes/projects in many cases are government mediated or sponsored, strategic alliance and industrial collaboration have their limit in terms of anti-trust legislation or competition policy. American antitrust law, for instance, holds that imperfect competition and inter-firm cooperation, including cartels, increase prices and reduce innovation (Best, 1990, p. 17). Therefore, it is widely recognised that the ability of innovating firms to cooperate by entering into alliances, often raises issues in antitrust as do other elements of business strategy (Jorde and Teece, 1992, p. 6).

As a matter of fact, international inter-firm collaboration extends beyond sharing the heavy financial (and intellectual) burden of R&D, and includes manufacturing and marketing (Dodgson, 1989, p. 5). In other words, collaboration can promote cartelisation and oligopoly and raise entry barriers to new entrants (Dodgson, 1993, p. 25). Even at the pre-competitive stage, inter-firm collaboration may have an anti-competitive element. Whilst the state is busy in supporting and promoting domestic inter-firm collaboration for the advancement of new technologies, they should always be alerted of the potential violation of competition rules and consumer interests by the industrial partnerships.

In the future, as Michalet (1991) suggests, the world economy will likely witness an even greater number of state entities participating in alliances alongside private firms on the one hand; and it is also likely that the state will be needed to guarantee or supervise the rules of the game developed by the members of the alliances and insure a minimal compatibility between the various standards set up by competing business coalitions on the other (p. 48). In other words, the state is likely to be both the rule maker and the player of the game.

Finally, multinational corporations represent an important force driving forward globalisation and technologies are becoming stateless. Given that the MNCs and new technologies, such as new information and communications technologies, do not show much respect for national borders, is there any significant role to be played by the state?

Michalet (1991) argues that the old internalised structure of multinational firms was based on hierarchy, whilst the 'network firms' or 'hollow corporations' favour horizontal relationships like those developed in Japanese companies (p. 46). Michalet (1991) concludes that, first, the complex structure of network firms and alliances will determine the emerging 'contractual economy'; second, competition will shift from firms struggling directly against one another for market shares to a new type of cartel structure based on technology; and, finally, market access for a firm will be determined by its position as a partner in network or alliance. If this argument is convincing, there is, perhaps, not very much room left for the state to manoeuvre, apart from that government agencies may have opportunities to participate in globally organised consortia or alliances led by private firms.

What implications may we draw upon the coming of the globalised network age? Does this mean the death of the much-advocated 'national innovation systems'?

National Innovation Systems and Globalisation

Recent debate centred on the 'national system of innovation' as opposed to the 'globalisation' argument constitutes another dimension for examining the process of governance for new technologies and innovation.

The theory of 'national system of innovation' suggests that the influence of factors such as the national education system, industrial relations, technical and scientific institutions, government policies, cultural traditions and many other national institutions are fundamental to successful innovation (Freeman, 1995, p. 5). It is argued that the economies that have benefited most from inward international technology transfer have national innovation systems that have strengthened their national absorptive capacity (Mowery and Oxley, 1995, p. 67). Although the notion of national innovation systems has been developed looking at industrially advanced countries, it does have important implications for developing and transitional economies (Archibugi and Michie, 1995a, p. 3).

In the meantime, another literature suggests that the process of globalisation generates great impact upon the process of innovation. In many cases the process of globalisation of technology and innovation is led by multinational corporations (MNCs), i.e. the technology leaders (Cantwell, 1995). Differing from the 'national innovation systems' argument, the 'techo-globalism' theory of innovation advocates that the international transmission of technology has become an effective alternative to the internal production of knowledge and, therefore, allows firms to avoid research duplication (Archibugi and Michie, 1995a). More specifically, the globalisation of technology and innovation means: a) *global exploitation of technology* – an increasing proportion of technological innovation is exploited in international markets; b) *global technological collaboration* – international collaboration between firms for sharing know-how with competitors from different countries, along with a parallel process of international collaboration between governments and the academic community; c) *global generation of technology* – firms, particular MNCs, are increasing the international integration of their research and development (R&D) and technological activities (Archibugi and Michie, 1995b, p. 125).

What seems most relevant to this chapter is the 'global exploitation of technology'. Multinational firms, and groups of them, with incompatible technical standards targeting the same international market have found collaboration, rather than head-to-head competition, is a less risky strategy. In the case presented in this chapter, the factors prompted the multinational firms to join forces are not technical or the burden of R&D cost on each firm or each group of firms. Rather, firms are more concerned with the possibility of losing out in the standard battle associated with a particular category of products.

By pursuing international collaboration with competitors, multinational firms have no respect for national borders. In the digital age, the information and communications technology sector is characterised by a process of digital convergence based on new digitisation techniques. This has made the ICT sector essentially a global industry and the individual national markets are being integrated into a global market. Globalisation is certainly a phenomenon largely created by global firms with ubiquitous global technologies/products and, therefore, very much favoured by these firms. When Microsoft has the opportunity to sell the same Windows operating system to a global market, there will be hardly any incentive for the company to invest in different operating systems for different national markets (apart from adapting its product to the local language environment with insignificant modification).

It seems that globalisation of technologies and market has made the 'national systems of innovation' increasingly less relevant to the process of technical change. If this is the case, could the innovation process in the world now be left entirely in the hands of market forces? Or, is the global innovation process already controlled by the allied commercial organisations? The case of Digital Versatile Disc innovation shows the degree to which allied commercial forces have staged a worldwide campaign for creating a global consumer market for the new technology. The implications of this process are significant to the understanding about the issues related to the digital revolution and governance.

Networks of Global Governance: Managing DVD Innovation

Standard setting for new communications technologies is one of the most important features of the ICT sector throughout history. In many cases, and increasingly, standard setting for new communications systems is achieved by competing groups of allied corporate organisations. The most recent stage of development in optical disc technology, i.e., Digital Versatile Disc

(DVD), appears to be an interesting case in which the innovation process was manoeuvred at the global level by international businesses through alliances. DVD is currently being promoted by leading consumer electronics manufacturers, the film industry and the computer industry.

With the size (12cm in diameter) of a standard compact disc, DVD discs can be used to store digitised film, video and multimedia programmes. Thanks to the high storage capacity, DVD is widely believed important to many domains of the digital communications sector (e.g. consumer electronics, the computer industry and the film studios).

The competition for DVD standardisation was initially between too rivalry camps: one side was lead by Philips and Sony, and the other side by Toshiba and Time Warner. This new format battle was reminiscent of the VCR (Video Cassette Recorder) format battle of the late 1970s and early 1980s, when incompatible formats competed fiercely for the same consumer electronics market. The format battle for VCR has ended with the global acceptance of the VHS system and the rejection of the Betamax and V2000 systems. The failure of V2000 and Betamax was a hard lesson for the companies that had developed the defeated systems.

Competition and collaboration for standardisation in digital media continued to provide valuable lessons for corporate strategic planning at multinational corporations in the 1980s and early 1990s. By pooling resources, Philips and Sony achieved huge success in launching the Compact Disc (CD) digital audio standard in the beginning of the 1980s. But subsequent developments of CD-based products/systems have been subject to format battles or lack of compatibility with each other. CD-ROM, the 'Yellow Book' standard, has many varieties to meet the computer industry's need for information/data storage purpose. CD-i (Compact Disc interactive), the third generation of CD-based technology jointly defined by Philips and Sony, was only one of the competing formats for the multimedia industry during the first half of the 1990s. Similar multimedia technologies, such as CD-i, 3DO (promoted by Matsushita) and CDTV (Compact Disc Total Vision, later changed into CD32, developed by Commodore), etc., were all capable of offering full-screen full-motion digital video mixed with other types of information stored on the same compact disc. The lack of industry-wide standard for digital interactive multimedia was largely to blame for the eventual failure of all of the competing systems.

The digital media sector is characterised by constant innovation. In the early 1990s, both Philips and Sony attempted to bring out a 'recordable' system for digital audio to complement compact disc, which was not recordable. This has led to another format battle between, this time, Philips and Sony – two collaborating partners for the CD format. More specifically, Philips has developed its Digital Compact Cassette (DCC) system, which was backward compatible with the analogue compact cassette. In Japan, Sony engineers reduced the size of compact disc from 12cm to 8cm in diameter and developed the MiniDisc (MD), a smaller version of CD but capable of recording up to 74 minutes of digital audio. The two new digital audio systems have been competing in the marketplace since the mid-1990s. Although Philips' DCC machine at one time reached the retailing stores, it has failed to become an established standard and has eventually become an unwanted product. Sony's MiniDisc system has, very slowly, found some niche markets (e.g. pocket-sized digital recording/playback products and in-car digital audio systems), it is not certain at all whether Sony could eventually claim a victory.

The arrival of DVD technologies in the mid-1990s heralded a new wave of global competition for digital video and interactive multimedia.

Having experienced the success in launching the CD format for digital audio, Philips and Sony wished to achieve a comparable victory with DVD. Multimedia CD (MMCD), jointly proposed by Philips, Sony and 3M as a new generation of computer data storage medium to replace CD-ROM but also has an application for the consumer electronics industry, was announced in 1994. Under the Philips/Sony/3M proposal, a single-layered DVD disc has the capacity of storing up to 3.7 gigabytes of data or 135 minutes of digital video of broadcasting quality. This is about five times the capacity of a standard music CD or CD-ROM – each offers 650 megabytes of storage capacity. It is also possible, as claimed by the MMCD group, a dual-layered DVD disc can double the storage capacity of the single-layered version to store 7.4 gigabytes of digital data.

The lucrative market potential promised by DVD immediately attracted competition. Shortly after the establishment of the MMCD group, a competing system, called Super Density disc (SD), was announced by an industrial consortium, the SD Alliance led by Toshiba and Time Warner in early 1995. The SD Alliance proposed a competing DVD standard using two super-thin discs, glued together, with half of the thickness of a normal Compact Disc. Two sides of the SD disc are capable of storing up to 10 gigabytes data — 5 gigabytes on each side.

Using similar technologies, both the MMCD and SD systems were backward compatible with CD digital audio. However, the MMCD and SD systems were not compatible with each other! It seemed that a new format battle would take place between the MMCD group and the SD Alliance in early 1995. Meanwhile, the two competing camps were faced with great uncertainties and pressures:

Firstly, a new format battle would likely confuse the market and, therefore, lead to the failure of the DVD technology as a whole without any winner. This is exactly what had happened to the CD-based multimedia technologies and, to a certain extent, the DCC/MiniDisc competition in the 1990s.

Secondly, having experienced the insufficient standardisation for CD-ROM, the computer industry wanted to have a single industry-wide system for DVD as a new generation of optical data storage product. A group of leading hardware and software companies in the United States, including Apple, IBM, Compaq, Hewlett-Packard and Microsoft, has specified their requirements that both the MMCD and SD formats should meet.[4]

The on-going digital revolution suggests that digital video, rather than analogue video represented by the VHS standard, will be the future. As a matter of fact, digital video was the 'Holy Grail', for which the electronics industry had been searching. With its technical and market potential, it would be a highly lucrative proposition for a single company or a single group of companies to become the technological owner(s) for DVD and, therefore, a format battle would seem a worthwhile risk. Meanwhile, because of the high stake associated with DVD, the risk of losing the format might be too high to be born by any single company or allied companies on either side. As indicated by the recent history of the consumer electronics industry, it is not impossible that the market would only choose one format and reject the other ones (e.g. the VCR format battle); or, even worse, none of the competing systems get accepted (e.g. the interactive multimedia format battle).

Faced with the great uncertainties associated with the DVD standardisation process, and under the pressure from the computer industry, the two competing groups – the MMCD group and the SD Alliance – eventually decided to end the format battle and work together on a single DVD standard. In December 1995, the DVD Consortium was established with 10 founding members as follows:

- Hitachi, Ltd.
- Matsushita Electric Industrial Co. Ltd.
- Mitsubishi Electric Corporation
- Philips Electronics N.V.
- Pioneer Electronic Corporation
- Sony Corporation
- Thomson Multimedia

- Time Warner Inc.
- Toshiba Corporation
- JVC (Victor Company of Japan, Ltd.)

Figure 7.1 The DVD Forum organisational structure

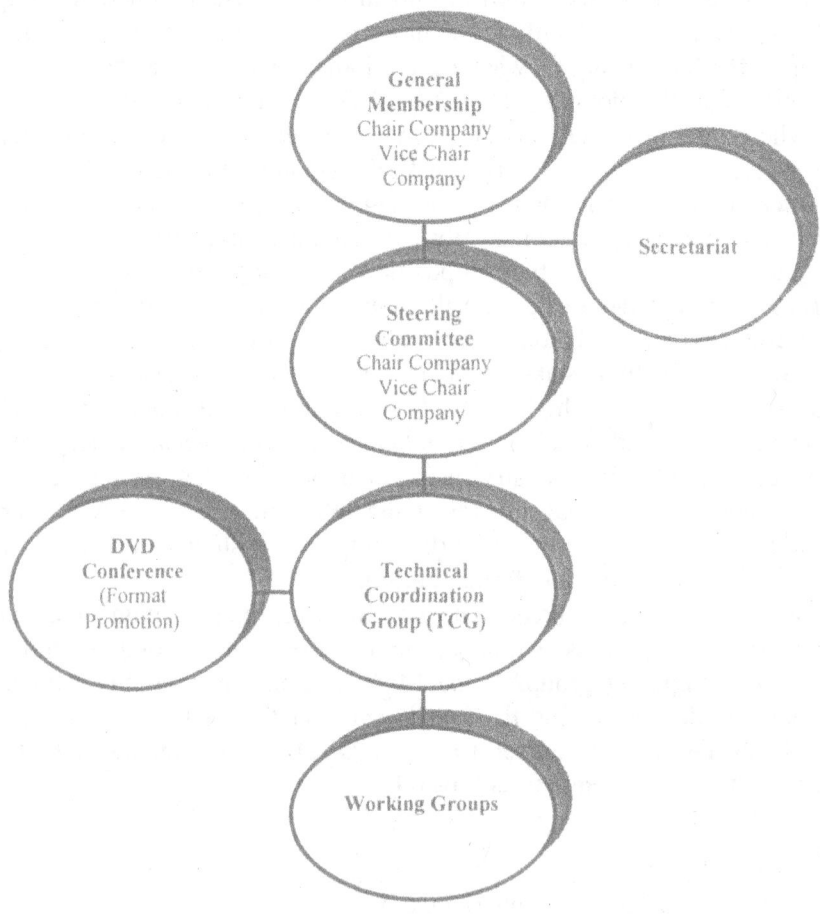

Source: Adapted from http://www.dvdforum.org/.

Upon the merging the two competing standards, the name of the technology, i.e. DVD, has been changed from 'Digital Video Disc' into 'Digital Versatile Disc'. The technical specifications of the single global standard for DVD would be derived from both the original MMCD and SD formats. From the outset the DVD Consortium has assigned itself the mission 'to establish the single DVD Format for each of the DVD application products, including revisions, improvements and enhancements, that would be in the best interests of consumers and users'.[5] In April 1997, the DVD Consortium decided to change itself into a more open organisation renamed as the 'DVD Forum.' The change was intended to attract more companies to join the international DVD association.

According to the DVD Forum, over 200 companies worldwide, including hardware manufacturers from consumer electronics and PC industries, software firms and media companies have become members of the organisation now.[6]

Within the DVD Forum, principal members, by paying an annual membership fee of one million Japanese yen, are entitled to participate in format-making activities in Working Groups, and to access to the technical information developed through the format-making activities. Associate members, each paying 300,000 yen per year to the DVD Forum, are entitled to access to Working Group activity reports, which are issued from time to time. In addition, associate members are entitled to participate in promotional conferences held by the Forum free of charge.

The core of the DVD Forum is the 'Steering Committee', which initially consisted of the 10 founding members. In May 1998, seven new companies, i.e., IBM Corporation, Research Institute for Industry Technology of Taiwan, Intel Corporation, LG Electronics Inc., NEC Corporation, Samsung Electronics Co., Ltd. and Sharp Corporation, also became members of the 'Steering Committee'.

The expansion of the membership in the 'Steering Committee', in particular the joining forces by IBM, Intel, NEC, Samsung and LG Electronics, suggests that the DVD Forum has now been strongly backed by both the computer and semiconductor industries. The original 10 founding members are mainly consumer electronics manufacturers plus one major Hollywood company (Time Warner).

DVD, backed by a large number of allied corporate organisations, is now poised to become the next most important consumer product. Hollywood studios, most of which initially rejected the new digital media format in fear of losing revenue from illegal copying, are now ready to use DVD as an important re-distribution format. By the end of 1999, no less than 4,300 DVD titles had been released in the United States alone.

The relationship, however, between the consumer electronic manufacturers from the DVD Forum and the Hollywood studios was a complicated one. The American film companies' reluctance in releasing their films through DVD discs was initially a major concern of the DVD

Forum. It is evident that the film industry did not want to lose control over the release of their films and they would not support any technology, which does not offer adequate copyright protection.

Figure 7.2   Map of DVD regional management code

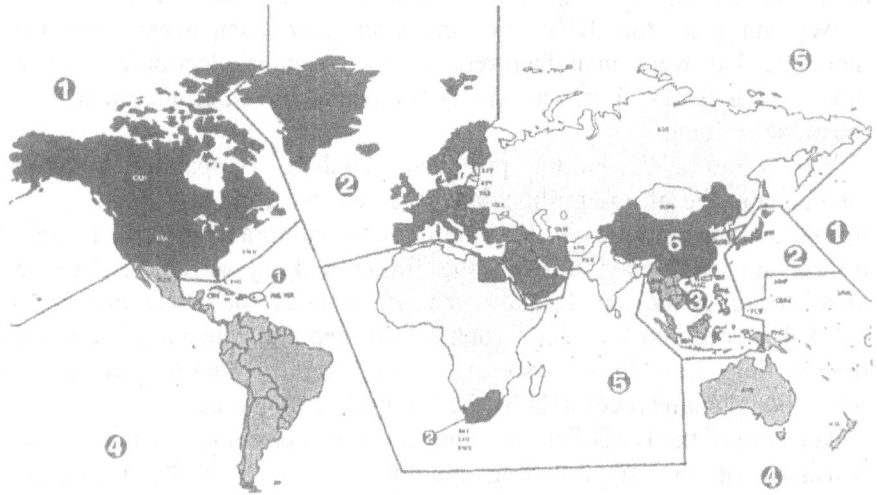

Source: http://www.unik.no/~robert/hifi/dvd/world.html.

Figure 7.3   DVD regional playback control code

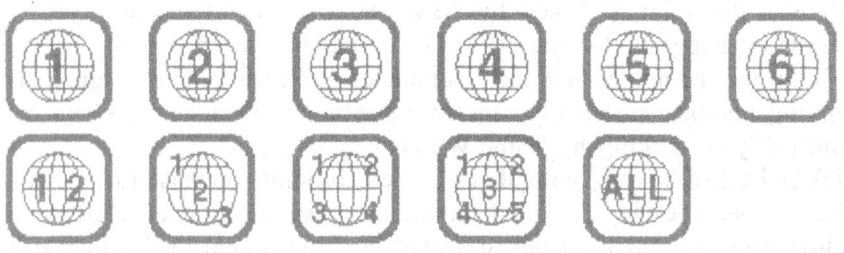

Source: http://www.epod-dvdvideo.com/.

Under pressure from the film industry, the DVD Forum agreed that the DVD players and discs would carry a unique 'regional code', which identifies the origin of the product with a particular 'region' and prevents it from being used in other 'regions'. Under the 'new deal' between the consumer electronics industry and the film industry, the world market has been divided into 6 different 'Regions' (or 'zones'). For instance, Region 1 is North America; Region 2 is Europe, Japan, the Middle East and South Africa, etc. Most DVD discs will have a 'globe' with one or more numbers on it to clearly indicate the region(s) in which the discs are playable. If the number(s) is different from that shown on the player, the disc can not be played with this particular DVD machine. In theory, if a consumer wishes to be able to enjoy any DVD disc bought from any part of the world, he or she needs to purchase six DVD players bearing six different regional codes!

Moreover, the film industry has demanded that DVD players should be made in line with division of the colour TV standards. Therefore,

> Most U.S. players only support NTSC video while most European players support both NTSC and PAL. In order to play a disc the player needs to support both the region and the video format. This means that most players in the USA can't play a European release even if the player has been modified to become a multi-regional player.[7]

In the UK, at the moment, most retailers only supply DVD video machines with a single European regional code. This means British consumers would not be able to use American DVD discs on their machine. A way to get round this restriction is to spend an additional £80 at some retailing stores to have a multi-regional chip set added (by special order) to the machine so that it can playback disc from abroad.[8] This suggests that the regional division of DVD manufacturing is purely a commercial consideration, rather than a technical necessity. Some retailers suggested that they had been promised by suppliers with a recordable version of DVD machines by the Christmas period of 1999 but this has been postponed by at least another two years.[9] Among other reasons, the delay of recordable DVD machines could be explained by the film industry's concern over copyright right.

Contrary to the DVD Forum's goal, which is to provide the world with a single standard, the world is firstly divided into six incompatible 'regions' or 'zones' and then further divided into two worlds according TV broadcasting standards (i.e., PAL/SECAM and NTSC). Protection of copyright in the information age is certainly an important issue to consider but the complicated regional management structure for the DVD industry might only add additional inconvenience and extra costs to the consumers. There is a need for further political debate on the balance between copyright protection and protecting consumer interest. As far as the result of the DVD standardisation process is concerned, DVD perhaps stands for 'Digitally Very Divided'!

Conclusion

Strategic alliances among corporate organisations have proved a key feature of the standardisation process at the global level. The DVD case shows that, due to the uncertainties associated with the outcome of the market, the standardisation process for new digital communications systems is likely more achievable by cooperation, rather than competition, among the key players. Under pressures from the computer industry, the two initially competing camps, the MMCD format group and the SD Alliance with the Super Density disc format, agreed to merge the two systems and create a single global standard for digital video. This is reminiscent of the creation of the Grand Alliance in the US in the early 1990s, which effectively ended the three originally competing consortia in developing a national digital TV standard. Competition will likely produce winners and losers whilst, in contrast, strategic alliance or inter-firm collaboration can in many cases avoid victimising any competitor – every partner could be winner to share the rent to be generated from successful collective effort in innovation.

With the rapid development of digitisation, technological/product convergence and market liberalisation, the new information and communications technology sector will be increasingly characterised by a growing number of corporate strategic alliances between firms. There will be continued concern over monopoly by a single corporate giant in certain domains of the new ICT sector. However, the growing size and changing pattern of the new digital communications world would make it increasingly unattainable for any corporate organisation to single-handedly control the innovation process and the global market. Big companies, such as Microsoft, AT&T, BT, BSkyB, etc., had to seek alliances with their competitors in order to survive the competition.

Although there are justifications for corporate strategic alliances in promoting new technologies and many governments, often with public subsidy in their hands, have extended their support to collaborative R&D programmes, it is worth noting that such ventures are sometimes achieved at the expense of competition and, therefore, consumer interests. The DVD Forum, involving over 200 firms, was established with the promise of creating one single standard for consumers worldwide. However, the standardisation process has ended up with the division of the world into six 'regions', and each is assigned with a 'regional code' incompatible with other 'regions'. In the DVD case, the leading consumer electronics manufacturers have colluded with the film industry and staged a remarkable campaign to manipulate the course of technical change and the development of the consumer market by means of standard setting.

Standard setting for DVD was a globalised process with leading players from many parts of the world collaborating in a well organised network. However, this globalised process is shadowed by the DVD regional code management structure. MNCs and new communications technologies are widely viewed the driving forces behind globalisation. However, when corporate powers, particularly allied or networked corporate powers such as the DVD Forum and the film industry, dictate the global agenda for technical change and innovation, this power is already beyond the control of any national government. Meanwhile, there is no alternative regulatory body at the global level to take on this kind of power. There is a widespread feeling that companies are assuming vast and unaccountable powers, while governments are losing their grip (Jackson, 1999). In politics, however, many governments and politicians continue to advocate that the private sector should play a leading role in the digital age:

> ... [T]he pace of change both in the technology and the marketplace frequently outstrips the ability of the government to anticipate the perils of a fast growing field. This is why I continue to believe that the private sector must play a vital leadership role.[10]

At a time when national governments, individuals and various non-governmental organisations are trying to come to terms with the impact of globalisation and the digital communications revolution, the case of DVD does offer some invaluable lessons.

Notes

[1] An earlier draft of this chapter was presented at the British International Studies Association (BISA) 24th Annual Conference, UMIST, Manchester, 20th – 22nd December 1999.

[2] Dodgson (1993) treats 'alliances', 'collaboration, 'cooperative agreements' and 'network' as synonyms.

[3] According to Levy and Samuels (1991), cooperative research consortia (each of them is often participated by more than dozens of firms) and other industrial alliances in Japan are also coordinated or/and funded by other public authorities such as the STA (Science and Technology Agency), the Ministry of Education, Mombusho (Science and Culture) (p. 122).

[4] These include nine requirements for DVD, i.e., single standard for TV- and PC-based applications; backward compatibility with current CDs; forward compatibility with future read/write and write-once discs; a single file system for both entertainment and PC-based content and for read-only, read/write. write-once discs; cost comparable to current CD-ROM drives and discs at equivalent volumes; no mandatory container (caddy or cartridge); reliable data storage and retrieval for read-only, read/write and

write-once media; high capacity extendible with future enhancement; high performance for both sequential (e.g. movies) and non-sequential (e.g. random-access computer data) files.

5. DVD Forum at http://www.dvdforum.org/.
6. http://www.dvdforum.org/.
7. http://www.unik.no/~robert/hifi/dvd/world.html.
8. The author's communication with electrical retailers Nuway (Hull), 13 December 1999. A Toshiba DVD player is currently priced at under £270 (product model: SD2109B) at Comet. The multi-regional chip set would increase the cost by almost one third. Nuway suggested consumers can buy this chip set themselves but as soon as they have fixed the component into the machine the manufacturer's product guarantee would become invalid.
9. The author's communication with electrical retailer Comet Group (Hull), 13 December 1999.
10. Al Gore, quoted in US Government (1999), *Towards Digital eQuality*, 2nd Annual Report by the Working Group on Electronic Commerce.

8 Conclusion

The aim of this book has been to investigate the politics of the digital age with a focus on the interplay between the changes in new information and communications technologies and governance. This has been achieved from two different but inter-related perspectives. First, in Part I of this book, the discussion was centred on what opportunities new information and communications technologies or, more broadly, the information society has brought with it for exploring new modes of governance. Second, in Part II of the book, the issue of who governs the process of the digital revolution was studied. The book, therefore, makes an up-to-date contribution towards the understanding about the impact of the digital revolution on governance on the one hand and the governance of the digital revolution on the other.

In order to achieve in-depth understanding about the impact of the digital revolution on governance, the European Union and China have been chosen as two case studies in Part I. Although both the EU and China have their unique characteristics in terms of their policies and strategies towards the digital revolution, they, to a certain extent, represent the western industrialised countries and the developing nations respectively. From the experiences of the EU and China it could be concluded that that the digital revolution does have a profound impact on the current power structure and public policy making process in both the industrialised and developing countries. What seems an interesting and noteworthy point underlying the first half of the book was the high level of awareness policy makers in both the industrialised and the developing worlds had shown of the potential of new ICTs to enhancing governance. The cases have shown that public authorities in the EU and China were not only fully aware of the process and potential of the digital revolution but also actively engaged in promoting the development and usage of new technologies to their advantage.

More specifically, Chapters 2 & 3 examined the extent to which the digital revolution has affected European governance since the early 1990s. Based on detailed analysis of the policy making process, Chapter 2 particularly argued that the launch and promotion of the information society programme in Europe was a concerted campaign to advance the course of European integration in the digital age. By putting forward its new vision and strategy on the so-called 'Common Information Area', 'European Information Society' and '*e*Europe', etc., the European Commission has played a remarkable co-ordinating role at the European level. As a matter of fact, the European Commission's vision has been responded in a very positive way by the public authorities at the national and local government levels in the Member States.

Further to the above discussion, it was argued in Chapter 3 that European politics has already been evidently characterised by the so-called 'network society'. In parallel with and on the basis of the new technological networks of digital communications, a large number of policy networks have been established under the EU's information society programme. The new policy networks, such as the 'erisa' (European Regional Information Society Association) and the TeleCities consortia were found to have constituted a new mode of European governance. Each of these new policy networks was joined by a large lumber of European regional or local governments with the political and financial support from the European Commission. These local and regional governments were able to engage themselves in not only a process of transnational collaboration with each other but also, in an unprecedented way, in the European policy making process *via* these policy networks. Meanwhile, with the prospect of offering the policy network members financial resources, the European Commission could effectively use these policy networks to disseminate EU policy and strategies pertinent to the information society.

Undoubtedly, the digital revolution and the emergence of the network society have provided a new opportunity for exploring new modes of European governance. New information and communications technologies are widely viewed throughout the European Union as a new source of dynamics needed for creating an 'ever closer Community'. However, the role of new ICTs should not be exaggerated; technologies might not be the panacea for all the economic, political and social problems the EU currently faces. Whilst new ICTs could be used for improved and new mode of governance, they have also brought with them new challenges for efficient governance. Among others, the transnational flow of digital information and communication as well as electronic commerce threaten to render the conventional pattern of governance at the national government level obsolete. In the meantime, there is a lack of EU level regulatory authorities dealing with the overall ICT sector. Apparently, there is neither the political willingness nor the necessary resources to create such a regulatory authority at the EU level.

In contrast with the European experience, the case study about China presented in Chapter 4 suggests that informatisation of the national economy has become an important feature of the Chinese government's new industrial policy. By constructing a high-speed information superhighway and promoting the applications of new ICTs within both the public and private sectors, China has embarked upon an entirely new course for economic development since the early 1990s.

In view of the accelerated trend of technological convergence driven by digitisation, the Chinese government undertook a major restructuring of its administrative structure. An important aspect of the government-restructuring programme was the creation of a super-ministry, i.e., the Ministry of Information Industry (MII). The MII has incorporated a number of previously independent (and sometimes competing) ministries such as the Ministry of Posts and Telecommunications, Ministry of Electronic Industry, Ministry of Broadcasting, Film and Television, etc. It can be said that the creation of the MII was in part an 'institutional convergence' in response to the technological convergence. Unfortunately, China's 'institutional convergence' has not led to more efficient governance as demonstrated by the case of IP telephony. When Internet users were able to make international telephone calls bypassing the MII's telephone exchanges, the MII felt its power and vested interests were threatened and the police responded by taking these users to the court.

The second set of cases presented in Part II of the book dealt with three major domains of the digital revolution: the Internet (Chapter 5), digital TV (Chapter 6) and Digital Versatile Disc (DVD, Chapter 7). The purpose of Part II was to analyse the role played by different players in manipulating the process of technical change contributing to the digital revolution. Among others, key players identified in these case studies included government forces (as manifested in policies and regulations), international business organisations (e.g. multinational firms and the alliances among them) and individual political activists (e.g. pro-democracy and human rights campaigners and their organisations). All of these players showed a strong interest and seemed to have a stake in the process and outcomes of the digital revolution.

With a focus on China, Chapter 5 demonstrated the growing importance of the Internet as a political tool for both government and anti-government forces. In order to maintain the current power structure (with the Communist Party being the absolute ruling authority) government forces were determined to put the Internet under their control. Given the nature of the Internet as a global network of digital media, the Chinese government has unilaterally imposed administrative and legislative measures to stipulate who should access the Internet, what information could be put on the Internet and how the Internet might be used.

Despite the fact that China has not enacted any telecommunications law until the time of writing, the government was quick to release a variety of Internet related regulations. Technical measures (e.g. 'firewall' technologies) were also used to erect virtual borders between the Chinese users and foreign websites. In the meantime, anti-government forces (e.g. human rights organisations and pro-democracy activists) have attempted to use the Internet to channel their voices and organise anti-government activities. *Falun Gong*, a Chinese spiritual movement, has successfully used the Internet and other new communications technologies to organise large-scale protests and disseminate information amongst its members and supporters. When the Chinese government outlawed the movement, *Falun Gong* has flourished within the cyberspace.

The Chinese government is now faced with a dilemma: it recognises the commercial potential of the Internet but it is not prepared to tolerate the political impact of the network, especially when the Internet was used by non-government forces against government wishes. Apparently, the potential of innovative technologies, such as the Internet, to contribute to economic development was sometimes compromised by the ruling regime's political interest. China is unique in many ways, but the fight for control over the digital information highway manifests two opposing views on the Internet at the global level: those in favour of *vis-à-vis* those against state regulation. It is perhaps still too early to say who will eventually control the Internet.

The case of new TV technologies (including High Definition TV and digital TV systems) presented in Chapter 6 threw doubts about the effectiveness of government regulation in promoting innovations *vis-à-vis* market forces.

During a global competition for HDTV technologies, the precursor of digital TV technologies, the European public authorities extended generous political as well as financial support to the allied European companies in the second half of the 1980s and early 1990s. However, the officially adopted European HDTV system, i.e., HD-MAC, flopped and gave way to, firstly, a US-led digital HDTV system (proposed by the Grand Alliance) and, then, indigenous European digital TV technologies, mainly the DVB standards family. The European Digital Video Broadcasting Group, a consortium of over 200 companies from mainly Europe but also many other parts of the world started as a private initiative, had hardly any substantial political and financial backing from the European authorities but managed to claim an overwhelming success. Now that a large number of countries within and outside Europe have already adopted DVB technologies and the American digital TV standard (ATSC) is faced with uncertainties, DVB has the potential to become a *de facto* global standard for digital TV broadcasting. As an open and flexible standards family, DVB includes digital terrestrial, digital satellite, digital cable delivery solutions and some other aspects of digital broadcasting technologies.

There are many lessons to be learned from both the collapse of HD-MAC and the rise of DVB. First of all, government regulation is often lagged behind technical change. When HD-MAC was first proposed in the mid-1980s, the European and international technology environment for broadcasting was still much dominated by analogue systems. But digital technologies became the norm of the 1990s. The EU rushed into legislation in order to protect the indigenous HD-MAC technology and was slow to recognise the potential of digital broadcasting technologies. The European public authorities eventually abandoned their official choice of HD-MAC but they only did so when they were pressurised to do it.

Secondly, there is potentially a great uncertainty associated with public policy makers' picking winners at a time when alternative technologies are competing at the global level. The eagerness to pick winner, usually an indigenous technology, might lead to backing the wrong horse. The reason is rather simple: when leading technology companies and their engineers could not be sure which specific technology would win the format battle, politicians and bureaucrats were not necessarily better informed of the technical details pertinent to the specific systems. Any premature decision by policy makers might result in wasting public resources.

Thirdly, some public policy makers' conviction that ownership of new technologies would lead to improved national competitiveness could be miss-leading. Japan did not invent the NTSC transmission standard but Japanese consumer electronics manufacturers are among the leading suppliers of TV sets in the world. Britain lost all of its domestic TV manufacturers but the country became the largest TV set exporter within the European Union in the 1990s, thanks to the plants set up by inward investment.

Finally, market forces should not be excluded from the recognised sources of dynamics for innovation. The European Commission now fully recognises the success of DVB but it did not do so until after the collapse of HD-MAC. With the wisdom of hindsight, the European Commission could have achieved more by doing less in terms of promoting new TV technologies.

In view of the lessons learned from the innovation process for new TV technologies, can we assume that the digital revolution is better managed by market forces?

Chapter 7 has analysed the impact of global alliances on the course of innovation at the global level in the absence of any government regulation. The empirical basis of the discussion presented in Chapter 7 was the global standardisation for DVD, which constitutes another important domain of the current digital revolution.

Having seen the failure of a number of competing and non-compatible multimedia systems introduced in the 1990s, companies in the ICT sector realised that a head-on format war for DVD should be avoided. Consequently, the two DVD groups, the MMCD group led by Philips and Sony and the Super Density Disc Group led by Toshiba and Time Warner, decided to merge their technologies and create a global standard.

Although a global standard for DVD was achieved (technologically speaking), the consumer electronics industry entered into an agreement with the film industry to divide the world into different zones in the name of protecting the film companies' copyrights. In the age of globalisation, the case of DVD shows that an important consumer electronics technology has been 'regionalised' in order to serve the film producers' commercial interest. The DVD Forum is a global alliance among corporate organisations, which is largely responsible for the global standardisation process for DVD. There is a lack of competent authority at either the national government level or the international level to intervene in the issues related to DVD standardisation. Therefore, consumer interest, in the case of DVD, has been largely ignored. Apparently, the substitution of 'state regulation' with 'market regulation' is not necessarily the right solution to the problems associated with the governance of the digital revolution.

The specific technologies analysed in this book, such as the Internet, digital TV and DVD, are only a fraction of the digital communications sector. We are now living in the beginning of the 21st Century, a time when digital convergence of telecommunications, computers, broadcasting, consumer electronics and publishing is still in its early stage. Undoubtedly, many new technological breakthroughs are to be added to the list of innovation. We are heading for an integrated network, which will connect all homes and enterprises by supplying them with a telephone, radio, television and telematic data, and a 'multimedia station', which will be used to read texts, listen to recordings and view images (Flichy, 1995).

Back to 1910, Theodore Vail, the then President of AT&T, described the company's strategy for merging telephone and telegraph as 'One system with a common policy, common purpose and common action; comprehensive, universal, interdependent, intercommunicating like the highway system of the country, extending from every door to every other door, affording electrical communication of every kind, from every one at every place to every one at every other place' (quoted in Pool, 1983). For Vail, 'every door to every other door' and 'every one at every place to every one at every other place' electrical communication remained an unrealised dream in his lifetime. Nowadays, the availability of digital technologies with the ease of use, and many more emerging at the horizon, promises to turn this 'American dream' into reality. In the digital age, multi-channel, multi-platform broadcasting are already offering viewers an unprecedented range of programme choices; digital broadcasting is poised to make analogue broadcasting a thing of the past; the Internet is offering new opportunities (as well as challenges) for individuals and commercial and non-commercial organisations.

It is often said that '[o]ne pleasing outcome of the information age is that more of us can enjoy the good things which life can offer without spoiling the world for everyone else' and '[t]here are some interesting possibilities on the horizon' (Handy, 1997, p. 255). To be sure, individuals, organisations and the state are all wakening up to the great potential of the information age and many of them are already benefiting from it. However, the coming of the new economy – the digital economy or the Internet economy or the knowledge economy or the information economy or the network economy – has not entirely divorced from the old politics. First of all, the old pattern of international economy is being replicated in the digital age. Although many developing countries, such as China, have committed to the construction of a national information and communications infrastructure, it is the western industrialised countries that own most of the technologies and dominate the process of digital revolution as well as having the necessary financial resources to support new initiatives. The digital revolution is indeed taking place all over the world, but it is rolling forward from the 'North' to the 'South' and the journey from the 'North' to the 'South' could be a long one.

Secondly, despite the fact that the 'network society' has the potential to offer more efficient and new modes of governance, it will be naïve to suggest that digital technologies are the panacea to all the problems associated with the democratic deficit in both industrialised and developing nations. In other words, new technologies can not be the substitute for fundamental institutional reforms. The information society is high on the European Union's policy agenda but '*eEurope*' cannot dilute the real politics determining the speed and direction of European integration. The

Chinese government's new technology policy has led to the construction of a high-speed communications infrastructure but it is not ready to accept any challenge to the totalitarian way of governing the digital age. New communications technologies might contribute to democratic change in the long-term but the impact of new technologies should not be exaggerated.

Thirdly, in the old economy of the industrial age multinational corporations have been the most powerful forces behind the global economic activities. This has not changed in the digital age. To a certain extent, the 'network society' is characterised by the rise of many internationally organised business networks consisting of mainly multinational corporations. In the new technologies sectors, such as digital TV and DVD examined in this book, global corporate alliances, i.e., business networks, are the key players in deciding what technology standards should be adopted and what products consumers could buy. 'Communications technologies are extensions of opportunities within the rules of the political economy that control the allocation of resources in society. It is naïve or worse to believe that computers, without reference to the larger context of power, can bring about new forms of economic, social, or political relationships' (Sussman, 1997, p. 285).

Finally, the global process of standardisation is producing global products, global services and global flow of communications facilitated by global networks. On the one hand, multinational corporations are welcoming the arrival of the borderless global market. On the other hand, the state is here to stay and would utilise every available means to maintain the *status quo* of its national sovereignty. This has enhanced the traditional weakness of international or global governance over the globalisation process in the digital age. There indeed exist many large-scale international organisations, such as the United Nations agencies, the WTO, the OECD, etc., but there is no evidence suggesting any of these international organisations is adequately equipped with the power and means to govern the increasingly globalised and, undoubtedly, commercialised network society.

Bibliography

ABN AMBRO Media Sector Research (1999), *Digital Television: New TV, New Growth*, London, January.
Alic, J. (1990), 'Cooperation in R&D', *Technovation*, Vol. 10, No. 5, pp. 319-332.
Ansell, C., Parsons, C. and Darden, K. (1997), 'Dual Networks in European Regional Development Policy', *Journal of Common Market Studies*, Vol. 35, No. 3, September, pp. 347-375.
Archibugi, D. and Michie, J. (1995a), 'Technology and Innovation: An Introduction', *Cambridge Journal of Economics*, Vol. 19, No. 1, pp. 1-4.
Archibugi D. and Michie, J. (1995b), 'The Globalisation of Technology: A New Taxonomy', *Cambridge Journal of Economics*, Vol. 19, No. 1, pp. 121-140.
Bakis, H. (1997), 'From Geospace to Geocyberspace: Territories and Teleinteraction', in Roche, M. and Bakis, H. (eds), *Development in Telecommunications: Between Global and Local*, Ashgate, Aldershot, pp. 15-50.
Baldwin, T. F., McVoy, D. S. and Steinfield, C. (1996), *Convergence: Integrating Media, Information & Communication*, Sage, London.
Bangemann, M. (1997), 'A New World Order for Global Communication', presentation at the *Telecom Inter@ctive '97*, International Telecommunications Union, Geneva, 8 August.
Bangemann, M. et al (1994), *Europe and the Global Information Society: Recommendations to the European Council*, Brussels, 26 May.
Barmie, G. R. and Ye, S. (1997), 'The Great Firewall of China', *Wired*, Vol. 5, No. 6, June.
Beniger, J. R. (1986), *The Control Revolution: Technological and Economic Origins of the Information Society*, Harvard University Press, Cambridge, Mass.
Benz, A. and Eberlein, B. (1999), 'The Europeanization of Regional Policies: Patterns of Multi-level Governance', *Journal of European Public Policy*, Vol. 6, No. 2, pp. 329-348.
Best, M. H. (1990), *The New Competition: Institutions of Industrial Restructuring*, Polity Press, Cambridge.
Bradley, S. P., Hausman, J. A. and Nolan, R. L. (1993), 'Global Competition and Technology', in Bradley, Hausman and Nolan eds., *Globalization, Technology and Competition: The Fusion of Computers and*

Telecommunications in the 1990s, Harvard Business School Press, Boston, Mass., pp. 3-32.

Branscomb, A. W. (1994), *Who Owns Information? From Privacy to Public Access*, Basic Books, New York.

Brinkley, J. (1997), *Defining Vision: The Battle for the Future of Television*, Harcourt Brace & Company, New York.

Brown, A. et al. (1992), *HDTV: High Definition, High Stakes, High Risk – A Report on High Definition Television*, NERA (National Economic Research Association), London.

Camilleri, J. A. and Falk, J. (1992), *The End of Sovereignty? The Politics of a Shrinking and Fragmenting World*, Edward Elgar, Aldershot.

Cantwell, J. (1995), 'The Globalisation of Technology: What Remains of the Product Cycle Model?', *Cambridge Journal of Economics*, Vol. 19, No. 1, pp. 155-174.

Castells, M. (1996), *The Rise of the Network Society*, Blackwell, Oxford.

Castells, M. (1991), *The Informational City: Information Technology, Economic Restructuring, and the Urban-Regional Process*, Basil Blackwell, Oxford.

Cave, M. (1997), Regulating Digital Television in a Convergent World, *Telecommunications Policy*, Vol. 21, No. 7, pp. 575-596.

Cawson, A. (1995), 'High Definition Television in Europe', *The Political Quarterly*, Vol. 66, No. 2, April-June, pp. 157-173.

Cawson, A., Haddon, L. and Miles, I. (1995), *The Shape of Things to Consume: Delivering Information Technology into the Home*, Avebury, Aldershot.

Cawson, A. et al (1990), *Hostile Brothers: Competition and Closure in the European Electronic Industry*, Clarendon Press, Oxford.

Centre for Information Infrastructure and Economic Development (CIIED) (1996), *China's Information Infrastructure, Policies, Networks and Services*, The Chinese Academy of Social Sciences, Beijing.

Ciborra, C. (1991), 'Alliances as Learning Experiments: Cooperation and Change in High-Tech Industries', in Mytelka, L.K. ed., *Strategic Partnership: States, Firms and Multinational Competition*, Printer, London, pp. 51-77.

Clinton, W. and Gore, A. (1997), *A Framework for Global Electronic Commerce*, http://www.iitf.nist.gov/eleccomm/ecom.htm.

Collins, R. (1994), *Broadcasting and Audio-visual Policy in the European Single Market*, John Libbey, London.

CommunicationsWeek International (1996), *A World of Communications* [map].

Coombs, R., Saviotti P. and Walsh, V. (1987), *Economics and Technological Change*, Macmillan, London.

Council Of the European Communities (1997), *Directive Amending Council Directive 89/552/EEC on the Coordination of Certain Provisions Laid Down by Law, Regulation or Administrative Action in Member States Concerning the Pursuit of Television Broadcasting Activities*, 97/36/EC, OJ L202, 30 July.

Council of the European Communities (1995), *Directive on the Use of Standards for the Transmission of Television Signals*, 95/47/EC, OJ C281, 23 November.

Council of the European Communities (1994), *Resolution on a Framework for Community Policy on Digital Video Broadcasting*, OJ C181, 2 July.

Council of the European Communities (1993a), *Resolution on the Development of Technology and Standards in the Field of Advanced Television Services*, OJ C209, 3 August.

Council of the European Communities (1993b), *Decision on an Action Plan for the Introduction of Advanced Television Services in Europe*, 93/424/EEC, OJ L196, 5 August.

Council of the European Communities (1992), *Directive on the Adoption of Standards for Satellite Broadcasting of Television Signals*, 92/38/EEC, OJ L137, 20 May.

Council of the European Communities (1990), *Decision Concerning the Implementation of an Action Programme to Promote the Development of the European Audiovisual Industry (Media) (1991-1995)*, 90/685/EEC, OJ L380, 31 December.

Council of the European Communities (1989a), *Decision on the Common Action to be taken by the Member States with Respect to the Adoption of a Single World-wide High-definition Television Production Standard by the Plenary of the International Consultative Committee (CCIR) in 1990*, 89/630/EEC, OJ L363, 13 December.

Council of the European Communities (1989b), *Directive on the Coordination of Certain Provisions Laid Down by Law, Regulation or Administrative Action in Member States Concerning the Pursuit of Television Broadcasting Activities*, 89/552/EEC, OJ L 298, 17 October.

Council of the European Communities (1989c), *Decision on High Definition Television*, 89/337/EEC, OJ L142, 25 May.

Council of the European Communities (1986), *Directive on the Adoption of Common Technical Specifications of the MAC/packet Family of Standards for Direct Satellite Television Broadcasting*, 86/529/EEC, OJ L311, 6 November.

Cullen International (1997), *PHARE Regulatory Observatory for Telecommunications, Broadcasting and Posts: Central and Eastern Europe*, Country Reports produced for the European Commission, January.

Curwen, P. (1995), 'Telecommunications Policy in the European Union: Developing the Information Superhighway', *Journal of Common Market Studies*, Vol. 33, No. 3, pp. 331-360.

Dai, X. (1997), 'State Regulation and the Commercial Triumph in the Age of Digital Broadcasting', *Communications & Strategies*, Issue 25, March, 1st Quarter, pp. 61-90.

Dai, X. (1996a): *Corporate Strategy, Public Policy and New Technologies: Philips and the European Consumer Electronics Industry*, Pergamon, Oxford.

Dai, X. (1996b), 'Technical Convergence and Policy Divergence in the European Information Society: The Case of New TV Systems', M. Wintle ed., *Culture and Identity in Europe: Perceptions of Divergence and Unit in Past and Present*, Avebury, Aldershot.

Dai, X. (1996c): *Challenges of the Information Society: A Vision for Hull*, Study report commissioned by the Hull Economic Development Agency, Hull City Council, July.

Dai, X., Cawson, A. and Holmes, P. (1996), 'The Rise and Fall of High Definition Television: The Impact of European Technology Policy', *Journal of Common Market Studies*, Vol. 34, No. 2, pp. 149-166.

Dai, X. and Gao, S. (1998), 'New Industrial Policy for the Digital Age: Implications of the Chinese Information Superhighway', *Communications & Strategies*, Issue 31, September, 3rd Quarter, pp. 11-52.

Davis, R. (1999), *The Web of Politics: The Internet's Impact on the American Political System*, Oxford University Press, Oxford.

Delapierre, M. and Zimmermann, J. B. (1991), 'Towards a New Europeanism: French Firms in Strategic Partnership', in Mytelka, L. K. ed., *Strategic Partnership: States, Firms and Multinational Competition*, Printer, London, pp. 102-119.

Department for Culture, Media & Sport and Department of Trade and Industry (1998a), *Government Response to 'the Multimedia Revolution'*, July, London.

Department for Culture, Media & Sport and Department of Trade and Industry (1998b), *Television: The Digital Future*, A consultation document, January, London.

Department of Trade and Industry (1999), *Regulating Communications: The Way Ahead*, Results of the consultation on the convergence Green Paper, June, London.

Department of Trade and Industry (1998a) *Our Competitive Future: Building the Knowledge Driven Economy*, CM4176, HMSO, London.

Department of Trade and Industry (1998b), *Converging Technologies: Consequences for the New Knowledge-driven Economy*, September, London.

Department of Trade and Industry and Department for Culture, Media & Sport (1998), *Regulating Communications: Approaching Convergence in Information Age*, Green Paper, London, November.

Dodgson, M. (1993), *Technological Collaboration in Industry: Strategy, Policy and Internationalization in Innovation*, Routledge, London.

Dodgson, M. ed. (1989), *Technology Strategy and the Firm: Management and Public Policy*, Longman, Harlow.

Dordick, H. and Wang, G. (1993), *The Information Society: A Retrospective View*, Sage, London.

Dorgan, M. (1997), 'Rewriting the Laws of the Information Age', *San Jose Mercury News*, http://www.sjmercury.com/news/asia/malaysia/stories/cyberlaws.htm.

Dupagne, M. and Seel, P. B. (1998), *High Definition Television: A Global Perspective*, Iowa State University Press, Ames.

Dyson, K. and Humphreys, P. (1988), *Broadcasting and New Media Policies in Western Europe: A Comparative Study of Technical Change and Public Policy*, Routledge, London.

European Commission (1999a), *eEurope: An Information Society for All*, Communication on a Commission Initiative for the Special European Council of Lisbon (23 and 24 March 2000), Brussels, 8 December 1999.

European Commission (1999b), *Towards a New Framework for Electronic Communications Infrastructure and Associated Services: The 1999 Communications Review*, COM(1999) 539 Final, Brussels, 10 November.

European Commission (1999c), *The Development of the Market for Digital Television in the European Union*, COM(1999) 540, Brussels, 9 November.

European Commission (1998a), *Public Sector Information: A Key Resource for Europe: Green Paper on Public Sector Information in the Information Society*, COM(98) 585.

European Commission (1998b), *Globalisation and the Information Society: The Need for Strengthened International Coordination*, COM(98) 50 final, Brussels.

European Commission (1998c), *The Digital Age European Audiovisual Policy*, Report from the High Level Group on Audiovisual Policy, Brussels.

European Commission (1998d), *Central and Eastern Eurobarometer*, No. 8, May.

European Commission (1997a), *Fifth Framework Programme for Research and Technological Development*, COM(97) 553 final, Brussels, 5 November.

European Commission (1997b), *Agenda 2000: For a Stronger and Wider Union*, Vol. 1, Communication, DOC/97/6, 15 July.

European Commission (1997c), *Agenda 2000: Commission Opinions concerning the Applications for Membership to the European Union*, 15 July.

European Commission (1997d), *Agenda 2000: The Effects on the Union's Policies of Enlargement to the Applicant Countries of Central and Eastern Europe*, 15 July.

European Commission (1997e), *Agenda 2000: Reinforcing the Pre-accession Strategy*, Vol. II, Communication, DOC/97/7, 15 July.

European Commission (1996a), *Living and Working in the Information Society: People First*, Green Paper, COM(96) 389.

European Commission (1996b), *The Information Society: From Corfu to Dublin the New Emerging Priorities*, Implications of the Information Society for European Union Policies, COM(96) 395.

European Commission (1996c), *Standardization and the Global Information Society: The European Approach*, Communication from the Commission to the Council and the European Parliament, COM(96) 359.

European Commission (1994), *The Action Plan: Europe's Way to the Information Society*, COM(94) 347 final.

European Commission (1993a), *White Paper on Growth, Competitiveness, and Employment: The Challenges and Ways forward into the 21st Century*, COM(93) 700 final, Brussels, 5 December.

European Commission (1993b), *Digital Video Broadcasting: A Framework for Community Policy*, Communications from the Commission and Draft Council Resolution, Brussels, COM(93) 557.

European Telework Development (1999), *Statistics Relating to Information Technology in EU & CEE Countries*, 8 June. http://www.eto.org.uk/eustats/index.htm.

Evans, B. (1992), *Digital HDTV: The Way Forward*, IBC Technical Services Ltd., London.

Farrell, J. and Shapiro, C. (1992), 'Standard Setting in High-Definition Television', *Brookings Papers on Economic Activity: Microeconomics*, The Brookings Institution, Washington D.C., pp. 1-93.

Federal Trust (1995), *Network Europe and the Information Society*, published by the Federal Trust, London.

Finnie, G. (1995), 'The Politics of Control', *CommunicationsWeek International*, 2 October 1995, p. 25.

Flichy, P. (1995), *Dynamics of Modern Communication: The Shaping and Impact of New Communication Technologies*, Sage, London.

Freeman, C. (1995), 'The "National System of Innovation" in Historical Perspective', *Cambridge Journal of Economics*, No. Vol. 19, No. 1, pp. 5-24.

Gao, S. and Dai, X. (1996), 'Zhanlue Jishu yu Zhanlue Xuanze: Gao Qingxidu Dianshi Guoji Jingzheng de Qishi (Strategic Technology and Strategic Choice: Implications of the Global Competition for HDTV)', *Strategy and Management*, Vol. 15, No. 2, pp. 110-120.

Gasman, L. (1994), *Telecompetition: The Free Market Road to the Information Highway*, Cato Institute, Washington DC.

Gerlach, M. L. (1992), *Alliance Capitalism: The Social Organization of Japanese Business*, University of California Press, Berkeley.

Gibbs, D., Dai, X. and Shahin, J. (1999), *An Audit of ICT-based Projects, Activities and Networks in the Humber Sub-region*, Report to Humberside Training and Enterprise Council.

Gibbs, D. and Tanner, K. (1997), 'Communications Technologies, Local Economies and Regulation Theory', *Journal of Economic and Social Geography*, Vol. 88, No. 1, pp. 29-40.

Gomes-Casseres, B. (1993), 'Computers: Alliances and Industry Evolution', in Yoffie, D. B. ed., *Beyond Free Trade: Firms, Governments, and Global Competition*, Harvard Business School Press, Boston, Mass., pp. 79-128.

Gore, A. (1991), 'Infrastructure for the Global Village', *Scientific American*, September, pp. 108-111.

Hagedoorn, J. (1993), 'Understanding the Rationale of Strategic Technology Partnering: Interorganisational Modes of Cooperation and Sectoral Differences', *Strategic Management Journal*, Vol. 14, 1993, pp. 371-385.

Hamel, G. and Prahalad, C. K. (1993), 'Strategy as Stretch and Leverage', *Harvard Business Review*, March-April, pp. 75-84.

Handy, C. (1997), *The Hungry Spirit: Beyond Capitalism – A Quest for Purpose in the Modern World*, Hutchinson, London.

High Level Group of Experts (HLGE, 1996), *Building the European Information Society for Us All: First Reflections of the High Level Group of Experts*, Interim Report, Brussels.

Hills, J. (1991), *The Democracy Gap: The Politics of Information and Communication Technologies in the United States and Europe*, Greenwood Press, New York.

House of Lords Committee on Science and Technology (1996), *Information Society: Agenda for Action in the UK*, 5th Report, HLpaper 77 session 1995-96, HMSO, London.

Hughes, G. (1996), 'Progress Report on the Achievements of the IRISI'. http://eris.epri.org/irisi/discussion/paper4.html.

The Information Society Forum (1996), *Networks for People and Their Communities: Making the Most of the Information Society in the European Union*, First annual report to the European Commission, Office for Official Publications of the European Communities, Luxembourg, June.

Information Society Project Office (ISPO, 1997), *Information Technologies, Productivity and Employment*, DGIII – DGXIII, Brussels http://www.ispo.cec.be/infosoc/promo/pubs/prodemp.html.

Information Society Project Office (ISPO, no date), *Financial Instruments for the Information Society Projects and Actions*, DGIII – DGXIII, Brussels.

Jackson, T. (1999), 'Capitalism Advances in a Climate of Mistrust', *Financial Times*, 14 December 1999.

Jorde, T. M. and Teece, D. J. (1992a), 'Innovation, Cooperation, and Antitrust', in Jorde, T. M. and Teece, D. J. eds, *Antitrust, Innovation, and Competitiveness*, Oxford University Press, Oxford,, pp. 47-81.

Kennedy, P. (1979), 'Imperial Cable Communications and Strategy', in Kennedy, P. (ed), *The War Plans of the Great Powers, 1880-1914*, Allan & Unwin, London, pp. 75-98.

Kitchin, R. (1998), *Cyberspace: The World in the Wires*, John Wiley & Sons, Chichester.

Kohler-Koch, B. (1996), 'Catching up with Change: The Transformation of Governance in the European Union', *Journal of European Public Policy*, Vol. 3, No. 3, September, pp. 359-380.

Kranzberg, M. (1985), 'The Information Age: Evolution or Revolution?', in Bruce R. G. (ed.), *Information Technologies and Social Transformation*, National Academy of Engineering, Washington D.C.

Krugman, P. (1994), 'Competitiveness: A Dangerous Obsession', *Foreign Affairs*, March/April, pp. 28-44.

Kynge, J. (1998), 'Is the Door Finally Opening?', FT Telecoms Survey, *Financial Times*, 17 March.

Laudon, K. C. (1977), *Communications Technology and Democratic Participation*, Praeger Publishers, New York.

Lebessis, N. and Paterson, J. (1997), *Evolution in Governance: What Lessons for the Commission? A First Assessment*, Report of the Forward Studies Unit, European Commission, Brussels.

Leonard, M. (1999), *Network Europe: The New Case for Europe*, The Foreign Policy Centre, London.

Levacic, R. (1986), 'Government Policies towards the Consumer Electronics Industry and Their Effects: A Comparison of Britain and France', in Hall, G. ed., *European Industrial Policy*, Groom Helm, London.

Levy, D. (1997), 'Regulating Digital Broadcasting in Europe: The Limits of Policy Convergence', *West European Politics*, Vol. 20, No. 4, October, pp. 24-42.

Levy, J. and Samuels (1991), 'Institutions and Innovation: Research Collaboration as Technology Strategy in Japan', in Mytelka, L. K. ed., *Strategic Partnership: States, Firms and Multinational Competition*, Printer, London, pp. 120-148.

Lin, H. (1997), 'Summary of Discussions at a Planning Meeting on the Effects of Information Technology on the Role and Authority of Government', National Research Council, 26-27 March, Washington DC. http://www4.nas.edu/cpsma/cstbweb.nsf/.

Link, A. N. and Tassey, G. (1987), *Strategies for Technology-based Competition: Meeting the New Global Challenge*, Lexington books, Mass.

Lovelock, P. (1996), 'The Role of the State on the Information Superhighway in Asia: Co-ordination or Control?', paper delivered at the 1996 British International Studies Association (BISA) Conference, Durham, 16-18 December.

Lyon, D. (1995), 'The Roots of the Information Society', in Heap, N. *et al* eds, *Information Technology and Society*, Sage, London, pp. 54-73.

Lyon, D. (1988), *The Information Society: Issues and Illusions*, Polity Press, Cambridge.

Ma, R. (1996), 'The Early Stage of the Golden Bridge Project', *Electronics Review and Policymaking*, No. 1, pp. 20-23.

Mackay, H. (1995), 'Theorising the IT/Society Relationship', in Heap, N., Thomas, R., Einon, G., Mason, R. and Mackay, H., *Information Technology and Society: A Reader*, Sage, London, pp. 41-53.

Madon, S. (1997), 'Information-Based Global Economy and Socioeconomic Development: The Case of Bangalore', *The Information Society*, Vol. 13, No. 3, July-September, pp. 227-244.

Marsden, C. (1997), 'The European Digital Convergence Paradigm: From Structural Pluralism to Behavioural Competition Law', *Journal of Information, Law and Technology*, No. 3, October. http://www.elj.warwick.ac.uk/jilt/commsreg/97_3mars/.

Marx, K. (1976), *Capital: A Critique of Political Economy*, Vol. 1, translated by Fowkes, B., Penguin, London.

Masuda, Y. (1980), *The Information Society as Post-Industrial Society*, Tokyo Institute for the Information Society.

McQuail, D. (2000), *McQuail's Mass Communication Theory*, 4th Edition, Sage, London.

Michalet, C. A. (1991), 'Strategic Partnerships and the Changing Internationalisation Process', in Mytelka, L. K. ed., *Strategic Partnership: States, Firms and Multinational Competition*, Printer, London, pp. 35-50.

Michalis, M. (1999), 'European Union and Telecoms: Towards a Convergent Regulatory Regime?', *European Journal of Communication*, Vol. 14, No. 2, pp. 147-171.

Miller, N. and Allen, R. eds. (1995), *The Post-Broadcasting Age: New Technologies, New Communities*, John Libbey Media, Luton.

Ministry of Science and Technology (1999), Development Report on China's New and High-Tech Industry, The Science Press, Beijing.

Mintrom, M. and Vergari, S. (1998), 'Policy Networks and Innovation Diffusion: The Case of State Education Reforms', *The Journal of Politics*, Vol. 60, No. 1, February, pp. 126-148.

Morgan, K. (1989), 'Telecom Strategies in Britain and France: The Scope and Limits of Neo-Liberalism and Dirigisme', in Sharp, M. and Holmes, P. eds., *Strategies for New Technology: Case Studies from Britain and France*, Philip Allan, Hertfordshire, pp. 19-55.

Mosco, V. *The Political Economy of Communication: Rethinking and Renewal*, Sage, London.

Motohashi, K. (1997), 'ICT Diffusion and Its Economic Impact in OECD Countries', OECD *Science Technology Industry Review*, No. 20, Special Issue on Information Infrastructure, Paris, pp. 13-45.

Mowery, D. and Oxley, J. (1995), 'Inward Technology Transfer and Competitiveness: The Role of National Innovation Systems', *Cambridge Journal of Economics*, Vol. 19, No. 1, pp. 67-73.

MPT (1995), *Provisional Regulation on the Open Telecommunications Services Market*, 10 November.

MPT (1993), *Guidelines for Approving Applications of Undertaking Open Telecommunications Services*, 11 September.
Mueller, M. and Tan Z. (1997), *China in the Information Age: Telecommunications and the Dilemmas of Reform*, Praeger, Westport, CT.
Mytelka, L. K. (1991a), 'Crisis, Technological Change and the Strategic Alliance', in Mytelka, L. K. ed, *Strategic Partnership: States, Firms and Multinational Competition*, Pinter, London, pp. 7-34.
Mytelka, L. K. (1991b), 'States, Strategic Alliances and International Oligopolies: The European ESPRIT Programme', in Mytelka, L. K. ed, *Strategic Partnership: States, Firms and Multinational Competition*, pp. 182-210.
Nakamura, K. (1998), 'Japan's TV Broadcasting: Digital Broadcasting Policy and Problems', Preliminary Draft for ITS 12th Biennial Conference, Stockholm, 21-24 June.
Negrine, R. M. ed. (1988), *Satellite Broadcasting: The Politics and Implications of the New Media*, Croom Helm, London.
Negroponte, N. (1995), *Being Digital*, Alfred A. Knopf, New York.
Nelson, J. (1997), 'Grappling with Crime Wave on the Web', *Los Angeles Times*, 30 November 1997, http://www.latimes.com/HOME/NEWS/BUSINESS/UPDATES/internet1130.htm.
NERA and Smith Systems Engineering (1998), *A Study to Estimate the Economic Impact of Government Policies towards Digital Television*, Report for Radio Communications Agency and Department for Culture, Media and Sport, January, London.
Noam, E. M. (1991), *Television in Europe*, Oxford University Press, New York.
Ohmae, K. (1990), *The Borderless World: Power and Strategy in the Interlinked Economy*, Collins, London.
Peng, H. A. and Nadarajan, B. (1995), 'Censorship and the Internet: A Singapore Perspective', http://www.info.isoc.org:80/HMP/PAPER/132/txt/paper.txt.
Peterson, J. (1997), 'States, Societies and the European Union', *West European Politics*, Vol. 20, No. 4, October, pp. 1-23.
Peterson, J. and Sharp, M. (1998), *Technology Policy in the European Union*, Macmillan, London.
The Policy Studies Institute (UK), City Liberal Studies (Greece) and CITI/INETI (Portugal) (1997), *The Impact of the Information Society on the Territorial Planning of the Less Favoured Regions*, A Report to the European Commission, Brussels-Luxembourg, May.
Pool, I. (1983), *Technologies of Freedom*, Harvard University Press, Cambridge, Mass.
Porter, M. E. (1990), *The Competitive Advantage of Nations*, Macmillan, London.
Qiu, J. L. (1999/2000), 'Virtual Censorship in China: Keeping the Gate Between the Cyberspaces', *International Journal of Communications Law and Policy*, Issue 4, Winter, pp. 1-25, available at http://www.ijclp.org.

Richardson, J. (1996), 'Policy-Making in the EU: Interests, Ideas and Garbage Cans of Primeval Soup', in Richardson, J. (ed.), *European Union: Power and Policy-Making*, Routledge, London, pp. 3-23.

Robillard, S. (1995), *Television in Europe: Regulatory Bodies*, Media Monograph 19, The European Institute for the Media, John Libbey, London.

Saxby, S. (1990), *The Age of Information: The Past Development and the Future Significance of Computing and Communications*, Macmillan, London.

Schumpeter, J. (1942), *Capitalism, Socialism and Democracy*, Harper and Brothers, New York.

Sclove, R. E. (1995), *Democracy and Technology*, The Guildford Press, New York.

Sharp, M. (1989), 'Corporate Strategies and Collaboration: The Case of ESPRIT and European Electronics', in Dodgson, M. (ed.), *Technology Strategy and the Firm: Management and Public Policy*, Longman, Harlow, pp. 202-218.

Sidjanski, D. (1997), 'Networks of European Pressure Groups', EURYOPA Articles et Conférences 4-1997, Institut européen de l'Université de Genève.

Standage, T. (1998), *The Victorian Internet*, Weidenfeld & Nicolson, London.

Stephens, P. (1999), 'Broken Borders of the Nation State', *Financial Times*, 3 December.

Sussman, G. (1997), *Communication, Technology and Politics in the Information Age*, Sage, London.

Tapscott, D. (1996), *The Digital Economy: Promise and Peril in the Age of Networked Intelligence*, McGraw-Hill, New York.

Teece, D. J. (1986), 'Profiting from Technological Innovation: Implications for integration, Collaboration, Licensing and Public Policy', *Research Policy*, 15, pp. 285-305.

The TeleCities Network (1998), *Annual Report*.

The TeleCities Network (1997), *Annual Report*.

The TeleCities Network (1996), *European Cities and the Information Society: Declaration to the European Commission*, Declaration of Antwerp, 27 February.

Thajchayapong, P. *et al* (1997), 'Social Equity and Prosperity: Thailand Information Technology Policy into the 21 Century', *The Information Society*, Vol. 13, No. 3, July-September, pp. 265-286.

Thomas, A. (1999), *Regulation of Broadcasting in the Digital Age*, Department for Culture, Media and Sport, May, London.

Tipton, F. B. and Aldrich, R. (1987), *An Economic and Social History of Europe from 1939 to the Present*, Macmillan, London.

Toffler, A. (1981), *The Third Wave*, Pan Books, London.

Tömmel, I. (1998), Transformation of Governance: The European Commission's Strategy for Creating a 'Europe of the Regions', *Regional & Federal Studies*, Vol. 8, No. 2, Summer, pp. 52-80.

Tyson, L. D'A. (1992), *Who's Bashing Whom? Trade Conflicts in High-Technology Industries*, Institute for International Economics, Washington, D.C.

US Government (1999), *Towards Digital eQuality*, 2nd Annual Report by the Working Group on Electronic Commerce.

van Dijk, J. (1999), *The Network Society: Social Aspects of New Media*, translated by Spoorenberg, L., Sage, London.

Wendland, R. (1998), *IP Telephony and Enterprise Network Convergence*, Durlacher, London.

Williams, R. (1999), 'The Technology and the Society', in *The Media Reader: Continuity and Transformations*, edited by Mackay, H. and O'Sullivan, T., Sage, London, pp. 43-57.

Xu, A. and Armstrong, P.(1995), *Chinese Telecom Market*, A Study Report by Northern Business Information, McGraw-Hill Companies, New York.

Yang, Z. (1998), *The Chinese Telecommunications Infrastructure*, Unpublished study report, The Chinese Academy of Social Sciences, Beijing.

Index

'863' Programme 98
3DO 231
Advanced Television Research
 Consortium (ATRC) 198
Advanced Television Systems
 Committee (ATSC) 178, 206
 Broadcasters' rebellion 203
Air France 6
Aldrich, R. 9
Alic, J. 11, 226, 227
Amazon 2
American Airlines 6
American Alliance 198
American Consortium 198
American Democratic Party 2
America Online (AOL) 145
American Sky Broadcasting (ASkyB)
 194
Ansell, C. 65, 67
Apple 233
Archibugi, D. 229
Armstrong, P. 106
ASDA 3
ASkyB *see* American Sky Broadcasting
Asynchronous Digital Subscriber Line
 (ADSL) 2, 109
Asynchronous Transfer Mode (ATM)
 109, 114
AT&T 104, 107, 114, 198, 221, 222
ATRC *see* Advanced Television
 Research Consortium
ATSC *see* Advanced Television Systems
 Committee

Bakis, H. 1
Baldwin, T. F. 20
Bangemann, M. 8, 37, 69, 94
Bangemann Report 37, 40, 57, 72, 79

Barclays Bank 4
Barme, G. R. 159
BBC 146, 193, 209
BDB *see* British Digital Broadcasting
Bell Labs 114
Bell telephone system 1-2
Benz, A. 67, 68
Berlin Wall 49
Best, M. H. 227
Betamax 183
BIB *see* British Interactive Broadcasting
'Big brothers' 159
Big character poster 162-63
Binary code 19
Bosch 176
Bradley, S. P. 221
Branscomb, A. W. 151
BRITE 11
British Airways 6
British Digital Broadcasting (BDB) 193,
 211
British Interactive Broadcasting (BIB)
 222
British Empire 8, 45
 'all red' cable telegraphic
 communications network 45
British Satellite Broadcasting (BSB)
 177, 191-2
British Telecom 29, 221
BMW 4
BSB *see* British Satellite Broadcasting
BSkyB 191-7, 211, 222
Bulgarian Telecommunications
 Company (BTC) 50

Cable & Wireless 107, 115, 137
CableLab 203
Calton Communications 211

Camilleri, J. A. 152, 159
Cantwell, J. 229
Castells, M. 5, 19, 66, 67, 89
Cathode Ray Tube (CRT) 207
Cawson, A. 213, 216n, 217n, 221, 224
CD32 231
CDA *see* Communications Decency Act
CEECs *see* Central and East European Countries
Central and East European Countries (CEECs) 47-56
Centre for the Chinese Information Infrastructure and Economic Development (CIIED) 109-10
CERNet *see* Chinese Education and Research Network
China-China-Foreign (CCF) 169n
ChinaGBN 141
China Democracy Party (CDP) 150
China Internet Network Information Centre (CNNIC) 141, 143, 144
ChinaNet 141, 142-3
China News Digest (CND) 149
China Telecom 107, 115, 116-8
China Unicom (Liantong) 103, 114
Chinese Education and Research Network (CERNet) 137, 138, 141
Chinese Institute of High Energy Physics 140
Chinese National Telecommunications Working Conference (CNTWC) 108
Clinton, W. 3
CND *see* China News Digest
CNN 141, 146, 158
CNNIC *see* China Internet Network Information Centre
Cold War 47, 48
Comdex computer trade show 3
Committee of the Regions 82, 83
Common Information Area 21, 24-28, 30, 36, 45, 46, 56, 67
Communications Commission 29
Communications Decency Act (CDA) 145
Communications gap 53
Compact Disc (CD) 231
Compact Disc-interactive (CD-i) 231
Compact Disc Total Vision (CDTV) 231
Competitiveness
  European 23
  national 36
  regions 69
Competitiveness White Paper 15n
CompuServe 145
Computers 2
Consultative Committee for International Radio (CCIR) 175, 176, 178
Continental Airlines 6
Convergence 29
  definition 19-20
  regulation 121
Coombs, R. 7
Corfu 37
Corporate strategy 3
Creative destruction 11
CRT *see* Cathode Ray Tube
CSTNet 141
Cultural Revolution 99, 157
Cybercops 158
Cyberspace
  definition 15n
  Falun Gong 155
  lack of law 150

DaimlerChrysler (DC) 6
Dai, X. 11, 61n, 146, 213, 216n, 217n, 218n, 223
Darden, K. 65, 67
Davis, R. 8
DBS *see* Direct Broadcasting by Satellite
Delapierre, M. 224
Delors White Paper 23, 37, 56, 57, 70
Delta Airlines 6
Department of Justice 10
Department of Trade and Industry (DTI) Information Society Initiative (ISI) 39
Detroit Exchange 6
DiBEG 197, 207
Direct Broadcasting by Satellite (DBS) 177, 185, 187
Digital Compact Cassette (DCC) 231
Digital economy 5, 19, 39, 144
Digital exchange 101
Digital Freedom Network 154
Digital goods 30-31, 161
Digital marketplace 46
Digital Satellite System (DSS) 202-3
Digital Sites 84
digital switch over 212
digital Terrestrial Television

broadcasting (dTTb) 201, 206
Digital TV
  Definition 216n
  Global competition 197-212
  introduction in EU 209
  Japan 207-8
  multi-channel 2
Digital Versatile Disc (DVD) 2, 12, 222, 230-7
  DVD Consortium 233
  DVD Forum 12, 234-5
  playback control code 236
  regional management code 236
Digital Video Broadcasting (DVB) 197, 199-207
  de facto standards family 208-12
  DVB-Cable 201
  DVB-Satellite 201
  DVB-Terrestrial 201
  European Launching Group (ELG) 199
  General Assembly 200
  Memorandum of Understanding 205
  Organisational Structure 200
  Specialised Modules 201-2
  Standards 204
  Steering Board 201
Digitisation
  definition 15n
D-MAC 191-2
Dodgson, M. 223, 224, 225, 226, 227, 228
Dordic, H. 19, 94, 127, 131
Dot-com 3
DSS *see* Digital Satellite System
dTTb *see* digital Terrestrial Television broadcasting
Dubrovnik 175
DVB *see* Digital Video Broadcasting
DVD *see* Digital Versatile Disc
DVD Consortium 233
DVD Forum 12, 234-5
  organisational structure 234

eBay 3
Eberlein, B. 67, 68
EBU *see* European Broadcasting Union
EchoStar 194
Economic development 9
e-Envoy 8
eEurope 19, 24-28, 36

democratic deficit 43-46
EIB *see* European Investment Bank
electronic commerce (e-commerce) 2
Electronic mail (e-mail) 2, 156
electronic marketplace 6
e-Minister 8
Empire
  European 8
  British 8
  News Corp. 191, 196
  Soviet 9
Ericsson 104, 108, 221
eris@ *see* European Regional Information Society Association
ESPRIT 11
EU95 *see* EUREKA 95 HDTV Project
EU-CEEC Information Society Forum 41, 42, 43
EU enlargement
  information society 47-56
EUMEDIS *see* Euro-Mediterranean Information Society Forum 41
EUREKA 11, 98
EUREKA-95 HDTV Project (EU95) 176-8
EUREKA-256 206
EUREKA-625 206-7
Euro-Mediterranean Information Society Forum (EUMEDIS) 41, 42
EUROPA 43
Europe Agreements 48, 49
European Broadcasting Union (EBU) 205
European Centre for Nuclear Research 140
European Commission
  1999 Communications Review 33
  Directorate-General-V 73, 81, 82, 83
  Directorate-General-XII 84
  Directorate-General-XIII 8, 40-1, 81, 84
  Directorate-General-XVI 73, 81, 82,
  HDTV 'Action Plan' 178
  Information Society Activities Centre (ISAC) 41
  International Charter 47
  selected policy documents 38
European Economic Interest Grouping (EEIG) 189
European Empires 8
European governance 36, 68

information society 36-7
new mode 78-87
policy process 36-40
European integration
deepening 14
widening 14
European Investment Bank (EIB) 28
Europeanisation 68
European Parliament 82, 83
European Regional Development Fund (ERDF) 73, 84-7
European Regional Information Society Association (eris@) 75
European Regulatory Authority 28-36, 29, 31, 59-60
European Social Fund (ESF) 73, 84-7
European Union (EU) 2
audiovisual policy 190
Common Information Area 21
enlargement 47
European activism 185-9
European Competitiveness 23
European integration 14
ever closer Union 45
Fifth Framework Programme 11, 24, 41
Fourth Framework Programme 24
Funding 84-7
Global Information Society 21
governance 46, 68
industrial policy 23
localisation of EU policy 68
Maastricht Treaty 26, 184
MAC Directive 185
policy dissemination 78-80
single European market 26
Special Council of Ministers 8
technology community 24
technology policy 23, 24
Treaty 25, 71-72, 182-5
TV without Frontiers 188-9
Virtual Europe 21

Falk, J. 152, 159
Falun Gong movement 154-5
Federal Trust 67, 70, 80, 88
Fifth Generation Computer 98
Flat panel display (FPD) 182
Flichy, P. 246
Ford 6
Four Modernisations 99

Freeman, C. 229
Freeserve 3
Fuzhou 101, 123
Fuzhou Municipality People's Intermediate Court (FMPIC) 123

Gasman, L. 11
GDP *see* Gross Domestic Product
General Instrument(GI) 171, 180
General Motors (GM) 6
Gerlach, M. L. 223
GI *see* General Instrument
Gibbs, D. 70
GII *see* Global Information Infrastructure
GIS *see* Global Information Society
Global governance 46
EU governance 46-47
Global Information Infrastructure (GII) 107, 215
Global Information Society (GIS) 21, 46, 59
Globalisation 7, 12
challenges 31
dynamic force 215
economy 69
global firms 230
technology and innovation 229
Global One 115, 116
GlobalPartnership 22
Global Standard for Mobile communications (GSM) 50, 108
Global Village 96
Golden Projects 94, 110
administrative authorities 120-1
Golden Bridge 94, 110-11
Golden Card 94, 111
Golden Customs 94, 111-12
Gomes-Casseres, B. 224
Gore, A. 25
Government Online 151
Governance
EU 46
definition 16n
global 46
new technology 10-13
technology 7-10
Granada 211
Grand Alliance 197, 198-9
members 219
Great Firewall 149-51, 155, 156

Great Leap Forward 97
Gross Domestic Product (GDP) 51, 52
   growth of ICT sector in China 142
GSM *see* Global Standard for Mobile
   communications

Hagedoorn, J. 223, 226
Hamel, G. 225
Handy, C. 247
Hausman, J. A. 221
HD-Divine *see* High Definition Digital
   Video Narrowband Emission
HD-MAC *see* High Definition
   Multiplexed Analogue Component
HDTV *see* High Definition TV
Hewlett-Packard 233
High Definition Digital Video
   Narrowband Emission (HD-Divine)
   201, 206
High Definition Multiplexed Analogue
   Component (HD-MAC) 177
High Definition TV (HDTV) 61n, 171
   Action Plan 178
   D2-MAC 186
   development in US 178-80
   EU95 176-8
   FCC policy 179-80
   global competition 172-81
   HD-MAC 176-8
   Hi-Vision 174-6, 207
   MAC Directive 185
   MAC/packet family 186
   Multiple Sub-nyquist Sampling
   Encoding (MUSE) 174
   second generation 176
   Vision 1250 189
Higher Education Funding Council for
   England (HEFCE) 137
High Level Group of Experts on the
   Social and Societal Aspects of the
   Information Society 41-42, 69, 80
High-Level Group on the Information
   Society (HLGIS) 37, 41
Hi-Tech 23
HLGIS *see* High-Level Group on the
   Information Society
Holmes, P. 213, 216n, 217n
Honda 6
Hong Kong and Shanghai Bank
   Corporation (HSBC) 4, 7, 222
Hong Kong Telecom 107, 115

Hughes 202

IBM 104, 233
ICANN *see* Internet Corporation for
   Assigned Names and Numbers
Independent Television Commission
   (ITC) 29
Indian Sky Broadcasting (ISkyB) 195
Information age 96
Information and communications
   technologies (ICTs) 1
Information economy 5, 94
Information infrastructure 94, 107
Information society 5
   definition 19
   European governance 36-47
   Europeanisation 68-78
   policy push 20
   user-friendly 24
Information Society Activities Centre
   (ISAC) 41
Information Society Forum 41
Information Society Initiative (ISI) 39
   Local Support Centres 39
Information Society Project Office
   (ISPO) 93
Information superhighway 144
   China 94, 104-10, 126, 146
   US 25
Information Technology Development
   Leading Group (ITDLG) 121, 127
Informatisation 19
   China 97
   industrialisation 96
   the National Economy 9, 95, 99, 121,
   151
Info Society 2000 (Danish government)
   39
Institutional convergence 116
Institutional reform 116-21
Integrated Services Digital Broadcasting-
   Terrestrial (ISDB-T) 207-8
Integrated Services Digital Network
   (ISDN) 2, 109
International Charter 47
International Telecommunications Union
   (ITU) 186
Internet
   a new media 159-63
   birth 2
   chat rooms 157

Chinese dissidents online 153-4
Chinese regulation 146-9
Chinese users 143
Democratisation 151-9
economy 2
.eu 31
global design and national control 158
Great Firewall 149-51
growth in China 140-5
hierarchical control 145
holes in the Great Firewall 155-9
lack of law 150
Netwall 149
Top level domains 31
Transnational Political Mobilisation 152-3
user registration 156
Web page 156
Wei Jingsheng 153
WTO effect 159-63
Internet Contents Providers (ICPs) 143
Internet Corporation for Assigned Names and Numbers (ICANN) 8
Internet Explorer 10
Internet Information Management Bureau (IIMB) 12
Internet Protocol (IP) Telephony 121-30
definition 122-3
Inter-Regional Information Society Initiative (IRISI) 66, 70, 71-6
funding 74
Memorandum of understanding 72
Network Bureau 73
Network Management Committee (NMC) 73
partnership 73
Regional Information Society Steering Group (RISSG) 73
Regional Information Society Unit (RISU) 73
Internet Service Providers (ISPs) 141, 153
China 141-142
CompuServe 145
Kingston Net 145
user monitoring 156
'Invisible hands' 216
IP see Internet Protocol
IRISI see Inter-Regional Information Society Initiative

ISAC see Information Society Activities Centre
ISDB-T see Integrated Services Digital Broadcasting-Terrestrial
ISI see Information Society Initiative
ISkyB see Indian Sky Broadcasting
ISO 199
ISPO see Information society Project Office
ISPs see Internet Service Providers
IT (Information Technology) Hub 2
ITC see Independent Television Commission
ITU see International Telecommunications Union

J18 152-3
Jackson, Thomas Penfield 10
Janet see Joint Academic Network
Japan Sky Broadcasting (JSkyB) 195
JHLC see Joint High Level Committee
Joint Academic Network (Janet) 138
Joint Conference for the Informatisation of the National Economy (JCINE) 120-1
Joint High Level Committee (JHLC) 41, 42, 43
Jorde, T. M. 225, 228
JSkyB see Japan Sky Broadcasting
JVC 183

KDD 107
Kennedy, P. 45
Kingston Net 145
Kohler-Koch, B. 65
Korea Telecom 107
Kranzberg, M. 10
Krugman, P. 61n
Kynge, J. 115, 142, 143

Laudon, K. 139
Leonard, M. 5
Less Favoured Regions (LFR) 84
Lettelekom 50
Liantong (China Unicom) 103, 114, 116-8
Lin, H. 70
Link, A. N. 225
Lithuania Telecom 50
Lobbying 81-4
London Stock Exchange (LSE) 5

Lucky Goldstar 180
Lyon, D. 19

Maastricht Treaty 26, 70
MAC-Directive
    loophole 192
MAC/packet family 186
Madon, S. 93
Ma, R. 99
Marconi radio system 2
Market regulation 12
Marx, K. 11, 161
    use value 11
Matsushita 199
Mawei District People's Court 123
Mawei Post and Telecommunications Bureau (MPTB) 123
MCI 107, 194
McQuail, D. 9
McVoy, D. S. 20
Merrill Lynch 7
Michalet, C. A. 228
Michie, J. 229
Microsoft 10, 104, 221, 230, 233
    Internet Explorer 10
Midland Bank 4
MII *see* Ministry of Information Industry
Millennium bug 4
MiniDisc 183, 231
Ministry of Information Industry (MII)
    formation 118
    regulate Internet telephony 124
Ministry of Public Security (MPS) 149, 156
Ministry of State Security (MSS) 149
Mintrom, M. 67
MIT 198
MMCD *see* Multimedia CD
MNC *see* Multinational Corporation
Mobile communications
    3rd Generation (3G) 2, 16n
    auction of radio spectrum, 16n
Morgan, K. 224
Morse Code 1
Morse, Samuel 1
Mosco, V. 12
Motorola 104, 108
Mowery, D. 229
MPEG-2 199, 205, 206
Mueller, M. 147, 153, 162
Multimedia CD (MMCD) 232

Multimedia Super Corridor 95
Multinational Corporation (MNC) 221
Multiple Sub-nyquist Sampling Encoding (MUSE) 174
Murdoch, Rupert. 3
MUSE *see* Multiple Sub-nyquist Sampling Encoding and HDTV
Mytelka, L. K. 223, 226

N30 152-3
National Information Infrastructure (NII) 20, 22
National innovation systems 229-30
National regulatory authorities (NRAs) 29, 33, 60
National Television Systems Committee (NTSC) 171, 72, 173
National Westminster Bank 3-4
NEC 114
Negroponte, N. 2
Nelson, J. 157
Net-generation 5
Netscape Communication 10
Netwall 149
Network 15-16n
    business (inter-firm) 222
    cable 8
    China's First Network Case 122
    global governance 230
    Internet 6
    new communications 8
    radio broadcasting 6
    telegraphy 6
    telephone 6
    Trans-European 26
Network Europe 15-16n, 67
Networking 6
Network society 5, 6, 7, 69
    policy networks 66-68
Newly industrialised countries (NIC) 173
News Corp. 104, 146, 191-7
N-generation 5
NHK *see* Nippon Hoso Kyokai
NIC *see* Newly industrialised countries
NII *see* National Information Infrastructure
Nippon Hoso Kyokai (NHK) 174, 180, 207
Nissan 6
Nokia 104, 108, 182

Nolan, R. L. 221
NRAs *see* National regulatory authorities
NTSC *see* National Television Systems Committee
NTT 107

Oftel (Office for Telecommunications) 29
Ohmae, K. 223, 224, 225
ONdigital 211-2
OpenCable 203
Oxley, J. 229

PAL *see* Phase Alteration by Line
Parsons, C. 65, 67
People's Liberation Army (PLA) 101, 117, 164
PerfecTV 195
Personal Computer (PC)
    children's education 144
Peterson, J. 66, 67
Phase Alteration by Line (PAL) 171, 172, 173
Philips 104, 176, 182, 183, 192, 198, 199, 231
PLA *see* People's Liberation Army
Policy community 65
Policy network 65, 67, 68
    network society 66-8
    pan-European 78
Policy push 20
Pool, I. 151, 166, 247
Porter, M. 227
Post-industrialism 19
Post-industrial society 5, 96
Posts and Telecommunications Administrations (PTAs) 107
Prahalad, C. K. 225
Prodi, Romano 24, 34
PSTN *see* Public Switched Telephone Network
Public Switched Telephone Network (PSTN) 110

R&D (Research and Development)
    cost 229
    HD-MAC investment 176
    HDTV 176
    hi-tech 98
    Inter-European collaboration 11
    management 23
    promotion 112
RACE *see* Research on Advanced Communications for Europe
RAI 207
Regional Information Society Initiative (RISI) 75, 81-7
    Funding 84-7
    Lobbying 81-4
Renault 6
Research Institute of Industrial Technologies (RIIT) 181
Research on Advanced Communications for Europe (RACE) 11, 206
Richardson, J. 66, 67, 68
RISI *see* Regional Information Society Initiative
Rom Telecom 50
Rover 4

Samsung 180
Satellite transponders 1
Saviotti, P. 7
SBC 107
Schumpeter, J. 11
    creative destruction 11
Sclove, R. E. 7, 139
SD Alliance *see* Super Density disc Alliance
SDH *see* Synchronous Digital Hierarchy
SDI *see* Strategic Defence Initiative
SDTV *see* Standard Definition TV
SECAM *see* Systèm Electronique Couleur avec Mémoire
set-top box (STB) 193, 206, 211
Shakespeare, W. 1
Sharp, M. 223
Sinclair Broadcast Group 203
Singapore One 95
Singapore Telecom 107
SkyDigital 211-2
SkyMCI 194
Small and medium sized enterprises (SMEs) 23
SMEs *see* Small and medium sized enterprises
Society of Motion Picture and Television Engineers (SMPTE) 178
Sony 174, 183, 199, 231
Soviet Union
    computerisation 8-9
    empire 9

Special Economic Zones (SEZs) 131n
SPECTRE 201
Sprint 107, 142
Standage, T. 9
Standard Definition TV (SDTV) 208
Star TV 146, 195
Star War 98
State Commission for Wireless Administration (SCWA) 120
State Council Information Office 12, 144
State Information Centre (SIC) 120
State Planning Commission (SPC) 120
State regulation 12
STB *see* set-top box
Steinfield, C. 20
Strategic alliances
  ICT sector 223-4
  reasons 224-6
  transatlantic, 16n
Strategic Defence Initiative (SDI) 98
Super Density disc Alliance (SD Alliance) 232
Sussman, G. 13, 248
Swedish Broadcasting Corporation 206
Synchronous Digital Hierarchy (SDH) 99, 106, 202
Systèm Electronique Couleur avec Mémoire (SECAM) 171, 172, 173

Tanner, K. 70
Tan, Z. 147, 153, 162
Tapscott, D. 19
Tassey, G. 225
Technological determinist 9
Technology policy
  China 98-116
  Eureka 98
  Fifth Generation Computer (Japan) 98
  selectivity and priority 112-3
  Strategic Defence Initiative (SDI) 98
  technology transfer and foreign investment 113-6
Teece, D. J. 225, 228
TeleCities 66, 70, 71, 76-8, 81-7
  Funding 84-7
  lobbying 81-4
  Manchester Declaration 76
Telecom Denmark 206
Telecommunications

China-China-Foreign (CCF) 169n
  exchange capacity (China) 100
  Growth (China) 100
  investment (China) 100
  liberalisation 26
  networks 1
  privatisation 26
  rule of law 119
  world league table 102
Telecom Norway 206
Telia Research 206
TEN-Telecom *see* Trans-European Telecommunications Networks
Teracom 206
Tesco 3
TEU *see* Treaty of the European Union
Thajchayapong, P. 128
Third Wave 96-7
Thomson 176, 182, 192, 198, 199
Thorn EMI 176
Tiananmen 153
Tipton, F.B. 9
Toffler, A. 96
Tömmel, I. 67, 68, 88
T-Online 3
Top level domains 31
Toyota 6
Trans-European Networks 26, 34, 56, 70, 72
Trans-European Networks of Telecommunications (TEN-Telecom) 27, 56, 70
Transnational cooperation 80-1
Treaty of the European Union (TEU) 25
  audiovisual 182-5
TV without Frontiers 188-9
Tyson, L. 213

United Airlines 6
United Nations (UN) 144
Use value *see* Marx, K.

V2000 183, 192, 231
VADIS 201
Value Added Tax 31
van Dijk, J. 5
VAT *see* Value Added Tax
Vergari, S. 67
VHS 183, 192, 231
Video-on-Demand (VoD) 109, 194, 211
VIP Reference 153

Virtual Europe 21, 43, 45, 46
Virtual surgery 137

Walsh, V. 7
Wang, G. 19, 94, 127, 131n
Warsaw Pact 48
Web browser 10
   Internet Explorer 10
   Navigator/Communicator (Netscape) 10
Wei Jingsheng 153
World Broadcasting Satellite
   Administrative Radio Conference (WARC) 186, 191
World Online 3
World Sky Broadcasting (WSkyB) 197
World Trade Organisation (WTO)
   China's membership 115
   global institution 222
   global protest 152-3
   implications of China's membership 160-2
   Information Technology Product Agreement 46, 59
   Telecommunications Agreement 46, 59
   trade rules 116
World Wide Web (WWW) 2, 142
   free economic zone 157
WTO *see* World Trade Organisation
WWW *see* World Wide Web

Xinren Information Technology 146, 195
Xu, A. 106

Yahoo! 3
Yang, Z. 106, 117
'year 2000 (Y2K)' problem 4
Ye, S. 159

Zenith 198
Zhirinovsky, Vladimir 9
Zimmerman, J. B. 224